GREAT WINEMAKERS OF CALIFORNIA

Great Winemakers *of* California

Conversations with
ROBERT BENSON

Foreword by
ANDRE TCHELISTCHEFF

CAPRA PRESS
1977
Santa Barbara

For my parents,
for Clea and Amy,
and for Lesley who gave me the idea.

Jacket print courtesy Firestone Vineyard, Los Olivos, California.

Winemaker's photographs by Wayne McCall with the exception of the following: Martin Ray by Alfred A. Knopf, Karl Wente by Leigh Weiner, Andre Tchelistcheff by Tim Crawford, Mary Ann Graf by C.T. Conway, and Don Alexander, Richard Peterson, Ely Callaway and Brother Timothy.

Typical winemaking operation drawing courtesy of Sebastiani Vineyards.

Production credits: Design and layout by Marcia Burtt, display type by Foster & Horton, typesetting by Charlene McAdams, printing and binding by R.R. Donnelley & Sons.

Library of Congress Cataloging in Publication Data
Benson, Robert, 1942-
Great winemakers of California.
Includes index.
1. Vintners—California—Biography.
I. Title.
TP547.A1B46 663'.22'0922 [B] 77-3888
ISBN 0-88496-107-9

CAPRA PRESS / 631 State Street, Santa Barbara, California 93101

CONTENTS

PREFACE

Nineteen thirty-three to nineteen seventy-seven: recovery from the traumatic injury of Prohibition, renaissance of the California wine industry, opening of the gates to the golden age. Robert Benson's *Great Winemakers of California,* in its very own individual and original form of personal interviews, brings the reader face to face with a gallery of winemakers who are leading California wine into its golden age.

These are the frontier men and women of California winemaking: winemaker composers, winemaker conductors, winemaker artist-performers—all so different, their wines so individual, so contradictive, in their own styles and in their own artistic images. And behind this select group, there are others, equally important and hardworking, with their own ambitions and dreams, their own viticultural and oenological philosophies.

Beneath the surface of the question and answer dialogue, Benson's book teems with historical facts perfectly combined with current winemaking ideology and, far more important, it opens the outlook for tomorrow. After all, we are dealing with a very young California wine industry which is just now accomplishing the breakthrough the author describes, just now reaching its intellectual and artistic maturity.

Every season brings new challenges to the winemaker. The economics of grape growing becomes more complex. New viticultural regions open, each a New World of winemaking possibilities, involving new ideas, new technological research and spiraling accomplishments. Each winemaker better understands ecological dogma than his predecessors. Through these interviews, the reader gains insight into these complexities and others confronting California vintners, such as principles of geographical appellation of origin, vintage denomination versus nonvintage philosophy, and the future of generic wines.

Yet the vintners do not confront these complexities alone. Powerful winds are blowing from different directions, with new energy springing from the expectations of young wine consumers, the new generation of wine buffs, wine merchants and restaurateurs. The book of Robert Benson is part of that new energy, written for that new generation of consumers. It is full of depth, full of reflections of winemakers struggling to open the gates to tomorrow. How fast and how far we will move ahead is very hard to predict, but the gates are already ajar. It is the power of you, the wine-lover, that will help us all to throw open wide these gates to our golden age.

INTRODUCTION

"Ah, back to France!" the French winetaster exclaimed as he sniffed a glass of white wine. Unknown to him, the glass held a California Chardonnay. The year was 1976, the scene the Académie du Vin in Paris, the judges: nine top French wine experts. They were blind tasting California Chardonnays with the finest white Burgundies, and comparing California Cabernet Sauvignons with some of the greatest red wines of Bordeaux. When the scorecards were in, California wines had taken first place in both categories and half the California entries had ranked above one or more of their French counterparts. In the spring of America's bicentennial year, a handful of California vintners had pulled a *coup* in Paris.[1]

The significance of that Paris tasting lay not in its rankings of individual wines, but in the fact that the judges were unable, across the board, to distinguish French from California wines. In recent years this had been happening with increasing frequency with other judges in other blind tastings. But until the 1976 Paris tasting the finding had never been confirmed by nine of France's best palates. In the final analysis, the Paris tasting was simply one of those convenient events which historians—anxious to pin things down in time and space—use to mark a watershed in history: in this case, the point when California became recognized as equal to the greatest wine regions in the world.

California wines have indeed come of age. And we Americans are no less startled than the French, for the quality breakthrough has been very recent and sudden. Fine winemaking began with a flourish in

California in the last decades of the nineteenth century when characters like Haraszthy, Krug, the Beringers, Niebaum, Wetmore, Lefranc and Masson had the bravado to set themselves up on grandiose winegrowing estates, pretenders to a European inheritance of opulent châteaux and two thousand years of winemaking tradition. Their pretensions produced some headlines and a few marvellous wines, but failed to put California on the map as a serious rival to European wine regions. After the devastating interlude of Prohibition, a new generation of vintners carried on the fine wine cause. You could count them on your fingers: Martin Ray, the Wentes, John Daniel of Inglenook, the Latours of Beaulieu Vineyards (aided by their great winemaker Tchelistcheff), Lee Stewart of Souverain, Fred McCrea of Stony Hill, Louis Martini and few others. This tiny post-Prohibition generation reached occasional peaks of excellence, but fame accrued to individual vintners and individual wines, not to California as a great wine region of the world.

Suddenly, in the late 1960s, something happened—an enormous groundswell of wine consumption in the United States. Between 1966 and 1975 adult per capita annual consumption increased from 1.6 gallons to 2.7 gallons nationwide, and from 3.6 to 5.8 gallons in California. California, which produces 85 percent of American wine, more than doubled its wine production in the 1960s; growers planted tens of thousands of new acres in fine wine grapes; nearly 100 new wineries opened. Most of the expansion was in the making of common, rather than fine, wine. A wave of large corporations was attracted by the fantastic investment potential. They eagerly bought out Inglenook, Almadén, Beaulieu, Beringer, Simi, Souverain and other high quality wineries; some maintained that quality while others let it plunge in the interest of profits. The wave of newcomers, however, also included dozens of individual enthusiasts, ex-urban amateurs seeking a country life, dedicated to making great wine simply as a romantic challenge. One newcomer explained, "We amateurs have turned winemaking into a competitive sport."

A competitive sport, quality competition for the sheer fun of it: is that what produced the quality breakthrough in California wines? Was it the infusion of big capital, purchasing sophisticated technological improvements? Could it have been the accumulated wisdom of 100 years of matching grapes, climates and soils? Whatever it was, virtually overnight the number and quality of fine California wines grew prodigiously. Wine critics began to announce, quizzically at first and then excitedly, that the quality of these new wines signaled a quantum leap in excellence that put California in the same league with Europe's greatest wine regions. Our reality today is as Robert Louis Stevenson prophesied in 1880 while traveling in the California wine country: "The smack of Californian earth shall linger on the palate of your grandson."

What do we know, then, about this fine wine region called California? Precisely where are the best vineyards? How exactly are their grapes made into fine wine? Most important, who are California's great winemakers and what sets them apart as makers of fine, rather than ordinary, wine? Little has been published addressing these questions in any depth. In contrast, we have long had such information about the European wine regions, starting with the detailed reports of Thomas Jefferson who stalked inquisitively through Burgundy and Bordeaux as American commissioner to France. This flow of information continues with many modern volumes about the French districts, the Rhine, and even the famous Italian, Spanish and Portuguese wine regions. We have book after book about the vintners, vineyards, grapes, cellar practices—in short, the whole story.

I wanted to learn the whole story about fine California wines, and tell it in this book—a fool's goal, perhaps unattainable. And yet this book does plow the field of California wine knowledge to a significantly greater depth than has been done previously, making it, I hope, a more fertile field for wine buffs and historians, and a more interesting one for casual wine drinkers or readers. My method was simple. Between the summers of 1975 and 1976, I tramped through vineyards and wineries with a tape recorder, and questioned vintners face to face. Then, instead of the usual practice of writing a book describing the *wines* and my personal taste preferences, I focused on *winemakers*, convinced that the people behind the wines were the most important factor in the California quality breakthrough. Moreover, I knew the information they possessed would have more lasting value than a mere diary of my palate's pleasures. I pumped them for that information, trying to be an amiable interlocutor, but pursuing the reasons each vintner was drawn into the craft of winemaking. I probed for how one vintner's wines differ from others', where the vineyards are, their soils, microclimates and viticultural practices, and how the wine is made, from picking grapes right through to bottling. I attempted to discover not only "what," but "why," to draw out the winemaker's own reasons or philosophy for doing things one way rather than another. As information poured into the tape recorder, I decided it would be a mistake to filter it into a summary of what the winemakers revealed. I wanted readers to see the winemakers' own words, to catch the flavor of their personalities and attitudes, to notice the nuances of information, to be in on the conversation. So, I transcribed the interviews as they were recorded. Manuscripts were edited for clarity and brevity, and a copy was sent to each interviewee for verification of accuracy and revision; only a few made extensive revisions. The following chapters, then, are my conversations with twenty-eight great California winemakers.

These vintners produce most of the wines that can honestly be compared with the world's best; that includes less than ten percent of California wines, just as it would include less than ten percent of French wines. It can be argued that there are great winemakers among the producers of the other ninety percent of California wine, but these are excluded here.[2] Even among those who produce the top ten percent, there are other winemakers who might have been included had space been more plentiful,[3] and among those included some make better wine than others. But these twenty-eight portray the full spectrum of approaches to the craft of fine winemaking. Included are great winemakers of the post-Prohibition generation, vintners from fine old family wineries in the business for generations, and many of the new wave of "amateurs" challenging the status of these older wineries. Also represented are wineries owned by large corporations, partnerships, and individuals. Some of the tiniest wineries in the state are here, along with some of the largest in the fine wine field, and all sizes in between.

This book can be read, I feel, on four different levels.

First, it is entertainment for any reader—even a teetotaler—fascinated by human nature and why people, especially artists or craftsmen, do what they do for a living. At this level, it stands somewhere between Studs Terkel's interviews in *Working* and the *Paris Review* interviews with poets and novelists.

At a second level, the book provides copious oral history, colorful verbal portraits by the winemakers of themselves and their industry. If I am right that the California wine industry has just made a quality breakthrough leading to its most important era, then this book should provide historians a rich harvest of material.

The third level is for the casual wine drinker, the person who enjoys wine and is not averse to learning more about it, but who is not about to enroll in an intensive study course. Such persons can dip casually and randomly into this book and be rewarded to the extent of their dipping. For them, above all, I have recommended a wine to drink while reading each chapter, and I wish them many sweet silent sessions of sipping as they read the words of the vintner in whose hands the wine was crafted. I confess, my heart is with them.

Finally, this book can be read at a much greater level of intensity by the true wine buff who thrives on knowledge of which grape varieties were blended in the wine, whether it was fermented in oak or stainless steel, and all the other details which go into fine winemaking. It is easy to belittle an interest in such details as a manifestation of snobbism, and certainly some oneupsmanship goes on among oenophiles. On the other hand, it is of such details that great wines are made, and knowledge of them fills the thinking and dominates the discussions of winemakers themselves. So it hardly seems intelligent to counsel one ardently interested in wine that detailed knowledge is to be shunned. In fact, ridicule of such knowledge usually comes from the connoisseur who prefers to keep such information exclusively within his own domain.

For the reader who tackles the book at this level, drinking the recommended wine with each chapter may not be entirely advisable, lest the ability to discern fine differences be blurred! Those fine differences appear from chapter to chapter and factors that determine wine quality will come into sharp focus. For example, if the reader considers each index entry under "fermentation . . . oak," the merits of oak barrel fermentation as a quality factor—and the vintners' views and practices in that regard—will become apparent. Likewise, the index might be used to compare thinking on whether quality is best achieved by doing little or no fining, filtering or centrifuging, or by using those techniques extensively. Other questions, to mention a few, are the role of soil, the practice of selective harvesting, the types of oak cooperage, and the relationship between quality and size of a winery. (For convenience, I have arranged the interviews within each region starting with the smallest winery and ending with the largest; the two exceptions are the late Martin Ray and the consultant Andre Tchelistcheff, who head the chapters in their respective regions.)

Growing numbers of consumers are interested in such details about the craft of wine, and if this book opens the floodgates of detailed wine knowledge, perhaps the domain of the wine snob will become less exclusive. Moreover, as consumers become more knowledgeable about wine, the market pressure for better quality will inevitably intensify, as will consumer demand for informative and truthful wine labeling laws which will also promote quality.[4] It is a pleasant prospect to contemplate: by the time we usher in the year 2000, we should be able to look back to our bicentennial year and say it marked the beginning of the golden age of California wine.

I want to add a word of true gratitude to Andre Tchelistcheff, who enlivened this book with his interview and graced it with his preface, making both contributions with characteristic warmth.

Finally, permit me to note that there were many pleasures in doing this book, but I did not know the nicest one would come when submitting the manuscript to a publisher. It seemed fated that a book on the craft of fine wine should be published by a fine craft press like Capra. Noel Young and Linda Rolens immediately lent their personal joy and concern to the project, greatly improving the manuscript and keeping the spark glowing in us all. The same book would not have been possible without these two lovers of language and wine.

—ROBERT BENSON
March, 1977

FOOTNOTES

[1]Wines were judged on a 20 point scale, and the judges' evaluations were added to give the following scores (California wines are in boldface). Whites: **1973 Château Montelena** (132); 1973 Meursault-Charmes, Domaine Roulet (126.5); **1974 Chalone** (121); **1973 Spring Mountain** (104); 1973 Beaune "Clos des Mouches," Drouhin (101); **1972 Freemark Abbey** (100); 1973 Batard-Montrachet, Ramonet-Prudhon (94); 1972 Puligny-Montrachet "Les Pucelles," Domaine Leflaive (89);**1972 Veedercrest** (88); **1973 David Bruce** (42). Reds: **1973 Stag's Leap Wine Cellars** (127.5); 1970 Château Mouton-Rothschild (126); 1970 Château Haut-Brion (125.5); 1970 Château Montrose (122); **1971 Ridge "Monte Bello"** (103.5); 1971 Château Leoville-las-Cases (97); **1971 Mayacamas** (89.5); **1972 Clos du Val** (87.5); **1970 Heitz "Martha's Vineyard"** (84.5); **1969 Freemark Abbey** (78). The judges were Pierre Brejoux, Inspector General of the Institut National des Appellations d'Origine Contrôllée; Michel Dovaz of the Institut Oenologique de France; Aubert de Villaine, co-director of the Domaine de la Romanée-Conti; Claude Dubois-Millot, a director of Le Nouveau Guide; Odette Kahn, director of the Revue de Vin de France; Pierre Tari, owner of Château Giscours; Raymond Oliver, owner of the restaurant Le Grand Vefour; Jean-Claude Vrinat, owner of the restaurant Taillevent; and Christian Vanneque, wine steward of La Tour d'Argent.

[2]It would be customary at this point to pay homage to the industry's myth that the ordinary wines of California are the "best in the world" of their class. But I find the only substance to that claim is that, unlike wines abroad, it is rare to find a vinegary or spoiled wine in California. With due respect for that accomplishment, I think it must also be said that California common wines are generally bland, like processed cheese, when compared with the dramatic range of character to be found in the cheap country wines of Europe.

[3]I excluded wineries specialized in sparkling or dessert wines, as well as several new wineries from which we will undoubtedly hear much in the future. Fred McCrea of Stony Hill Vineyard, who produced some of the best California wines for many years, preferred not to be included, and I deferred to his privacy. He passed away as this book was going to press. In addition, there is sometimes more than one "winemaker" at a winery (the owner and a technical winemaker both qualify) and in such cases, I interviewed the person who seemed to dominate in determining the winery's style and techniques.

[4]Labeling laws that have existed since repeal of Prohibition have been scandalous in their dishonesty, expressly permitting misrepresentation of grape variety, origin and producer. For 40 years, the federal agency which regulates wine labeling has treated the consumer as if he had George Orwell at his elbow to advise him that the words on the label do not mean what they say. With increasing consumer pressure, however, there is some chance that by 2000 we will have labels as honest as the wines are great.

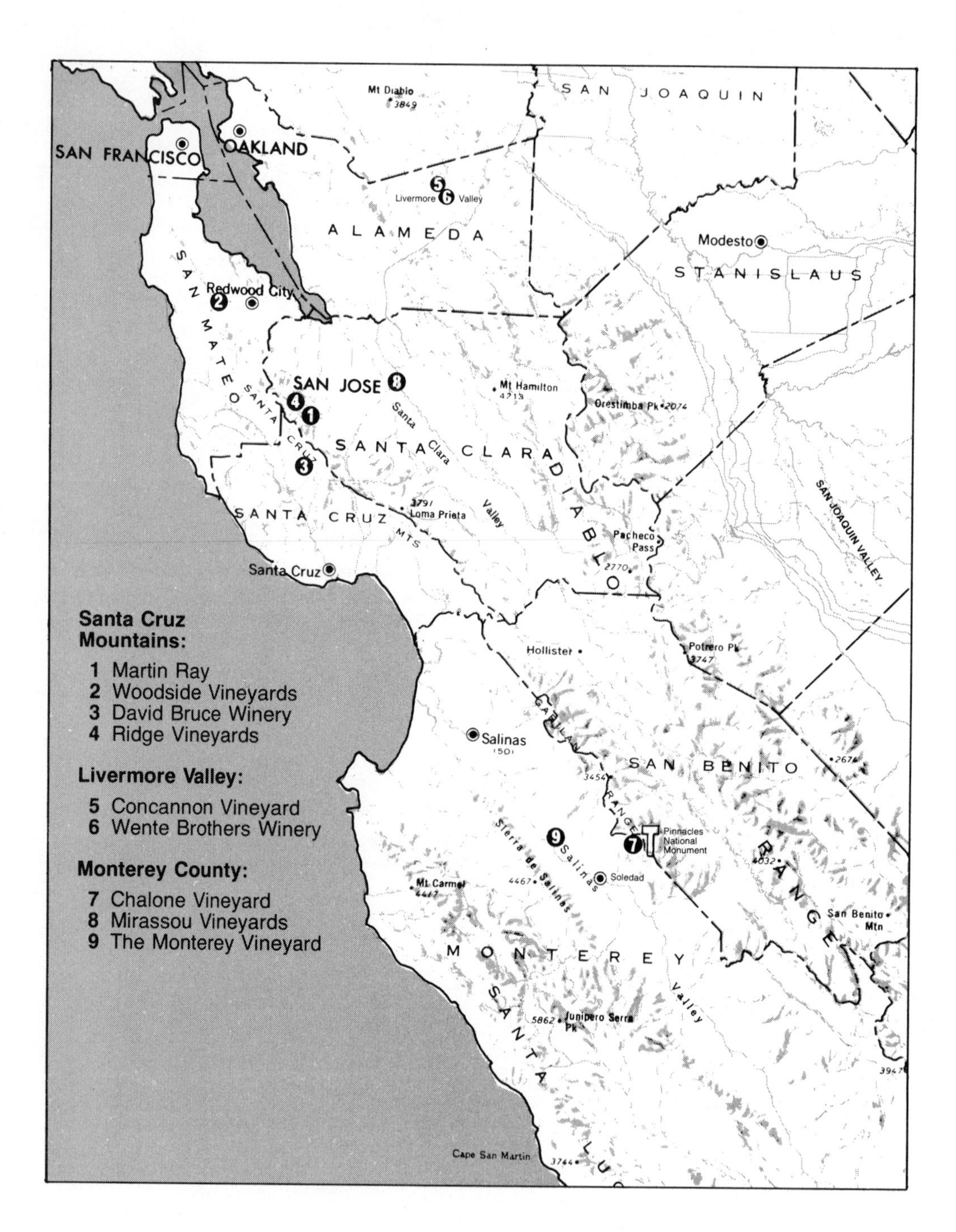

SOUTH OF SAN FRANCISCO BAY

Santa Cruz Mountains:

CRADLE OF INNOVATION

Flying south from San Francisco you see bedroom communities strung along the peninsula, the Stanford University campus and the inevitable freeway carrying its congestion up and down the sprawling suburban system. Only if you look very carefully may you see occasional vineyards dotting the landscape. Unlike the Napa Valley, where travelers are greeted by a landscape entirely dominated by viticulture, few who drive south from San Francisco are aware of passing through one of California's most extraordinary wine regions. The vineyards are hidden in crannies and peaks of the Santa Cruz Mountains. A finger of these mountains rises gently in mid-peninsula, then becomes a sharp hunched back reaching to three thousand feet as the peninsula ends and the mountains become a massive range running south to Monterey Bay.

These mountains have cradled a remarkable succession of individualistic, innovative winemakers. No doubt the area's climate and topography contribute to the big, rich style of the wines. But something else in the mountains' atmosphere must breed winemakers with appetites for experiment and individualism. Among them were Etienne Thée, who came from Bordeaux in 1852, his French son-in-law Charles Lefranc and Lefranc's son-in-law, the splashy Burgundian Paul Masson. Also included must be the intellectual Emmett Rixford who wrote *The Wine Press* and the colorful Dr. Osea Perrone. All were assertive personalities in the early days and their influence still reverberates in the mountains. (The Paul Masson and Almadén wineries, both descended from Thée, are now mass-production wineries owned by Seagrams and National Distillers, respectively. Their far-flung operations no longer represent the Santa Cruz Mountain tradition described here.)

The individualist tradition has been carried through to our own day. San Franciscan Louis Benoist, who once owned Almadén, maintained the tradition, as do the tenacious owners of Mt. Eden Vineyards, whose winery rests on part of Martin Ray's mountain top, won from Ray in financial litigation. Four extraordinary winemakers of the Santa Cruz tradition are interviewed in the following pages. I spoke with the indomitable Martin Ray, who throughout his life loudly refused to compromise wine quality; the hobbyist Robert Mullen, who quietly tends Emmett Rixford's old vineyard; Paul Draper, the purist who questions compromise with tradition; and the creative David Bruce who develops new tastes from old styles. By defining individual approaches to winemaking and believing in them wholeheartedly, these vintners and their forebears have made the Santa Cruz Mountains the source of some of our greatest and most interesting wines.

Martin Ray

We add nothing to our wines, nor do we take anything from them. With infinite care we leave them alone.

Martin Ray passed away a few months after this interview, and with him passed a legendary era in American winemaking. He was the legend. Viewing himself as the artistic heir of Paul Masson, the flamboyant French immigrant of the pre-Prohibition period, Martin Ray made his first vintage immediately after Prohibition and for the next four decades was unique as a vintner in America. He planted his vineyard and built his home and winery atop 2,000 foot Mt. Eden, overlooking the Santa Clara Valley at the southern tip of San Francisco Bay. The view of the valley changed over the course of his life from farmland to suburban sprawl, but Mt. Eden remained serene, and fragrant with the smell of the vineyards from which Ray produced limited quantities of handmade wines. He was an uncompromising perfectionist, an autocrat of the winepress, and he produced some of the finest wines ever wrought from California soil. At the beginning of Ray's career, he received a telegram from wine connoisseur Julian Street: "Your Pinot Noir 1936 tasted tonight is first American red wine I ever drank with entire pleasure . . . I am astounded." The acclaim continued over the years. Alexis Lichine proclaimed Ray's wines to be "the great wines of California." Angelo Pellegrini declared: "Comparable in character and quality to the finest European growths in their greatest years."

Near the end of his life he was involved in epic legal battles with investors on Mt. Eden. His lifelong battle, however, was for higher quality in California wines. A contentious individualist, he accused other California vintners of falling below his standards, and challenged them to join him in a voluntary quality control system. He chided them for making anything less than 100 percent varietal wines, alleged that many of their wines contained less than the legally required 51 percent of the varietal grape named on the label, and declared that the 51 percent requirement itself was as deceptive as allowing margarine to be labeled butter. More than one winegrower tangled with Ray over the years and wound up outraged, but until recent years few could meet the challenge of his wines.

I drove up the long and dusty road which winds to the top of Mt. Eden one morning and found Martin Ray in robust spirits. He, Mrs. Ray and I sat around a big kitchen table and shared a bottle of his Chardonnay while he talked. Though retired, he was outspoken, and passionately, romantically involved in the life of wine. When I left hours later, he accompanied me outside, explained his custom of "ringing out" guests, and commenced to clang a large bell that stood outside. It was still ringing as I approached the bottom of the mountain.

A few months later, Martin Ray died. A new partnership took over the winery and the Martin Ray label, with Ray's step-son, Stanford professor Peter Martin Ray, as winemaker. In accordance with his instructions, Martin Ray's ashes were scattered among his grape vines on Mt. Eden.

Recommended wine to drink while reading this chapter:

MARTIN RAY
CABERNET SAUVIGNON

You've frequently been called "controversial" within the industry. How did you earn that reputation?

You have correctly said "within the industry." I never hesitated to speak out against malpractices in the industry—and that's "controversial!" Evils carried over from Prohibition days, and new evils developed right after Prohibition. When I became a winegrower, right after Prohibition, little interest in fine wines had survived. So I had to create that interest. I entertained, I talked, I wrote. I challenged the old standards, urged improvements. Particularly, I championed the supremacy of keeping fine varietal wines from being blended out with lesser wine.

In those early days I was the only winegrower in the country making and selling strictly varietal wines—at prices that were many times what others were getting for their wines! Others noted that and jumped on the varietal bandwagon—even though they might have none of the varietals they were labeling! I fought against all that kind of mislabeling. So, since the majority of winegrowers didn't agree, or couldn't afford to, they took to labeling me "controversial." But that was among themselves. No knowledgeable customers for fine wines ever fall victim to trade propaganda—it's to those people I have always been dedicated.

You have made 40 vintages?

Yes, I made my first vintage in '35, and my last vintage in '74. I made wine in '35, we bought Paul Masson in '36, sold it to Seagrams in '43, and then came here to Mt. Eden.

Who has been your staff, who helped you make the wine?

Well, we're going back to right after '43 when I sold Paul Masson. The idea was to have it small. Paul Masson had about 60 acres in grapes, and we planted ten. And we figured the family could do all the work ourselves—Mrs. Ray, our two boys, and our daughter—and thereby cut down the labor, to make it economically feasible, providing us with a fine way of life; but we did not ever intend to make a great deal of money. I made my modest means in real estate. Paul Masson, I might add, lived the same way. In my 40 years I actually made a substantial profit from winemaking in only two years. And Paul Masson's books showed, when I bought his corporation, that he had made money only two years in a lifetime! So the idea is to provide a way of life—there's none better, or I would have turned away from this. I like it very much.

And were you able to operate the winery with your family?

We were able to do just as we planned, to a certain point, but the boys grew up. They became Ph.D.s, professors, and pretty soon they were taking trips to Europe and couldn't be on hand. They were both here with their families a few days ago. They're interested, but they're not available! Around 1960 we formed a group of investors, and we set upon 25 couples, organizing them and developing more new vineyards and bringing them under cultivation.

And with that group you attempted to form what you've called the first appellation control in California?

Yes, we formed an appellation control here because we had tried unsuccessfully to get the entire, well the cream of the industry, to join in such a venture. I worked with Dr. Winkler, particularly, at the University of California at Davis, trying to get them to appoint him as the one to oversee it all but it didn't work out that way. The others were devoted to another thing and that comes right back to the business of making money.

I can tell you a little story to illustrate what I mean, as I had a winegrower sitting on my front porch at our old vineyard next door one afternoon, at the time when I was first thinking of forming an appellation control, and our truck came around front, went down to the winery's lower cellar and picked up a load of cases and pretty soon returned, and this fellow winegrower said to me smiling, "Well, that's a nice shipment going out, Martin. It always makes me feel good, and I guess it makes you feel good, when you see those shipments going out. I shipped 100 cases to one consignee last week and I felt very good about it." And I said, "Well, I don't feel that way, I wish to God that I never had to sell any of my wines, that we could keep all the reds here as long as I live, because I know that *they'll* still be alive." He just shook his head, he didn't understand it.

It's a matter of just how you look upon winegrowing. You see in Bordeaux, for instance, speaking of the French growers, almost everyone is interested in growing wines for profit, for making money and the more the better. But in Burgundy, it's different, at least with the foremost growers. From my long friendship with the Latours, Louis Latour of Beaune, and his brother Jean, I know for a fact that they are not primarily interested in making wine that will bring them a fortune, but rather in making the best wines they can.

The appellation control you attempted to set up would have regulated planting practices, pruning.

The one up here was to regulate everything. If it was virgin land anyone was planting, the vines had to be at least ten feet apart. If it was replanted, they had to be 12 feet apart. I just gave you an example relative to planting, but pruning was the same way. In other words, the number of canes that you leave and replacement spurs, as we provided, had to be limited and, it's difficult to go into detail, but suffice to say that we controlled through the planting, pruning . . .

Harvesting as well?

The sulphur dusting, and even the picking.

I imagine you wouldn't have allowed any mechanical harvesting, but then it's too steep here anyway, isn't it?

Unless your land is level, there is no equipment to take care of it. Anyway, you can't ever get satisfactory results with mechanical picking of grapes. But let me add that when you're growing thousands of acres you're jolly well obliged to pick mechanically, there's no other way. What can you do with vast vineyards, scarcity of labor and the cost of labor always going up? You must bow to certain things if you operate on a large scale. But we must develop more small acreages where the owners are able and willing to care for the vineyards themselves. And as I understand it, that is going on now, but a good number of people still don't want to do much physical work, and there's lots of physical work in making wine!

Do you think we will have or should have an appellation control system by law?

I'll answer first that we should have if we want maximum quality, but I'll answer just as positively that we're not going to have it!

And why not?

Today most grape acreage is owned by large estates devoted to making wine with the sole purpose of making money. They're so large they can't operate within rules and regulations laid down by any worthwhile appellation control.

Could it happen if the small premium wineries got together?

Yes, those fellows should get together when the most recent plantings of fine varietals come in. Grape prices have already fallen to half what they were, and of course, wines are dropping. When all these new plantings bear, that will force them, or rather, will provide an opportunity for these fellows to get together and form an appellation control. Only by having very superior wine, are these small vineyards going to be able to sell it.

Are all your vineyards located here on Mt. Eden?

All the wines in our cellar have been made from grapes grown here on this mountain—vineyards I personally planted. There were no vineyards here before we came.

Do you think Mt. Eden, in the coast range at Saratoga about 50 miles south of San Francisco, provides your wines with special characteristics?

Let's put it this way. All this land is known as Franciscan shale formation, which is almost like rotten rock. When it's wet, fracture a piece in your hands. It always fractures more or less horizontally and vertically at a right angle. It's just like a first class, authentic Parmesan cheese: it breaks up. So every time you work that land those little particles become smaller, and, ultimately, after 20 or 30 years, it gets so it's almost chalk. If you don't roll that land after working it, why you sink down over your shoe tops. One of our sons is a geologist and he told me this Franciscan shale extends from the south side of the Golden Gate Bridge on down toward Hollister.

What about climate on Mt. Eden?

Well, if we have 23 to 24 inches of rainfall we consider it sufficient but a little bit of a dry year. Such years, however, are when you get your best grapes—not your heaviest crop but the berries are a bit smaller, so the seeds and skin surface are larger proportionally and they get a little more sugar because there's less moisture. Twenty-five inches of rain, if it doesn't all fall at one time, is ideal. We've had up to 70 inches one or two years, and you get an enormous crop but also a poor vintage.

In the U.C. Davis classification, is this a Region I up here?

They labeled this as Region I, based on Dr. Winkler having a recording device in the vineyard which recorded temperatures 24 hours a day. But I note now that they don't speak of these hills which range from 1,500 to 2,000 feet, but of Santa Clara Valley. That's quite a different thing, it's but slightly above sea level, and that is, and always has been, classified as Region II—warmer at the valley level, as in Napa and Sonoma.

Do you think yourself as a "traditional" winemaker?

Yes, traditional—that is, classical. It's simple, as contrasted with what I term "sophisticated," which is away from the natural. I think you will find still in Dr. Amerine's office, a letter I wrote him on his request many years ago that he wanted his students to see. I said we add nothing to our wines nor do we taking anything from them. And that is a pretty simple way of going about it. You might ask what is it you don't add, well: no chemicals, no sugar, no concentrate—that's the worst thing ever to hit the industry! It's hard to buy even a California Cabernet today that is not a bit on the sweet side from concentrate. If you could see the circularization we are subjected to, offering us tankcar loads of concentrate! You know they're selling it somewhere. And now we're even getting ads, believe it or not, from France, offering us grape juice concentrate in 100 gallon drums! It's become *the* thing.

May I ask you about each of the major steps of winemaking—what kind of approach you have, starting with crushing and stemming?

Well, with your consent, I'll go into the vineyards for picking first. We pick with little scissors, not grape hooks, because to cut with a knife a tough stem like the Cabernet, you squeeze the bunch a little. You break a few berries maybe, the juice starts running, it gets messy and it attracts flies and bees and whatever they carry. We always instruct our pickers to let the bunch lay in their open palm and cut the stem with scissors. Then don't throw the bunch into the box, but lean over and place it in carefully. As fast as they're picked, we place those boxes on the concrete slab with our stainless steel crusher, which crushes and stems the grapes. If it is a very hot day, we space those boxes, so the evening air cools them off, because those grapes come in from 80 to 100 degrees. Yet, we have cool evenings at this altitude, and this sets the time of crushing, always 5 a.m. We do this for two reasons: to crush them before the sun comes up, with a good handy crew—we've used the same people for some 20 years, one man has dumped every box of grapes that has gone into our crusher for 20 years. He does it for *fun*, he's a friend. Once crushed, the reds in the portable fermenters go immediately into the cellars. We crush the whites directly into the circular basket of our press, a large old handpress no different from those used 100 years ago. In fact, Paul Masson's father-in-law, Lefranc, brought this one around the Horn. I've long since put a stainless steel tub in it and also a stainless steel sleeve on the big stem, so that the grape must goes directly into that press basket. Now, I said there were two reasons for crushing at 5 a.m.; the second reason is to get them before the flies come out. Before sunup there are no vinegar flies, no yellowjackets, no bees, wasps. We always crush more or less the same amount of grapes—it may take several mornings, but on a given morning, one press full. We always try to have the last box crushed just as the sun is coming up over the eastern mountains, and at that point—Mrs. Ray, whom we call Madame Pinot, and two or three of the other gals have ready Champagne on ice. Madame Pinot makes big three-egg omelets for everybody, and we have Champagne, we have our omelets and our toast and our coffee, and the "crush" is already in the cellar and our cellar men are getting ready to start pressing. I generally get away very quickly and watch over *everything*, and direct *everything*, as I always have. No one but myself has ever made a vintage here or at the old property.

Could you be more specific on the different treatment of the reds and the whites?

A red wine does not go into the press basket but into portable oak fermenters. Each holds 200 gallons, and we fill them 100 gallons because they swell up and boil over otherwise. They're instantly covered with clean white cloths made of fresh sheets so if any flies do develop before the day is over, they cannot have any contact with the must. Now if it is the white grapes, everything is identical except beneath the crusher is not the fermenter, but the press basket. After the crush, we push the press basket and the press into the cellar and the hand pressing commences. Then the juice from the pressing is drawn into 60 gallon closed casks, filled only half full, and closed with a cotton gasket, to protect them from flies. They start to ferment right away. . . .

These are oak casks?

They are oak casks—French White Burgundian oak. I do not have the botanical name for the oak, but it is *not* Limousin oak! That's all you read about today, Limousin oak! I don't know whether the people who talk about it know what they're talking about. Limousin oak is what they make Cognac in. I get my casks from Louis Latour in Beaune. His own cooper makes them for me. I asked him, what is the oak? And he said, "I don't know the botanical name, we just call it Burgundy oak." Our son visiting over there saw a great pile of the oak planks from which the casks are made. If you were a lumber man you'd know what I mean by their being "sticked," meaning there's a pile of them with an inch airspace between each one, then there's a stick put crosswise, and another, so that the air passes freely between them. Seven years they stay outside, sun, rain, snow, cold, heat. By that time you have no oak flavor left, and you don't want oak flavor. You can't have it. And yet, oak is very important in helping to clarify your wine, I can't get into the technical thing, but for white wine: always *new* oak casks.

Why don't you use stainless steel fermenters?

Burgundian oak contributes something to the fermenting wines. Stainless steel does not. Stainless steel is for utensils or your crusher or even hoops that hold the basket on our press. There's nothing else you can use, it's the best. But fermenting in stainless steel, well, it's just the easy way to do it. It's no job to care for a stainless steel cask, like a stainless steel pot in the kitchen—much easier than cleaning something made from wood. People operating on a vast scale, fermenting hundreds of thousand gallons at a time, running into millions of gallons during a single vintage year, for them stainless steel is the only thing. Of course, the best small French growers have not gone to stainless steel. But the last time our son was in Bordeaux he reported that one of the first growth class wineries was taking out oak casks and putting in stainless steel! It's the thing for the big boys. But there you must understand the conditions forced upon them. Labor costs and the necessity of making controlled fermentation are essential to volume production. They can cool it or they can heat it. Whereas a small cask requires no control, it just can't overheat.

Really? With white wines aren't you interested in fine-tuning your temperature control?

Oh, no, and here you'll find probably no one to support me, but I have positive proof over a lifetime, that if you have clean grapes come in for crushing and fermenting, the hotter the fermentation you have, in the case of a red wine where you're trying to extract color and flavor from the skins, the better it is right up to the point where it's even close to pasteurizing itself. I can show you charts we kept of our finest vintages and they fermented up to the high 90s. Today you hear about fermentation of white wines in the 50s and 60s. Well, our whites ferment in the 80s and 90s and that's where they get their flavor. It's no different from cooking in the kitchen, goddamit, there are things you can soak forever and get no flavor but if you boil them you'll get the flavor. It's as simple as that.

What about the cap? Do you submerge the cap, or punch it down?

That's punched down manually, generally every three hours, so it never dries out.

And do you fine or filter?

We do absolutely nothing to the red wines. We don't even rack them. Now here's something. I know of no one else who in any way agrees with me about this. But we say if you bring your red grapes in clean—that's the reason for careful picking, cutting off any bad berries, and not allowing any vinegar flies in—if you are careful, you don't have to do anything, and the wine gets its great flavor off the lees, which is solid matter, albuminous material, some tannin, some tartaric, which settles out. We never bottle the red wines before they've been three years in the cask. But once we kept the wine in casks ten years deliberately, and our 1946 was one of the greatest Cabernets we ever made. Generally, though, three or four years. It's a matter of tasting and watching the color. You can't let the wine start to oxidize. But if it has plenty of alcohol, tannin, and tartaric and you keep the air off by keeping the casks filled, it won't oxidize. Bottle the wines right off the lees. We add nothing to our wines, nor do we take anything from them. With infinite care we leave them alone.

Now with the whites, it's quite different. We bottle them when they are three, four, five, six or eight months old. They get quite clear by themselves, clear enough so you'd have no objection to drinking a little glass. But they are not really crystal clear. About 35 years ago, I decided on the Seitz German-made asbestos filter, and we filter all whites, whether we make them later into Champagne, or sell them as still wines. That's all we do to them, we filter them.

Do you initiate fermentation by yeast inoculation?

Yes, I believe firmly in that. I've done it all 40 vintages. I add yeast immediately as the wines are drawn off the press if it's the white, or to the fermenters for the red. And that culture, you might like to know, is the true Montrachet.

Yet most of the French wineries allow spontaneous fermentation with the natural wine yeast.

That isn't true. I had Davis graduates tell me in the last year, "What, you use pure culture? You know the French never do!" All I can tell you is that Louis Latour always uses a pure culture. My sons have been there and helped him inoculate, and I know that that's the case.

You have restricted yourself to producing the four noble varieties—Cabernet, Pinot Noir, White Riesling and Chardonnay.

Yes. Actually, as far as customers are concerned, we've restricted ourselves to three: Pinot Noir and Cabernet Sauvignon in the reds, and the Chardonnay in the whites. We have made a little Riesling, but thus far we've drunk it all ourselves! I wanted to find out if we could make a first class California Riesling comparable to the best German. I have made it. Therefore others can make it.

Were you the first to put out a varietal label after Prohibition?

We were the first, in 1937. And the government has the records of our label approvals to prove it. We had Cabernet Sauvignon, Pinot Noir, Gamay Beaujolais, which is superb when grown at our high elevation—and incidentally was the *only* authentic Gamay Beaujolais planting in California for many, many years. By 1939 we had Chardonnay, Pinot Blanc which I designated Pinot Blanc *vrai*, not to confuse it with Pinot Chardonnay which is not a correct name—it's Chardonnay, period. At the old property I had a White Claret—that was the name of the grape, and I sold it as such. I had a Folle Blanche. Folle Blanche is actually a grape of Cognac, but in California if you can get it to 21 or 22 sugar, you've a delightful, refreshing, high acidity, but very lovely dry table wine. And it also makes a second class Champagne. In the old vineyard I was selling Folle Blanche, and a Burger, and a Verdal—all of these white wines.

Do you think the 51 percent varietal requirement should be higher?

Oh, I think it should be thrown out, for God's sake. Dr. Amerine has told me of cases where someone had 51 percent of the variety and they sold it and somebody blended it again, a third time, and there was finally a fourth owner, all of them having blended it. You see what they ended up with.

I'll tell you a story of my own. When I sold Paul Masson, I assumed I could always buy some of my own wines until my new vineyards came in, but they got into an internal hassle, and for two years they sold nothing. I said, "Well, my God, let me have a few cases of my Chardonnay. If you can't sell them give them to me. I'll give you cash, you can put it in petty cash." They said, "Oh, no, no, no, we must take inventory every month, and copies go to New York, copies to Kentucky, copies to San Francisco. We can't do it." So I asked Amerine if he knew where I could buy some Chardonnay. This was in 1943. He said there just wasn't any. And there wasn't, at that time, excepting my plantings. Same with Pinot Noir, no one had any. Finally he said, "By the way, do you know Garatti over by Mission San Jose? Do you know about the Chardonnay he has on his fence, a little growing there?" That's the old Theodore Gier vineyard, and Theodore Gier before Prohibition made the finest white wine in California. He had a vineyard in Saratoga and one in San Jose. I asked how much there was and Maynard replied, "Oh, I think you could get a barrel out of it, it doesn't mean anything to Garatti."

So I went over to see Garatti and we had a little conversation. Finally he said, "What do you have on your mind?" I said, "Amerine tells me you have some Chardonnay out on your fence." His face kind of clouded. I asked, "How much wine do you make every year?" "Oh," he said, "a couple million gallons a year." And I said, "Amerine said you might have enough Chardonnay to make 50 gallons," told him the problem and said, "How about my having those, I'll pay you whatever you want." And then he became quite restive, "I just can't let you have those, Martin." I was amazed, "What do you mean, you can't let me have them? You make two million gallons a year, what the hell does 50 gallons mean to you?"

"Martin," he said, "those grapes are the basis for my Chardonnay blend." And I said, "Your Chardonnay blend, what the hell is that?" "Well," he said, "I make it every year, I sell it to Cook's Imperial." I asked him how big that blend was. "Well," he said, "it's 10,000 gallons!" I said, "Do you mean to tell me that 50 gallons in 10,000 gallons means anything?" "God yes, Martin," he said, "I couldn't call it Chardonnay otherwise!"

Well, there it is. And that's the way with most California varietals today. I want to emphasize: no one polices it, no one keeps any records and they're very careful to see to it they don't. No one knows a thing about it. Ernie Peninou wrote a nice little book on wines some years ago. He was a graduate student at Davis and in the summertimes he worked at a weighing station, where you weigh fruit. He'd drop in to see me every year or so, and one time he said, "Martin, do you know how they determine varieties now? They come in and they have 20 tons of grapes on board. I say 'What do you have there?' They say 'Pinot Noir.' I write down 'Pinot Noir' and put the stamp on it." It becomes officially Pinot Noir, that's the proof of it!

Speaking of Pinot Noir, why is it so difficult to make great Pinot Noir in California?

To begin with, if it's grown anywhere other than in Region I, and possibly even then, it doesn't produce sufficient acidity. That's the big problem. It turns brown when it's a year or so old. If you don't have three-quarters of one percent total acidity as tartaric, the wine won't keep very long. Tartaric is relatively expensive if you operate on a large scale, and growers tell me they use citric acid, which doesn't belong in wine at all. I don't think Pinot Noir should be grown in California except in rare places and I don't know of any other than here, although I do believe there are such places. The other extreme is Cabernet Sauvignon, it's the natural red wine.

Your wines have always been quite expensive; why is that?

The only reason we've continually raised the price of our wines is so we won't run out of inventory, to keep within our guideline of not selling more than we made the previous year. If we hadn't raised our prices way out of line from what they were—some reds now go at $600 a case, for God's sake that's $50 a bottle! You just eliminate some of your best customers, they can't afford it! But you're able to keep your inventory. Otherwise, you'd be out of business.

You couldn't simply sell the wine at a lower price and release a smaller portion?

If you want to make enemies. I tried it years ago, and if you want to make enemies, try selling just to your friends. It is for all comers providing they pay your price, real supply and demand.

That means only those comers with a lot of money can pay those high prices.

Well, there is a new class of people who have money. Professors used to have no money; now our best outlets are in university towns—Pasadena, Cambridge, Palo Alto. And in the Middle West, practically nothing. Only in the sea coast towns will people pay for really fine wines. They are a different class of people.

The professors don't have more money, but we would rather spend the money on wine and then drive Volkswagens instead of fancy cars.

That's right, they're doing that too. Our sons are both full professors; one is chairman of his division at Cal Tech, and I saw him arrive the other day in a jeep, for God's sake! The other one has a Volkswagen. And yet both serve fine wines. Don't overlook the medics. Everyone knows they're grossly overpaid and they're spending a lot of it on wines. I don't know what's the matter with attorneys, they evidently think liquor is quicker; I never did have very many attorney customers!

I have one last question. Do you think the best California wines are equal to the best European wines?

I assume you're limiting them, you say "the best"? I could say this, California wines were best in 1939. Times were hard and for the first time merchants like Frank Schoonmaker and Freddie Wildman, people who'd never bothered to come to California, who had dealt solely in French wines, became desperate and came out here. They were willing to pay whatever we asked for wines if we could deliver fine wine.

But today, do you think the very best California wines do compare with the European?

I started to say I think the French are going backward. They've gone crazy too in these last few years. They're in the same position as California, they have vast quantities of wine on hand. Their prices are tumbling although they're using all kinds of propaganda to make it appear otherwise—rigged auctions and that sort of thing. But their wines have deteriorated. The best Chardonnay from Europe, the one for years I hoped to match, was that grown by Marquis de Laguiche, a Montrachet. It's under the same owner, the same distributor today, but today there are California wines in addition to those grown in our vineyards which are better. On the other hand, there is Joseph Drouhin, owner and shipper of Burgundy wines. He has on the market two white wines, definitely Chardonnays and unblended, selling at $3.00 to $3.99 a bottle, and they are better than most California Chardonnays. That gives the California growers something to think about.

Pinot Noir I've covered, no, I don't think they should grow Pinot Noir here unless they can turn out something that will taste like Pinot Noir. In the case of German White Riesling, Stony Hill grew some Riesling a few years ago I thought was very first class. What I liked was that it was dry, yet full of Riesling flavor, had plenty of body, and the glycerine tears you see when you swish the glass—very rare in California. All ours have it—I don't know what produces it but it's in all great wines, and it doesn't come from low sugar content grapes, I can assure you that. As to Cabernet Sauvignon, there has been no Cabernet Sauvignon grown in California outside these vineyards to stand up with the first growth Clarets made in years like '28, '34 and '45. But since then the French have been replanting and blending more and more. And I think there are Cabernets made in California today as good as most of the so-called French Cabernets.

Robert Mullen

WOODSIDE VINEYARDS

I don't rely on this for a living; in fact it's a liability to us. So we're in a position to consider it a complete art.

Bob Mullen's tiny operation is proof that fine winemaking in California is sometimes a cottage industry. Mullen is literally a home winemaker, though legally a commercial one. His home, in the wealthy town of Woodside, is in a residential neighborhood of lawns and trees, but the Mullen property is landscaped with hundreds of grape vines. His winery is a cellar under the garage. It is his hobby shop: there he spends evenings, weekends, and vacations from his regular occupation, turning out miniscule amounts of wines highly acclaimed by the critics who have been able to taste them. Because he is not commercially motivated, my interview with Bob Mullen showed me winemaking as a purely artistic endeavor. It also showed me the personal satisfactions of winemaking as a hobby, and hearing Mullen tell it is enough to turn you into a home winemaker. Mrs. Mullen supplied a tray of good cheeses, and we drank Woodside wines as we talked on a patio overlooking the vineyard.

Recommended wine to drink
while reading this chapter:
WOODSIDE VINEYARDS
PINOT NOIR

Winemaking is a labor of love for you, isn't it, just a hobby?

Yes, it has to be a hobby, because it's a commercial disaster and I'd hate to try making a living at it. I'm western regional sales manager for the Armstrong Cork Company—building materials. This is one of the complications we have today. I'm traveling much of the time, and it's been difficult to make sense out of both doing business and creating an artistic success of the winery.

I take it your staff consists of just your family?

Well, the family is just my wife Polly and I. Our staff is a lot of very good friends. We have a couple of high school boys who do the dirty work like lifting barrels, hoeing the vineyard, that sort of thing. But this would not run without the friends. We've been at it since 1961 and it amazes us we have friends who never miss a vintage; they show up to help not just one weekend but two or three. If the red wine is ready to press on a Thursday night, four or five guys or gals show up right away. Polly and I are quite active in the Village Church, and most of our friends and helpers are from the church. One Sunday during each vintage we have the ministers over and the whole group gathers in the vineyard for a brief service to bless the vintage and read Bible passages relating to wine and vineyards. We keep track of the grapes picked specifically for the blessing and when they're made into wine we supply the church with the communion wine. The Woodside Village Church is probably unique in having 100 percent Cabernet Sauvignon or Pinot Noir for communion. We've even sold a little wine that way!

Is Woodside Vineyards the smallest bonded winery in the state?

That's no longer our main claim to fame. I know of at least three or four that are smaller, but for years we were the smallest. When we were first bonded we were producing about 400 gallons a year, and we bonded because we wanted to make more than 200 gallons legally. We just discovered we had a lot more than we could drink in a year. Now we're producing around 1,500 gallons a year, and this is our maximum. It's all the building will hold, and also it's all the time we have to work on it.

How did you become such an enthusiastic home winemaker in the first place?

When we moved to California, we had scarcely tasted wine and that was all we knew about it. We drank an occasional beer and had a very, very occasional highball. We just weren't interested in drinking. The first day I was in California, one of the fellows at the office took me out to lunch, ordered a bottle of wine, and poured some for me. I said, "Oh, I'm sorry I don't drink." He said, "You're a Californian now, you'll drink wine!" It happened to be a Charles Krug Grey Riesling, by the way. I drank it, liked it, bought a bottle for my wife the next night and we decided wine was all right. Years later, a friend here in Woodside who owned half an acre of grapes invited us to help make wine. We thoroughly enjoyed the experience. At that time I was playing a lot of tennis, on a court on the far side of this property, and a road cut through where the winery is now. There was also an old vineyard of Zinfandel, a little Petite Sirah and some Alicante Bouschet, and grapes hung heavy on the vines. The place was for sale, so we contacted the owner, who said, "Sure, pick them." So I took a day off work, and several of us picked as many grapes as we could that day and made our first wine. That was 1960. We bought the property in '61. The following year we built the house and the winery. The whole orientation of our house relates to the winery. We picked the best spot to have the winery underground, and then the landscape architect oriented the house to the winery, to the vineyard, and so forth. So this is how we started, as a hobby, just something fun to do.

Where are we geographically, and what climatic conditions prevail here?

Woodside is 30 miles south of San Francisco in a small valley, about 400 feet in elevation. A small ridge separates us from Redwood City, creating a distinct climatic difference. For example, we get another 15 to 20 percent more rainfall each year. We average 38 inches a year. Right on the top of the ridge they get another 20 percent more rain than we do. That ridge is 2,000 feet high, 13 miles from the ocean. This puts us in a climatic zone that Dr. Winkler defined many years ago as a Region I. We seem to be in a high Region I, almost out of Region I on the cold side.

And yet you're at such a low elevation.

This ridge of mountains seems to make the difference. Now Ridge Vineyards, Martin Ray, David Bruce—Dave is actually on the other side—they pick up an extra hour of sunshine each day, and that would be enough to make the difference. We find the only grapes we can guarantee to ripen here are Chardonnay and Pinot Noir—they're the earliest producers. Cabernet Sauvignon has been planted here for years and normally it will ripen, but we've had cold years when it is marginal. Chenin Blanc is a disaster in this area, it just doesn't belong here and we've never had it ripen. In fact, we're grafting all our Chenin Blanc vines to Chardonnay. Our Cabernet in a good year will develop a nice 22 or 23 sugar, never as high as 24. In a bad year, we're lucky to get 21, though we'll settle for 21 any time we can get it. But that isn't what you want for a big wine, so when you taste our wine I think you'll find it is a little lighter bodied than most good big Cabs on the market today. So this is our style, we'll make a light Cab, and not worry about it. Ridge and some of the others make the really big wines, and we'll just take a different approach to it.

What about the soil here? You've attributed most of the special characteristics to the climate. Do you think the soil is an important factor?

Knowledgeable wine people tell us they could pick a bottle of our wine if they were drinking it in Miami or New York City, because they can taste the Woodside soil. It is basically adobe. From the standpoint of workability, it's just about the lousiest soil you can have. Yet almost anything seems to grow in adobe, it retains moisture, and we feel it imparts a definite character to the wine, an earthy, clay-like character. With better soil we would probably get a little better production and run closer to the norm of the Napa Valley.

Are all your vineyards located right here around your home?

No, we get grapes from eight different vineyards in Woodside. The largest is two acres, the smallest belongs to our pastor emeritus at the church who lives on the site of the old Rixford home. Pat told us he had always wanted grapes on his property, so we planted 156 Cabernet Sauvignon vines. We also use all the Cabernet still growing on the old vines of the La Questa property, plus an acre of new vines we planted there. All our Cabernet comes from there.

La Questa got its name because it was on the little crest of the hill that runs between Woodside and Redwood City, and there must have been 30 acres of Cab grapes planted on that hill prior to Prohibition. La Questa was a very successful winery in that era, owned by the Rixford family since 1883, and of course shut down during Prohibition. Emmett Rixford died or was too old to do anything with the winery when Prohibition was over, so his two sons tried to start it up on a part-time basis, but my information is they never really made good wine. When they quit, the property was subdivided. Happily, four families kept a quarter to a half an acre each on their properties, and one at a time we have acquired the use of the grapes from those parcels.

The original arrangement was that everyone would take care of his own grapes on these and the other vineyards. We would pick them in the fall, bring them over here to make the wine. Over a period of time, properties have been sold and in every case the new owners were delighted to let us harvest the grapes, but wanted nothing to do with caring for them. So now we have the responsibility for every vineyard but two, and even on those we do much of the work.

How far apart are your vines planted?

They're all planted to the old standard of eight by eight. The vineyards are quite demanding. We cultivate in the spring, sulphur dust in summer, irrigate the young vines the first two years, train them out on wires the second or third year, prune in the winter. Then there is the chore of netting all the vineyards in August to protect against birds. We bunch thin the Chenin Blanc because it doesn't ripen, to see if we can get the sugar up a bit, but the Chardonnay and Pinot Noir are fairly sparse producers so we don't thin them and there is no problem getting the sugar we need. The Cabernet vines are all older and their production is falling off, so in effect they thin themselves. The Rixford vineyard of Cabernet was originally planted in 1883, but I have trouble believing those vines are 90 years old. The oldest natives we can find here though, cannot remember the vines being planted, or being very young vines, so we put the planting date sometime ahead of 1920.

How do you pick grapes at harvest?

We use shears, and it's all done by friends. Typically we'll have a crew of 20 or 30 people on Saturday or Sunday morning, and around noon we load the grapes on a truck and bring them back to the winery. We stop and have lunch; Polly puts on a pretty fine spread. People come because they know it's fun and they're going to get good food and sippings from last year's harvest. In the afternoon we crush and the wine starts fermenting that evening.

Do you consider yourself a traditional winemaker, one who uses older techniques?

Well, I suspect I'm going to say much the same as the other winemakers say, but maybe we mean it a little more than they do since we don't have a commercial responsibility. If we don't sell a bottle of wine next year we won't go out of business, since I don't rely on this for a living; in fact it's a financial liability to us. So we're in a position to consider it a complete art. While I don't even begin to contend we make the finest wine in the state, we think it is unique because we really do the absolute minimum to it.

When you started making wine, what kind of training did you give yourself?

The bulk of our training was trial and error, and we've made about every mistake there is. We had a knowledgeable friend connected with a winery who worked with us the first few years, and then, early in the game, I took a one week course at Davis, and have taken a couple more since. We've also had a good deal of advice from Dr. Julius Fessler, who used to own the Berkeley yeast lab. Now his business is dealing in wine supplies for small operations. We used to bring Julius down on a consulting basis.

Also, you learn a lot in discussions with other winemakers. It's always amazed me that people like Bob or Mike Mondavi, Justin Meyer from Franciscan Vineyards, and others tell you anything you want to know. There are no secrets. If we have a problem, we could take samples up to the big wineries and they'd tell us how they read it and what to do with it. Technically, I'm probably the least proficient winemaker in the state, and I have to rely on other people for advice.

Nevertheless, some wine writers have compared your wines to some of the best in California.

Well, I honestly think it's our strict adherence to letting the wines make themselves. It makes a wine that's different, and I think when you taste them you'll say you've never tasted any exactly like them. In many cases, people compare them more with European wines than Californian.

Well, how does your notion of "letting the wine make itself" translate into operations in the winery?

To begin with, we have an old hand crusher we inherited from an Italian family who owned one of the Cabernet vineyards; it handles one box of grapes at a time. It's just a crusher, and the stems are taken off in the next step when the crushed grapes drop down into the winery where we have a big box sitting across the top of the 300 gallon vat. The box has one-inch holes in the bottom, an inch apart; four or five people stand around it and rub their hands over it like a scrub board and the grapes and juice fall through, but the stems are too big and remain. It was invented for us by a friend who is an airline pilot. We do it for the fun of it, as much as anything. But I think it also means our grapes get a gentler treatment than those put through a stemmer-crusher.

Do you inoculate with yeast, rather than relying on the natural wine yeast on the grapes to start fermentation?

I do inoculate, though I'm confident some of our batches have started themselves. Few people actually rely on natural yeast, and I haven't experimented with that.

What kind of a press do you have?

We have a quarter ton basket press, a half ton basket press, and a two and a half ton basket press. All hand operated, but the largest one is also hydraulic. We get a very light pressing from all of them. I guess we throw quite a few gallons of juice into the vineyard when we're done and put the skins out there. We ferment in wood and plastic. We pump the whites from the press into a 400 gallon plastic tank. We chill the whites to about 60 degrees by a little stainless steel coil dropped into the wine, and it takes about two weeks to complete fermentation. All of the reds are fermented in 200 and 300 gallon redwood tanks. We punch down the cap about three or four times a day, and fermentation is finished in five to seven days.

Any fining or filtration?

No, we don't own a filter. We used to fine some of the wines but could detect no improvement so we stopped. We're fortunate, our wine falls quite clear, and we get very little sediment in the finished wine. We sometimes get tartrate settlements because we don't cold stabilize, other than letting cool air run through the winery at night.

Do they go through a malo-lactic fermentation?

No, definitely not on the whites, and any on the reds has been accidental. We don't encourage it as Ridge and some of the other wineries do.

How long are the various wines aged?

We give our reds two years in the barrel and two years in the bottle. Originally we had them three years in barrels and one in the bottle, but we had a problem with too great acidity, and found they smoothed out faster with more bottle aging. All the barrels are American oak.

How often do you rack them?

Three times the first year, and maybe twice the second year. The Chardonnay is a year in the barrel and a year in bottle. The Chenin Blanc gets about six months in wood before bottling.

You've stuck to three of the four "noble varietals" so far. Have you had any thought of making other varietals?

No, I really think even four varieties are too much for a winery as small as ours, and as I mentioned we're grafting the Chenin Blanc over to Chardonnay now. If I had it to do over again, I might go to just Chardonnay and Pinot Noir. But we've built our reputation on Cabernet Sauvignon. We must be doing something right with our Pinot Noir, too, which is just coming into production.

Why have you been successful with Pinot Noir, when so few in California have been?

Well, my personal opinion of our Pinot Noir had not been so high, except for some critical acclaim from a few people I respect. But a couple of people told me when people drink a California Pinot Noir they're looking for something that compares with a great Burgundy. The great Burgundies are not necessarily only Pinot Noir. Besides, their soil and climate are slightly different. So the wines are hard to compare. But I have had our wine compared to certain Burgundies. Then too, it's a more sensitive grape than others, and it's hard to get good color from it. Maybe it's such a delicate grape that it needs minimum treatment to draw the best out of it.

You don't make any generic wines, but what is your view of California generic wines named after European geographical areas?

Oh, I think it's a mistake, but it's an accident of history. Maybe it'd be possible to phase it out, prohibit it after a certain date in the future. The American wine industry is on its feet now so we can use our own names.

Let's build a reputation of our own. The average wine drinker says, "Oh, I just love Chablis." What's that mean? In America it's the complete spectrum of cheap white wines, so they really haven't learned to love anything. How much better if they said, "I sure love Santa Clara Valley whites better than Napa Valley whites," or vice versa. I think we owe it to ourselves to eventually get around to our own regional terminology.

Will the best future wines in California come from small wineries?

That goes without saying. The larger you get the more processes you must use to be competitive. They can make technically fine wines for the price, but for the quality you and I and a small percentage of the wine consumers are looking for you have to come to a small winery.

My last question for you is, do you believe the best California wines are as good as the best European wines?

We recently took our first European trip and visited some of the finest wineries in Bordeaux and Burgundy, and a few in Germany. Their very best wines probably exceed all but one or two outstanding California wines. Why not? They've had 400 or so years of practice! But our fine wines—Ridge, Mondavi, Heitz and dozens of smaller operations—match or exceed the average production of even those finest vignerons. On average, it's darned near a toss-up, as some significant comparative tastings have recently shown.

David Bruce

DAVID BRUCE WINERY

California is making some superlative wines now, but it's like a newly wed husband, he's sort of groping, he's really not sure what he's up to, but he's learning fast.

Dr. David Bruce is one of the new winemakers of the 1960s who began making wine as an amateur. An individualist pursuing his own vision, he has rapidly become known for producing wines of surprising strength and character in unorthodox styles. On the way up Bear Creek Road to his winery at 2,000 feet, I passed Christmas tree farms and thick woods with an Alpine air. Bruce's vineyards start almost at road's edge and nestle in a bowl on the side of steep hills. The winery is a plain, unpretentious structure beside the vineyards. Bruce's home sits on a hill immediately above. Just before I arrived, a pump broke on the well supplying water to the winery and house, and Bruce was engaged in a several hour emergency repair job. Our conversation was recorded as we hiked back and forth through the vineyard between a tool shed and the well site—a striking illustration that winemaking is not all romance.

Recommended wine to drink while reading this chapter:

DAVID BRUCE
PINOT NOIR

You got your start as a home winemaker, didn't you?

That's right. I made 11 gallons of Concord in 1959, came back to California and made 200 gallons of wine. I still have some of those early wines—some were damn good wines. And then I set up my office—I'm a dermatologist.

Do you still have a medical practice in San Jose?

Oh yes, I continue on in that endeavor. I enjoy it very much. I probably will continue, unless this liability insurance gives me a lot of problems. It's nice to be able to go in a couple of directions if you really are pushed hard enough I suppose.

How much time are you able to spend at the winery?

About half and half. I try to preserve Sundays for myself but that really doesn't work. I used to work every day. I try to work three days at the office, three days here and then get Sunday off.

Is this your own operation, do you have partners?

It's my own. I have two full time workers; one works in the vineyard and another works in the winery. That's really all I have as far as help.

About how many cases a year are you putting out?

About 5,000 cases.

Do you think of your wines as having their own style, or character, different from other California wines?

Well, to a degree. I handle them less than other wineries, and I think this brings out some of the flavors more. In other words, by handling wines a great deal—fining, filtering, racking—the more you do of that the less flavor there is because they get more aeration. The more you use various chemicals—large sulphur dioxide—the more this influences the flavor. The less I tamper, the more flavor.

More flavor and what else? Bigger? More body?

That goes without saying, because aeration knocks down the body. That's part and parcel of the same thing, you see. You get certain grapes in from the field and they have a certain quality. You can't make better quality wine, but everything you do in the winery reduces the potential quality. So you handle it as little as possible.

Do you think of yourself as a "traditionalist?"

Well, I like to think I can be innovative. Nobody else hangs the barrels on the walls. I also made the first Zinfandel white in California. When I made that late harvest Zinfandel in '69 I wasn't aware that anybody else had done it, though later I discovered Mayacamas and Ridge had. I guess you'd have to call me somewhat innovative.

Where are we geographically? About 15 miles from the ocean and 2,000 feet high?

That's about right; 2,000 feet elevation, in the Santa Cruz Mountains several miles beyond Los Gatos. And we're facing south to southwest. It's a natural amphitheatre looking down on the San Lorenzo Valley.

What about the climate, is this classified Region I by Professors Amerine and Winkler?

I think it's probably what you'd call a middle Region I.

How much rainfall?

Well, between 40 and 80 inches a year.

That's quite a lot, isn't it?

Yeah, it's a lot all right.

Are there micro-climate factors you think make a difference here?

The Santa Cruz mountains are loaded with micro-climates. I think the amphitheatre effect here conserves much of the heat lost in other areas. We look down on Monterey Bay, they are under loads of fog all the time but we rarely get that. This year's an exception. We've had lots of fog this year, that's why I was worried about maturing this year. If we have a late fall we'll be okay though.

Do all of your grapes come from these vineyards?

No, I have four here: Pinot Noir, Chardonnay, Cabernet Sauvignon and a little White Riesling, 25 acres all told. I buy Zinfandel from other sources, mainly the Santa Cruz mountains. I also purchase Petite Sirah, Grenache and others when I can get good grapes.

Carignane?

Yes, I made the Carignane in 1970. But I only have those four types right here.

What percentage of your wines come from these vineyards?

I would say about five-sevenths, by last year; maybe 12,000 gallons.

What kind of soil do you have here?

It's called a Hugo Loam—a very fine, sandy loam with an underbase of sandstone. There were areas when I came which were absolutely bald sandstone. I ripped it up and planted it and you can see how lively those vines are. I decided the important factor is the presence or absence of water. In the area up there, they don't get enough water and they must struggle, but on this side, they grow tremendously vigorously. And they're all planted on their own roots.

Do you think your vineyard soil has special characteristics that others don't?

No, I've always wondered if heat isn't a more important factor than actual soil types. I'm not inclined to think soil types are as important as many people think. Maynard Amerine commented that around the world he felt maybe there were a couple of areas where he couldn't explain the wine other than on soil type. I was trying to think where that might be. Cognac? Perhaps. But heat is certainly a tremendously important factor.

Do you think it would be a good thing for California to have some sort of an appellation control system?

That would be marvelous, but it never would be possible. In the California wine industry there are vast holdings by just a few people and all this goes into a big melting pot. How can you really know what the quality of wines in those areas could possibly be? The San Joaquin Valley areas, and what have you. However, in small vineyards where you have a lot of people doing their own thing the way they want for love of the art of winemaking, then it's possible to find what the qualities actually are. But it would be hard for me to comprehend how we can get an *honest* appellation control in this country with the exception of some of the coastal areas. There's not enough involvement of the little fellows.

On the vineyards you own here, have you certain practices with respect to distance between vines, how you prune and so forth?

I've planted them from 9 to 12 feet apart just to see what would happen. I'm very particular how they are pruned, especially cropping practices—we've just gone through and spent a couple weeks bunch thinning the entire vineyard. That is immensely important.

Are you able to control those practices in the vineyards from which you buy grapes?

Not nearly as much as I'd like. You can say, "Well, I want grapes from that vineyard," and sometimes you can get those. And you can see how they've been controlled.

Do you buy regularly from certain people?

This varies from year to year. A few years ago it was very hard to buy decent grapes, now it's getting easier. I bought very good grapes from the Santa Cruz Mountains. They are no longer available so I've gone to other sources. I'm still very pleased with what I've gotten from them. My '72 Zinfandel comes from Amador County and I've made some wines from Lodi which are certainly better than I would have expected.

Are any of your grapes mechanically harvested?

No.

How do you pick the grapes here in your own vineyard? Do you have any special practices?

No, except that the *time* of picking is extremely important.

Do you use grape hooks?

No, we use scissors, pruning shears.

Would you buy mechanically picked grapes, or do you think there's a problem with them? At the last American Society of Enologists conference there were five relevant papers submitted and they showed mixed findings, they went all ways on it.

I don't think I would like them as well. One problem is that they pick all the grapes, regardless of maturity. We pick from the standpoint of maturity.

Do mean you select bunches?

Yes. Last year, we went over the Pinot Noir three or four times.

Do you take selected berries within the bunch?

No, that would be *quite* a problem. We don't go to that extent.

Which varieties interest you most?

I'm a Burgundy man, and I'm of the impression the greatest wines ever produced are Pinot Noir, and Chardonnay a close second. So I find Pinot Noir an exciting challenge. Unfortunately, in the past decade Pinot Noir has lost any snob appeal it ever had in California and now it's in the position where Zinfandel was ten years ago.

I remember in 1964 there was only one problem with Zinfandel, it had no snob appeal; you couldn't sell it for anything, though it was good quality wine. Now we have the same problem with Pinot Noir and we are making some superb Pinot Noirs. I think that Mt. Eden '72 was lovely, Sterling '71 was very nice, beautiful, and certainly some of Martin Ray's old wines—his '53, his '54—were superb wines.

Why is it more difficult to make great Pinot Noir than great Cabernet?

Pinot Noir is very difficult to stabilize bacteriologically. The wines do not finish off their malo-lactic fermentation easily. The organisms which are satisfied to stop at a certain acid level with other wines just keep merrily on their way munching more and more of the acid. They don't know when to stop, you see. I was recently in New York, sitting across from a fellow named Bill Massee, co-author of *Wines of France* with Alexis Lichine, and he just happened to make a comment which was vital to me—something I'm deeply concerned with and interested in. He said the Burgundians are having conferences now on how to make a complete malo-lactic fermentation. This is precisely our problem with Pinot Noir. And here they've been at it for centuries and are having the same problem! Cropping is also tremendously important: overcropping, undercropping. To make a decent Pinot Noir you need an essentially undercropped situation, where everything that that vine does goes into those grapes.

You make a number of varietals that not many others do.

Yes, such as the Carignane, the Grenache made into red Grenache, that sort of thing?

Right. Are they all 100 percent varietals, by the way?

Yeah, 100 percent.

Are they just experiments, will they make great wines? How do you rank them with your Pinot Noir and Cabernets?

One of the most exciting wines I've ever produced is the Grenache '71. Seventy was bigger, but the '71 made a delightful wine with an immense amount of fruit, and from my past experience with Grenache that fruit is going to hang on for a long time. It's big bodied wine, that sits on the tongue, not with that velvety quality you expect of a Pinot Noir, but with a robust quality. Perhaps that's why Grenache is used more in the Rhône. Incidentally, I have tasted a Rhône with no indication of varietal content but it had to be close to 100 percent Grenache. They do that in Rhône, and it's the only wine close to my '71 Grenache.

I'd like to ask you about the steps of winemaking, starting with crushing and stemming. What kind of a crusher-stemmer do you use?

It's a homemade job, does a good job, actually. It's a stemmer-crusher. I don't stem white wines—I crush them gently, then let them sit on the skins for more flavor. With the reds I usually crush and stem and get rid of most of the stems. Some wines, such as Zinfandel, achieve a better balance if you leave in half your stems. You get a little more tannin which it needs, particularly when you're making big wines.

What kind of a press do you use?

A small batch press. Holds a ton at a time and it runs at three different programs, very nice. It has the patience I don't have, and runs at a quick, medium or a slow speed if I want to press out something like Chardonnay.

Do you make any wines wholly from the free run juice?

Well, you're talking about reds, it's ridiculous to do that with whites, because the flavor's in the skins. If you use the free run juice with whites you get a wine without much flavor. The fermentation process in red wines removes most of the flavor in the skins. Then the free run would have all the flavor without the heavy press tannin effect. But my pressing is not that heavy. So what one person calls free run and what another person calls free run may be two different things. You have some of these continuous presses that really get 180 gallons per ton. Now that has some of the real press in there! For sure. Whereas, with these small batch presses we get 150, 160 gallons at the most.

How do you ferment the whites?

In stainless steel, then I put it into oak—in the case of Chardonnay, new French oak.

Do you temperature control it?

I usually keep it at 60 to 65 degrees.

Some vintners ferment whites lower than that, don't they?

Oh, I've heard of stories of some fermenting in the 40s, to just see how much fruit they can retain. I'm not sure there's much advantage to that. I've never—well, it's very difficult to do that unless you've got expensive equipment. I don't think there's that much value in fermenting that cool. You probably preserve a lot of things you'd like to be rid of, tannin and stuff of this sort, which might drop out during fermentation were it just a little warmer.

What about your reds, also fermented in stainless steel?

Yes, and around 80 to 85 degrees.

Do you always begin fermentation by inoculation with a yeast culture?

Not always, but usually. I've done experiments using natural inoculum on the bloom of the grapes, but it's easier and safer to do the other. I ruined one batch of Pinot Noir that way.

What kind of fining and filtration do you do?

I don't ordinarily do that. Basically, I give my wines, both reds and whites, a light filtration at bottling and that's all.

You do that only for clarity in the bottle?

Yes, I've had problems clarifying my Chardonnays, because they don't clarify readily when they undergo malo-lactic fermentation. Fining doesn't touch them. I've tried fining with bentonite and it doesn't do a thing for them. Unfortunately, the organisms are smaller than the size filter I like to use, so I'm resorting to other methods. A millipore filter takes them out but I refuse to strip the wine that badly.

How long do your various varietals spend in wood?

The whites are in wood as long as a year, in a few cases longer. The reds are generally in two years. The Chardonnay goes into new Limousin oak, the Pinot Noir into used Limousin, and the Cabernet generally is aged in Nevers oak. For the Zinfandel, I've used a mixture of things, including American white oak and Portuguese brandy barrels which I like very much.

Tell me about your innovation of barrel storage. Why do you put them on the wall?

So you can get to each barrel at any time. You go around topping them all the time. If you have a stack of barrels on the floor and you want to rack off the wine on the bottom row, you have to pull down the whole stack. Whereas I can get to any barrel I wish.

How often do you rack your big red wines?

I don't rack too often, I try to keep it down—two or three times a year.

When you rack you wash it out with hot water?

Generally, I soda ash. It's a nice cleansing agent. Rinse it out and put your wines back in. This removes all the sediment, if it's properly drained. Many larger wineries have racks and they go along with a siphon affair which siphons the wine. Then they come through with another affair which swishes water around and siphons that out, but you know very well they're probably leaving half a gallon of water in the bottom. And they do it at a specified frequency during the year—it has nothing to do with the quality or state of the wines as far as I can tell. They repeat this process four or five times a year, so you know they're adding probably two gallons of water each year to fifty gallon barrels. Now that's not exactly what I'm interested in, diluting down my wines with water.

Do you think the best California wines will come from small wineries, or does size have nothing to do with it?

They'll come from small wineries. It takes a fair amount of control to make fine wine. You have to control the yield, pick the grapes at the right time, do everything right. How can you do this with vast quantities of grapes? The most difficult thing for a large winery would be to get vast quantities of really high quality grapes. That makes it almost impossible for a really big winery to make first rate wines.

In your judgment, are the best California wines equal to the best European wines?

Well, you must remember that California hasn't been at it as long. I think that California is making some really superlative wines now, but it's like a newly wed husband, he's sort of groping you know, he's really not sure what he's up to but I think he's learning fast.

Paul Draper
RIDGE VINEYARDS

It was an intriguing idea to be able to take something from the earth and make of it as sophisticated and complex a thing as fine wine.

Paul Draper is affable, garrulous, and as down-to-earth as a ranch hand, yet probably has the most intellectual approach to winemaking in the state. He is a serious student of traditional winemaking techniques, and few wines in California are made with greater reliance on natural, rather than manmade, processes. The result is the distinctive Ridge style, famous among legions of Ridge adherents: huge wines, rich in nuances of variety and geography, at once intense and subtle. The nuances of geography are especially interesting. Ridge has led the way in exploring differences in wines made from the same grape variety grown in different vineyards, and regularly searches all over northern California for individual vineyards of promising grapes. Ridge has also led the way in sharing vineyard and other information with consumers on its labels.

My interview with Draper took most of a day, with interludes while Paul discussed a lab report with his inhouse chemist, conferred with his partner Dave Bennion on the number of cases that could be promised to a buyer who wanted too many, helped a home winemaker friend load some used Ridge barrels onto his truck, and checked progress on renovation of an old wooden house Draper is moving into next to the winery. We ended our conversation over a leisurely lunch of bread, cheese, cold cuts and Ridge wines on the porch of the rustic farmhouse that serves as the winery's office.

Recommended wine to drink while reading this chapter:

RIDGE GEYSERVILLE
ZINFANDEL

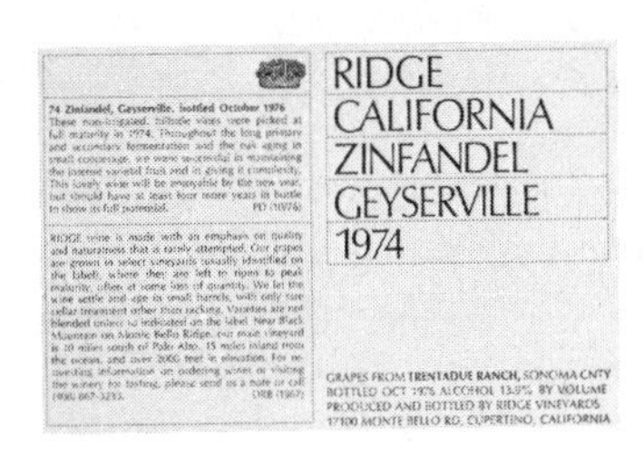

You once described yourself in a Wine World *magazine article as more of a traditionalist than many winemakers. What did you mean by that?*

Long before I was a winemaker, I was an intemperate lover of fine wine. I had been impressed by the richness and complexity of the few sound, pre-Prohibition California Cabernets I was fortunate to taste, as well as a number from the 1930s and 1940s that had been produced by what I call traditional techniques. I was also much impressed by fine Bordeaux, and most of them are still made by those same techniques, though some of the wines are not as big as they used to be. But what really interests me is what these methods have produced over the last 100 years, and what I think can be done in the future.

I have singled out the traditional practices of Bordeaux because of all the wine regions there seem to have been more books on winemaking written in the last 100 years by oenologists in Bordeaux than any other area. These books contain very detailed descriptions of the methods and how they affect the quality of wine. I began to study those techniques. I do read French, and those books were available to me.

Is there nothing similar available in English?

No, not really. Those books lay out very carefully, in the words and descriptions of oenologists from different periods, what the practice was, step by step, just exactly what was done and why: how they physically racked a barrel, and why they were racking, right on down through all their techniques, from crushing on, what acidity they were getting, what they preferred and why, the kind of maturity they were getting, how long the wine was held on the skins, how it was fermented, whether it was punched down, pumped over, or whether a submerged cap was used, all of those things. There is no such information in English.

There is a book which was published about 1882 called *The Wine Press*, which is in fact a compilation of writings of many of the French oenologists and the practices of California winemakers of the day. It was compiled by the owner of La Questa Vineyards here in California, and though there is a lot of folklore in there, it does discuss detailed technique more than most wine books do. The available books in English discuss theory and general practice, particularly practice as applied in the larger wineries of California and not much of the day-to-day practice in a small fine winery.

In addition to reading the books, did you go to France to study the techniques?

I really became interested in winemaking when I was living in Europe. I had gone to school at Stanford and I had really begun to collect wines then, but the experience of four years in Europe swung it for me. After completing my degree, I worked in Europe, though not in the wine industry, for about four years, first in Italy and then in France. And, perhaps not by chance, it happened that a number of my friends both in northern Italy and in Bordeaux were in the wine business, and either owned negotiant firms or their own vineyards and wineries. I spent much of my free time, particularly during harvest, in these operations, still having no intention of becoming a winemaker. I never had done any home winemaking. But I had grown up in the country on a farm, and it was an intriguing idea to be able to take something from the earth, to carry it a step further through artisan ability, and make of it as sophisticated and complex a thing as fine wine—and to have that also be something that would give pleasure.

I came back briefly to this country, then traveled extensively abroad again, and in the process helped set up, with one of my best friends, a foundation in South America working in a number of areas, including agricultural development. Chile was the principal country involved. Our intent was to fund very limited programs we hoped would have high impact, and would fill in gaps where larger programs, such as Rockefeller and others, were not interconnecting. One of our principal efforts in this area was involved with high protein meal, and the introduction of and experimentation with a whole series of soy bean varieties the length and breadth of Chile.

Was this connected with the Peace Corps?

No, there was no connection with the Peace Corps, but we ended up using some of their fine people to carry on our program. What it meant was that within a year I had worked myself out of a job and we were looking at what we could do in Chile that would bring some benefit to that country, and would also be something we were interested in. We decided to go into the wine business, hoping we could increase the amount of wine exported, provide foreign exchange for Chile, and employment for ourselves. We leased a vineyard and winery in Chile; I flew back to California to spend a few months here in some of the smaller wineries whose wines I had admired, then returned to Chile and ran that operation as winemaker for roughly three years. We were producing Cabernet Sauvignon from mountain vineyards in the coast range—very similar actually to our situation here at Ridge—and using traditional techniques.

The economic situation in that country, however, necessitated our closing down the business, and the wines were sold off in bulk. I brought some back with me, and we had a rewarding experience when we were asked to provide some wines for a '67 St. Emilion/Pomerol tasting at which all the best wines, including Cheval Blanc and Petrus, were being tasted. We put in a bottle of our '67 and it came out first, blind, against five or six of the best of that area. So there were some pretty good wines to be made in Chile.

Now, during that time in Chile, I was able to get back to Bordeaux for one extended trip of three or four months and spent about a week apiece at each of my favorite châteaux. In 1969, I returned to California, joined Ridge and then became winemaker, succeeding Dave Bennion. Dave manages the vineyard and as president of Ridge carries the responsibility for the day-to-day operation of the business.

Who does own Ridge?

There are eight principal people involved now. It was started in 1959 by a group of four partners, all connected with Stanford Research Institute, and three of those partners are still principals—Dave Bennion, Hew Crane and Charlie Rosen. The other principals are Dick Foster, Carl Djerassi, Alex Zaffaroni, George Rosenkranz and myself.

There was an original winery on this site in the 19th century, wasn't there? Who owned that?

Yes, in fact on what is now Monte Bello Ridge there were, at one time, as many as ten wineries. This was the largest, to my knowledge, and was also the farthest up on the Ridge. A San Francisco doctor by the name of Osea Perrone built the winery in the late 1880s or early 1890s. He operated the winery until his death in 1912 from an accident in which his carriage went off the winding road here. His nephew, who had come from Italy in the meantime, carried it on up until Prohibition.

Can you locate us geographically?

Yes. We are on Monte Bello Ridge whose highest promontory is Black Mountain, which stands over 2,900 feet, and is in the Coast Range, about ten miles south of Palo Alto, and within sight of the Pacific 15 miles to the west. At this point, the Coast Range divides into two ridges, along one of which runs Skyline Highway; that's to our west, between ourselves and the ocean. Monte Bello Ridge is relatively short, running from the Stevens Creek Dam north beyond Page Mill Road, paralleling the Skyline Ridge, and in fact is higher at this point.

But only a few of your vineyards are up here, I know, because nearly all of your wines carry individual vineyard appellations and they indicate you seem to enjoy making wines from vineyards all over northern California.

My feeling is that the Europeans, at least with their finest wines, still have a situation where each vineyard produces wine made separately, so fine distinctions can be made in terms of soils, location, and climate. Here in California we generally lost our ability to closely distinguish what grapes of the same variety would do in different vineyards because the larger wineries that opened or reopened after Prohibition purchased their grapes from a broad area and typically put them together in the different varietals and generics they were making. It is difficult to say, the way a Bordelais could, that a St. Julien tends to have this character, whereas St. Estèphe tends to have that character, and the reasons given are the soils or the climate or whatever. So one reason we keep our vineyards separate is that the grapes themselves seem to have a different character when made into wine. And we thought that we would learn more about the different areas, and fine wine lovers would too.

Do the Regions I through V of professors Winkler and Amerine explain most of the differences?

I think those regions are extremely important, but they're loose definitions, of course, and you have to keep records yourself or they only give you a very general guideline. The problem is that within every area there are micro-climates and there's no way to lump together the Monte Bello Ridge or the Santa Cruz Mountains, for example, with the Santa Clara Valley, nor to lump together some of the hill vineyards above Napa Valley with the valley floor. You could go up on the top of Spring Mountain above St. Helena and be in a different region than you would be down in the valley. I tend to think that with the same varietal, as the climatic conditions become more nearly equal in two different areas, the soils have a greater importance than they otherwise would. We definitely do get a certain type of spiciness and certain flavors in the Zinfandels grown on Monte Bello Ridge that we do not get from Zinfandels grown in most other locations. We find a particular intensity of flavors from the Coast Range in Sonoma County that differs from other vineyards in the same climatic region but not in the Coast Range.

For example, up on the hills that separate Dry Creek Valley from Alexander Valley, such as the Lytton Springs vineyard or our Geyserville vineyard, the one is not as distinct from the other as both are from the Fiddletown vineyard in the Sierra foothills. But all of them are old vines. We prefer to get grapes from low production vineyards. We strive for that because it seems in practice that when you are making wines from grapes that have been grown with low tonnage per acre, you get an intensity of flavor and aroma you do not get from grapes produced in two or three or four times the volume, from a rich, fertile, valley location.

Let me pursue that theme. How can you have control over the vineyards which you do not own? How can you control overcropping and irrigation and other practices?

Well, of course, it's quite difficult. There are some growers who are interested in your striving for quality, and we attempt to pay premiums for high quality grapes. However, a grower is in business to grow grapes and sell them. There is a basic price per ton offered, which is affected by premiums for quality, but not as greatly as it should be. What it means is that a valley vineyard with deep, fertile soils and plenty of water to irrigate, is able to increase production.

There are many grapes of very high quality grown in some valley floor vineyards, but it's easier for us to turn to a man who has a vineyard in the hills, and therefore has, in general, poor, shallow soils, with little or no water for irrigation, and so has no choice. He has no way to increase his production even if he might like to; consequently, his grapes are going to be more of the type that we want. We will not have to worry so much about arranging with him not to irrigate as heavily, or arranging with him to try not to overcrop, because in those cases these people have little choice, at least on an ongoing basis. Of course, they can prune the vines so they overproduce one year, but then they will suffer the next, so that what he gains one year, he'll lose the next. It works out with the hill vineyards almost automatically.

About how many cases a year are you producing now, and what is your planned maximum?

For the last three years we have been producing between 16,000 and 18,000 cases a year. We have long planned to keep our maximum between 20,000 and 25,000 cases. And with the exception of a handful of cases of Chardonnay sold only at the winery, all that production is of red wine varieties.

Would you describe to me how you actually make your different wines, and how your "traditional" techniques come into play?

To begin with, traditionally in small operations the grapes are crushed gently, and even when a stemmer-crusher is used, as it is now used nearly universally, the grapes are fed into that machine by hand, pushed in from a hopper so that they fall in whole and undamaged. This is true at places like Latour, Lafite, Mouton, etc. A good stemmer-crusher is an implement carefully designed to avoid cutting stems, crushing seeds, or macerating the grapes while it destems them and breaks the skins. You may often see the use of helical screw conveyors to bring the grapes into the stemmer-crusher, and sometimes these can do damage to the grapes which the machine itself has been designed not to do. So that's one very small point where we would use the excessive care inherent in the traditional method.

When it comes to fermentation, though, you use stainless steel tanks and that's not traditional.

Yes, that's true. We have ten 2,000 gallon stainless steel fermenters, two 3,000s and two 1,000s. They're considerably better than wooden fermenters because during fermentation you're getting no aging, you're getting no effect from the wood—either from the air penetrating through the wood into the wine, or from the wood giving a flavor to the wine, and it's difficult to keep the wood from deteriorating during the rest of the year when the tanks are not in use. Stainless steel doesn't deteriorate and you can clean it with chemicals and be sure it's very clean. You cannot use those same chemicals on a wooden tank because it would soak into the wood and affect later wines. So there is no question in my mind, at least, that for fermentation, stainless steel is probably the best single advance that has been made.

Do you inoculate with a yeast strain to start fermentation?

That's something we do a little differently here at Ridge from most California wineries, but it may not be a very significant difference. Most of the Bordeaux châteaux and the fine Burgundy estates ferment on the natural wine yeast, and the natural sequence usually involves two yeasts, whereas with inoculation you use only one. Since 1969, we happen to have used the natural yeasts every year. Needless to say, we have a commercial strain on hand and if we could not get a fermenter started within, say, 12 hours, we would use a commercial yeast, though it hasn't yet been necessary. We have no proof that there is any difference in quality between the natural yeasts and a good commercial yeast, but since the natural yeasts are there and have worked as well or better for us, we prefer to use them.

Another difference at Ridge is an old European and Californian technique called submerged cap fermentation, which uses a grid to hold the grapes below the surface of the liquid. This allows us to minimize pumping over and to let the grapes macerate after they have fermented dry, without worrying about the cap acetifying. We then press our skins very lightly so that we can add back the first press entirely. The wine goes into a tank for malo-lactic fermentation, and we rely on the natural lactobacillus that is present in our winery to get that started. Only a few others do that. Most wineries here who want to get malo-lactic fermentation use the bacteria that's available commercially. The better wineries in Bordeaux and Burgundy, however, rely on the natural bacteria, and we prefer to do it that traditional way although, again, its effect on the quality of the wine is unproven.

Of course, most wineries do not want a malo-lactic fermentation because the majority of the grapes are not high enough in acidity to take the reduction it causes and still be well balanced. Only the finer producers who have suitable grapes actually seek it, and for most, their conscious seeking of it is fairly recent. So we're really talking about a fine wine technique. We get it in every one of our wines, including, when possible, in the tiny amount of Chardonnay we produce. Now that's unusual in California, but the fine white Burgundies—according to their makers and by analysis—have usually had the malo-lactic in any good year, and the great white Burgundies are made of Chardonnay. Burgundians seek it actively, because they consider that it adds a noticeable complexity and quality in the Chardonnay as well as in their Pinot Noirs, and, of course, it is equally sought after in Bordeaux.

Another thing that makes for big wines and is essential for us, is to hold the wines as long as possible on the skins. Our Zinfandels average 12 days on the skins; our Cabernets average probably 16 days and sometimes three weeks or more. In a warm, big year, you need less time on the skins than you do in a sound but cool year. We then press gently. We have two presses, one a Willmes, one a Howard.

Are those the pneumatic bladder type?

No, those pneumatic presses have their principal use with white grapes, where you really want that delicacy of pressing, although they work very well with red grapes, too. But ours are the piston type horizontal basket presses, and we control the pressure and consequently can keep pressing to a minimum. The quality we get is what you might call first press. We don't do a harder pressing because we don't use the filtration required to clarify those pressings. We therefore can add the press juice right back into the free run juice itself. In only one or two cases have we felt the press juice was not of sufficient quality to include. To us, and this holds true in Bordeaux as well, the high quality press is essential not only for pigments and tannin, but for the complexity it adds; it can contribute greatly to the richness of the wine.

And most of your wines are neither fined nor filtered, I understand.

Traditional Bordeaux practice, of 100 years ago, held that there was no need to use egg whites or some other fining agent if the wines were already stable and clear. We believe basically in that technique. We only use fining when there is a real reason, such as lack of clarity or cleanness on the palate or a potential for instability, and we experiment each time to determine the minimum fining needed to achieve the desired quality. The main advantage others see in fining every year is that there will be little or no sediment laid down in the bottle for the first five or six years. Today, the Bordelais fine every year whether they need it or not because they think it is more acceptable commercially to avoid that sediment.

As far as filtration is concerned, we are probably one of the only California wineries that does not filter its wines as a matter of course. In current practice you would give your wines a rough filtration or centrifuging soon after being made and then normally would go on to give them a polish filtration before bottling. Once again, we think if you can get clarity and stability in your red wines without filtration you tend to have a bigger, richer wine with more character, more nuance. We do have a limited capability to filter the wines and anytime we cannot get the clarity or stability we want, we have no compunction about turning to fining or filtration. But over 70 percent of our wines in any given year are not fined, and less than 10 percent have been filtered.

It certainly isn't the case that proper fining or filtration in any way lowers quality. Perhaps the real reason I avoid these very useful aids whenever possible is that in attempting to do without them I'm forced to take far better care of the wine than might otherwise be required. We top the barrels every ten days and rack every three to four months, using CO_2 to avoid oxidation. We constantly taste and analyze the wines for increases in volatile acidity, for amount of free SO_2, for the presence of various bacteria, and for developing off-odors and off-flavors. Some of the petty details we so assiduously pursue may eventually be shown to have no positive effect and in fact may be unnecessary risks. But what I'm seeking is complexity of character and I know no more proven way than to use the finest grapes, treat them gently, and make and age the wine with the care reserved for a living thing.

We get our malo-lactic fermentation immediately after the primary fermentation, so by December of the vintage when the gross dregs have settled out we rack the wines off those dregs directly into the barrels. There is a tendency in California not to put wine which is going to throw much sediment in a barrel, so most wineries centrifuge or rough filter them at this point. We attempt to take full advantage of the natural process. The Zinfandels spend approximately a year and a half to two years in oak, the Cabernets about two years on the average. During that time, we rack the wines off the sediment about seven or eight times, and wash the barrels, which is one reason many prefer to avoid it, but we believe that one of the advantages of careful aging is to get that natural settling.

What types of oak cooperage do you have?

Well, we began to look for alternative sources of fine oak when we saw the price of French oak increase, and then were informed by the principal Bordeaux supplier that he would not be able to provide oak of the quality he had in past years. One of my closest friends in Bordeaux had done his thesis on oak aging, and had depended greatly on a French study from around the turn of the century that had used the best oak available, which at the time came from Latvia, Germany, Yugoslavia, France, and the United States. These were long term studies, done by making two barrels of wine in each oak at six different châteaux. The very highest ratings came from the Baltic, that is, first from Riga in Latvia and second from Stettin, now in Poland, and third from Lübeck in Germany. And following those came the American oak, then the Yugoslavian oak, and last of all the French oak. And this was done by French oenologists in Bordeaux.

So we experimented with American oak, that is, *Quercus alba,* buying air dried staves from five different areas, and continuing to buy some of the best French oak for parallel experiments. For our Cabernet Sauvignon and Zinfandel, we've now narrowed it down to two areas in this country which we have liked best in blind tastings of the young wines. As of now, we principally have American 50 gallon oak barrels from these two areas. We'll continue to experiment as time goes on and see ultimately if we were right, or if we're kidding ourselves.

Ridge has produced a greater range of Zinfandels, and I should add, greater Zinfandels, than most wineries. In fact, you have helped give Zinfandel a status equal to Cabernet in the eyes of many. Why are you so interested in Zinfandel in particular?

We would be buying Cabernet grapes if 80 or even 30 years ago, a great deal of Cabernet Sauvignon had been planted throughout the cooler, low production areas of California, such as the hills in the central and north-coast counties. But it happens that they planted Zinfandel in those days, and there are Zinfandel grapes from older vines on the market, and wines made from those grapes can be very high quality. Much of the

Cabernet planted in recent years has been planted in more fertile, irrigated soils by growers who economically must seek a better yield than the two to two and a half tons per acre obtained at, for instance, Château Latour, and it is simply not as intense and rich in varietal character. So, we don't feel there are many Cabernet grapes on the open market that are of the quality of some of the Zinfandel available.

It's amusing that Zinfandel is not listed as a "premium" varietal. The wines made from the best Zinfandel are of higher quality in every way than most any Pinot Noir produced in California, which is considered to be a premium varietal! I'd go so far as to say the best Zinfandels produced in a given year are better wine than 80 percent of the Cabernet Sauvignons produced in California in the same year.

My last question is, do you think the best California wines are as good as the best European wines?

Especially since the comparative tasting in Paris, in which the French experts rated some California wines so high, this has become a somewhat delicate subject. My feeling has been that in Pinot Noir and White Riesling, with a very few notable exceptions, California does not come close to its European counterparts in complexity and overall quality. On the other hand, in Chenin Blanc, Petite Sirah, Cabernet Sauvignon, and Chardonnay it would seem that a number of California wineries have shown the potential for wines of at least equal complexity and quality. We do not grow the varieties of Italy, so there is no direct comparison, but in the more moderately priced wines California has shown it is more than the equal of Europe.

I don't think we should avoid comparing California wines with the European ones, but it is only instructive if the wines are of the same age and from a year of agreed excellent quality in both countries. For example, in Cabernet Sauvignon I believe the 1970s could be compared, and, with a number of exceptions, the 1971s. In general the 1972s in California and France suffered too much to make the comparison particularly interesting and later vintages must mature a bit before we will know.

For me, comparative tastings are especially useful and even necessary if the grapes are of the highest quality and if the wines are made with the degree of care and ability needed to produce a truly fine result. When those factors are comparable in the two wines, there is an absolute standard of quality being considered, and a fine St. Estèphe is not necessarily any more different from a Monte Bello or a Spring Mountain Cabernet than it is from a Graves.

Livermore Valley:

PATCH OF GRAVEL

Livermore, once a picturesque wine area, suffered from its close proximity to Oakland and San Francisco. Lacking steep terrain to discourage building, it became another victim of suburban sprawl in the '50s and '60s. Only the old Concannon and Wente wineries survive, viticultural islands in a sea of tract homes.

Even Wente has moved many of its vineyards to Monterey County. However, it is likely the two wineries will cling to their historic Livermore base, directly across the road from one another.

Their reasons are not all sentimental, either: they are reluctant to yield the unique patch of gravel under their vineyards, said to resemble that of Graves or certain sections of the Rhône Valley. And they are reluctant to forfeit the widespread belief that this gravel produces superior California white wines. That belief started in the 1880s when Charles Wetmore brought cuttings of Sémillon, Sauvignon Blanc and Muscadelle Bordelais from Château Yquem in Sauternes and planted them in Livermore. His Cresta Blanca Winery (a label now used by another winery) grew famous largely on the basis of these vines, and the varieties have been deservedly celebrated in Livermore ever since. But the *goût de terroir* claimed for Livermore wines is elusive at best. And the greatest Chardonnays and White Rieslings, for many of today's winetasters the noblest whites, do not grow in Livermore. For these reasons and because so few vineyards remain, Livermore is something of a step-child among California wine regions.

James Concannon

CONCANNON VINEYARD

The Archbishop suggested to my grandfather over a few dinners: "Jim, why don't you make wine, altar wine for the Church?"

Jim Concannon was warm and intense as he talked with me in his office near the winery, just a few feet from the old Concannon home. The winery is a small affair, where tourists gather around a tasting table set up directly next to the bottling line, and whose equipment is an ironic mix of very old and very new. The laboratory, where Jim has been known to sleep overnight on a cot while supervising a fermentation, is bright and modern. Jim and his brother Joe are the current heirs and operators of one of the few wineries in the country to be handed down from the 19th century through successive generations of the same family. Since its inception it has made wines for the Church. It survived Prohibition that way, and even today enjoys a significant altar wine business. Altar wines are usually sweet, so, not surprisingly, dessert wines are the keystone of the Concannon reputation, although the reputation also rests on moderate success with certain table wines, such as the Concannon Petite Sirah which was the first varietally labeled Petite Sirah in California, or the new, unusual Zinfandel Rosé.

Recommended wine to drink while reading this chapter:

CONCANNON
ZINFANDEL ROSÉ

Growing up in a winemaker's family, I imagine you started your oenological training even as a child.

That's right. My home we can see out the window here is the one I live in today, and it was built 93 years ago. As little fellows Joe and I were exposed to the profession we were going to go into, not knowing it at the time. From 10 or 12 we started being fairly seriously helpful, washing bottles and tanks, always the dirtiest jobs.

During my college years, I'd come home and work in our lab. Our winemaker, a German-Hungarian named Mrs. Vajda, was really my tutor. Talk about women's lib. She was the first woman admitted to the technical advisory committee of the Wine Institute. A very precise individual, she didn't let the boss's son get away with anything, but still had compassion and charity. So I learned from her. My college training was not in chemistry, but business administration and accounting at St. Mary's College—easier courses! I did attend Davis for short courses in oenology over many years. If my son and Joe's have the capability and interest, they should obtain the academic training plus the on-the-job experience. My son helped install the electrical wiring on the bottling line the other day. He was up until 11 o'clock, didn't even come in for dinner. The interest is there. Especially if they don't work with Dad—that'll come some day you know, but to get right with the other men who know what they're doing, they love that.

How long have the Concannons been here in the Livermore Valley?

My grandfather founded the winery in 1883. He was, of all things, an Irishman who immigrated, lived in Boston and Maine and came across the plains to settle in San Francisco. He had different jobs, thinking always of improving himself. He became quite friendly with Archbishop Alemany, the first Archbishop of San Francisco, and over a few dinners the bishop suggested, "Jim, why don't you make wine, altar wine for the Church?" That's how he got started. I think we're still the only Irish people in the wine business.

When grandfather passed away, my Dad, Captain Joe, took over. He wanted to stay in the service with General Pershing's elite First Cavalry unit, but he came back to carry on. Grandfather had ten children but they all either died or sold out to Dad, and he became sole owner. Since Dad passed away around ten years ago, Joe and I have carried on. Our two sisters also have equal shares in the business.

The Concannons survived Prohibition by making sacramental wines, right?

That's right. We're not the oldest winery in California but we've kept it in the family and continually produced wine since 1883, even during Prohibition. The Prohibition years were very difficult, but we sold wines to the Catholic Church, Lutherans, Episcopalians and others who used it in their services. And doctors prescribed wine for their patients, more prescriptions written then than ever! Dad ran cattle and sheep to keep bread on the table, but he kept his wine grapes—most people pulled their wine grapes and put in shipping grapes which they transported east to home winemakers.

You and your brother Joe divide responsibilities—Joe takes care of the vineyards and you make the wine?

That's correct. Joe is manager and takes care of viticulture. We have 250 acres around the winery. Through the '75 vintage we leased about 20 acres of Cabernet and Riesling at the Hallcrest Vineyards in the Santa Cruz mountains. And we're getting Zinfandel from the Sierra foothills of Amador County, a younger vineyard called St. Amant Vineyard. This is the vineyard from which we made our '74 Zinfandel Rosé that's receiving tremendous press. Most wine experts believe some of the finest Zinfandels in California are presently coming from Amador grapes.

What percentage of your wine comes from your own vineyards?

Probably 80 percent comes from our own 250 acres. We're a small operation; our target this year is 40 or 50 thousand cases. But we feel this is the way to go, we're interested in quality and in keeping the varietal character up in the wine.

What about the character of your wines, how do you think of your wine's style?

Coming from Livermore, they develop the fullness of the varietal character. Livermore soil is some of the most unique in the world. It's about 60 percent rock or gravel which goes down hundreds of feet. The Graves district in France is like this, and the Hermitage, and the Côte Rôtie where they grow Petite Sirah.

Vines are like humans, and when they have to struggle for themselves from the day they're born and they manage to survive in that rock, they produce a beautiful grape. So I think this is why our Sauvignon Blanc, Riesling, Sémillon and Petite Sirah are some of our better wines. Our red wines are lighter bodied than those from Napa but they have complexity to them. The whites have fruit and full bodiedness you might not find in other areas. They don't have as high acid as Monterey and the cooler areas. We are in a Region III.

Do you think soil makes the biggest difference in Livermore grapes, or climate?

Here it's the soil conditions. You know about the stones in Graves, and I hear that in Germany they pack slate up in particular hillsides and lay it around the vines for warmth and drainage. Andre Tchelistcheff emphasized the soil when he came down here. Incidentally, Andre is a great man, great man. I consider him probably one of the finest winemakers, like the late Herman Wente, the kind that comes along once in a light year. I have a reverence for the man, it's that bad. They ought to lock all of us winemakers in a room and let him lecture for an hour or so. We would learn a great deal.

Are your varietals 100 percent of the grape named on the label?

We have blended down to 75 or 80 percent, but in recent years we've shot for 100 percent, maybe one to three percent of something else got in there when we topped off. Petite Sirah has its own blend which we can't divulge. It has a little bit of something which makes it distinctive, and uniquely Concannon. We were the first ever to make a varietal labeled Petite Sirah. A retailer in southern California, Denny Caldwell, urged us to bottle Petite Sirah as a varietal. It was always used as a blending wine, very robust, nondistinctive and rough. But in Livermore, it makes a lighter wine, with a great deal of complexity.

We also have one experimental acre of a Russian grape, the Rkatsiteli, which Joe obtained from the University of California at Davis.

They brought the cuttings back from the Vavilov Institute in Leningrad. It has a taste all its own. It has a pinkish tint when harvested, but white juice and high acid. We have a way to go on it, but they say it's the finest variety in Russia. We'll see, and the public will be the judge.

You also have a reputation for your generic and dessert wines.

Many people feel our Chablis is one of our better wines, and tell us we ought to label it as a varietal. It's Chenin Blanc and French Colombard, a very dry, high-acid wine. We also make a Burgundy, a Rosé, Flor Sherry and the Muscat de Frontignan which is a dessert wine and one they use for altar wine. We have our Château Concannon which is a dessert wine of Sémillon and Sauvignon Blanc. Charles Wetmore brought those vines from cuttings of Château Yquem in the 19th century.

Do you get any botrytis on those grapes?

No, it's not cool enough here, but we're going to experiment with that.

What tonnage per acre do you get on your vineyards?

Around three to four tons, not any more than that. My brother Joe will have the men cluster thin in the springtime. This year we lost ten percent of the crop to sunburn during a hot spell. Before that time Joe had actually dropped every third bunch. Our grower in Amador County dropped about half his crop, even when grapes were in short supply. That's probably what made the '74 Zinfandel Rosé so great. I don't think it was our winemaking techniques.

Who does the picking?

We have about 12 Filipino men who have been with us anywhere from 5 to 30 years. They're mostly single men. They are very dependable, and they're pros, employed all year round. We've thought about mechanical harvesting. At first we couldn't justify it with our limited acreage. Since then we've heard mixed reports about the quality of the wines. Some say it's great, and some say they get leaves and a chlorophyll taste in the wines. Hand picking also avoids bunches that aren't particularly developed. With the mechanical harvester you take a good portion of those. The harvester has advantages; you can crush right in the field and cap with CO_2 so the grapes won't oxidize. If a contractor does it on piece work, you have to be careful they don't harvest the grape stakes or sprinkler heads. And I understand the yield isn't always what it should be, sometimes around 140 ton gallons when it should be 170. It gets a little sloppy.

So we will still pick by hand. We put the grapes into small plastic containers which drop into one ton bins. These motorized units are transported to the row ends. Here we pick them up and take four to six tons at a time to the crusher. They're generally crushed within two hours after they're picked.

And the gondolas are dumped into a crusher-stemmer?

Yes. And then we ferment in temperature controlled stainless steel. We just increased capacity by 140,000 gallons. Those fermenting tanks are insulated so we use them for storage at about 45 degrees and we can cold stabilize in them. We have to cold stabilize to get out the excess tartrates. The public does not want a bunch of foreign material in their wines. I don't like to process any more than I have to, so we can leave the wine in the tanks and refrigerate them right in place at 25 degrees for about three weeks. We have a mixing unit from West Germany which moves the wine in the tank to get a uniform temperature. This avoids the pumping and possible aeration of the wine. It's a big breakthrough.

Do you always start fermentation by inoculation with yeast?

Yes, we use either the Montrachet or Champagne type yeasts.

Do you make any wines wholly from the free run juice?

We do. We follow the old Bordeaux method of keeping separate the free run and the press juice. If the press is of good character we'll blend it back in or else ferment it separately. In some cases it's not good enough for the free run, so we sell the wine in bulk.

Do you have to adjust acid on the Livermore Valley grapes?

At times we do; we use tartaric acid, the acid naturally in grapes. We don't use citric acid, and we do it right at fermentation. You can't add sugar or water to California wines. It's a natural product, and we try to keep it that way.

Do the red wines go through the malo-lactic fermentation?

They do, we monitor it very closely in our lab with proper chromatography.

When do you use the centrifuge?

This is our first year. I suspect we'll centrifuge the whites right after they're finished fermenting, the reds after the malo-lactic. We won't filter them, the centrifuge will replace filtration except right before bottling. The centrifuge takes less character out of the wine than the diatomaceous earth filtration.

Will you fine also?

We'll probably continue to fine the white wines with bentonite. The reds are unfined. Then, before bottling, we'll filter all the wines using millipore filter on the whites.

You centrifuge and fine but eliminate one of the filtrations. Some winemakers do more than that, some less. Do you worry that these procedures may take character out of the wine?

I'm in the middle on that. But you know you're talking about a lot of dollars and you have a responsibility, you know the bank talks to you. And also you are obligated to give the consumer a good, stable bottle of wine that he can put down in his cellar for years. Filtrations themselves don't always take character out of wine, you may have slight color removal but that's all. I don't want bacteria or yeast in a bottle, and even centrifuging isn't that precise, you must have an absolute type of filter at the time of bottling. People who are making some of these unfiltered wines can get away with more—the wines are dark and you can't see the clouds. The other night I tasted such a Cabernet, and it was right to the legal limit of volatile acidity. If you don't have a healthy wine, the bacteria start working on it.

We believe in not handling wine any more than you must. And we don't add preservatives that affect the taste. Sulphur dioxide is the only thing we use, you have to have it in whites or they'll oxidize. We have about 130 parts per million total which is very low at the time of bottling. When you sniff it, you know if they have too much in the wine.

What kind of wood aging do you give your wines?

Our whites and rosés are young and fruity, no oak, no oxidation. They are stored in stainless steel. As Andre said to me: make the wine your own way, don't start putting a lot of oak in it, that's not what Concannon is known for. I feel very strongly about oak. On a recent tasting panel I criticized Cabernets so overpowered with oak you couldn't tell the varietal character! A lot of oak makes a more complex wine, but it can cover a multitude of sins. A little oak is fine in the reds, but that's all. Our reds spend some time in oak, but we have a minimum amount of barrels, to say the least, and it's older cooperage and therefore you don't have that distinct oak character coming through. I think we might lose three or four points in a tasting because of that. Tasters are affected by oak, and by color; if it has high color they call it a "big wine." God, it could be a press wine and they would like it. I think a wine has to have good varietal character to be classed as a good wine.

How long would the Petite Sirah spend in oak?

From two and a half to three years, but it's in cooperage ranging from 400 gallons to 1,200. We always age our Cabernet Sauvignon four years in wood and one in the bottle. It's always five years old and priced at eight or nine dollars a bottle, but we have no problem selling it each year.

Do you think the best wines come from small wineries?

I think you can reach a point, and I don't know what that point is, where winemaking gets out of hand. The smaller operator can produce a better wine particularly when he specializes. You can't mass produce a top quality wine. And another thing, of course we're partial: we believe the family winery does well because it's a very personal thing. If you are a big outfit with a constant turnover in personnel you can't have that involvement. They can hire great chemists, but the chemists may be poor winemakers. I think the family wineries who produce quality wine will survive. Most people said my Dad was a fool for staying in the wine business during Prohibition, but he stuck it out. Our business is holding well. We must make better wines—the competition is highly selective, but that's what life is about.

In your view, are the best California wines as good as the best European wines?

It's difficult to compare European wines with California wines. It's like comparing apples and oranges. The great Bordeauxs may be only 65 percent Cabernet Sauvignon and a blend of other varieties. Many California Cabernets are in many cases made almost entirely from that one grape. You thus come up with very different wines. The region and soils differ a great deal in the two countries and therefore you have different tasting wines. I do believe in very great years it's difficult to touch the Europeans in quality—the first growths, possibly every 10 or 11 years. These are very rare wines and command especially high prices, so most people in America can't afford them. In the price range of three to six dollars, which is what the average wine buyer is willing to spend, I believe the California wines are very much superior.

Karl Wente

WENTE BROTHERS WINERY

I think the use of oak is like the use of garlic in cooking. We're here to make wine that has the flavor of a grape, not a two-by-four.

Karl Wente, his voice resonant and imperturbable, speaks to me from behind his desk in the winery's business office. He has reason to be calm; he is the third generation head of an establishment whose renown was already great in the second generation, whose business has grown in his, and whose future is secure in the hands of the fourth generation sons now active in the winery.* The business office is plain, while next door a showcase tasting room is filled with tourists, and in back the winery building gleams with modern equipment. Wente wines have been available for years in restaurants and markets all over the country, and the winery is still growing. It is almost exclusively a white wine producer, and it has made secondary white varietals like Grey Riesling and Sémillon particularly popular. The Wentes were among the first to make botrytised Johannisberg Rieslings in California, and also among the first to plant vineyards in Monterey County, thereby earning a reputation for being at the forefront of new developments in the industry. It is a winery which undoubtedly has a future as well as a past, but it is hard to foresee whether that future will emphasize mere growth or greater wines.

---

*Tragically, Karl Wente died of a heart attack in 1977 at age 49.

Recommended wine to drink while reading this chapter:

WENTE BROTHERS
GEWURZTRAMINER

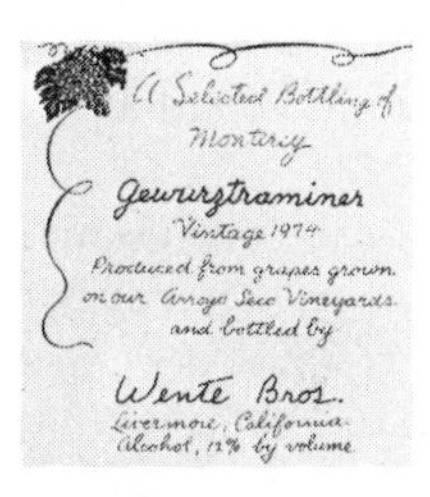

The Wentes have been in Livermore for several generations, haven't they?

About 92 years. My grandfather started here in 1883. He immigrated from Germany, spent some time up in Lake County, then worked in the Napa Valley for Charles Krug, and eventually settled here on 40 acres.

What attracted him to the Livermore Valley?

He was intrigued by the gravelly soil. He felt this was rather like the Bordeaux area, the soil much like Graves. He was basically right in terms of temperatures, too, though we're a little warmer. They're the middle of a Region II in Bordeaux and we're the top of Region II or just into III.

Was the Wente winery the first in Livermore?

No, Cresta Blanca was here in 1882, then ours and the Concannons came a year later. There were other wineries at one time, this valley was just covered with grapes. Prohibition spoiled that. The Concannons sold wine through the Church during that period, but we were the wrong denomination—Lutherans didn't use wine. So we shipped grapes, and we kept the winery alive by making sweet Sauternes for Georges de Latour at Beaulieu who had a very good relationship with the Catholic Church. This worked well for a few years, then it collapsed. We actually spent most of the 1920s and 30s raising cattle, sheep, pigs, barley and hay.

We started again from scratch with a little winery. We had retained the same land all this time, so we replanted vineyards. We now have about 800 acres of vines here in Livermore. In 1962 we planted vineyards in Monterey County. It's different from here. Just as grandfather found that this area was a little warmer than he thought, we found it a little cooler in Monterey than we expected. It's on the low end of a Region I.

In what part of Monterey did you plant your vineyards?

We're near Greenfield, on the Arroyo Seco Road. We have about 650 acres there, 550 in vines.

What percentage of the grapes you use are from your own vineyards?

About 75 percent. The rest comes from growers who have been growing for us for years here in Livermore, some newer ones in Monterey, and two growers up in Mendocino, who grow Grey Riesling and Chenin Blanc for us.

Have you come to any conclusions as to which grapes do best in Livermore and which in Monterey?

Sauvignon Blanc does better in Livermore, gives a fuller, richer wine. The Grey Riesling does better here too, softer and fuller, whereas it tends to be thin and sharp in Monterey. We have our Pinot Blanc principally in Monterey. The Johannisberg Riesling is best in Monterey, full of flower and blossom, where here it's rather flat and flabby. Pinot Noir does much better down there too, more color, more body. Petite Sirah grows better in Livermore, it's too big and harsh and too dark in color in Monterey. We're trying out Zinfandel and Cabernet down there too. In Monterey it makes a very heavy wine which takes a long time to age.

We think eventually we'll have a Merlot-Cabernet blend, with more Merlot than Cabernet because the Cabernet is just too strong. Chardonnay does quite well in both places, makes two different wines and we're going to have to rationalize this. Right now we're blending the two. The Livermore Chardonnay is much fuller, even has a more golden color; the Monterey one is much sharper, higher acid, fruitier, closer to a traditional Chablis.

You've mentioned some interesting differences between Livermore and Monterey. Are they almost wholly explained by the temperature differences?

Almost wholly explained by that. There's considerable soil difference, but in my opinion the temperature and the peaks of temperature explain it. Monterey is never as hot or cold as it is here.

What about differences in rainfall and soil?

We're short on rain in both areas. Monterey was never a big viticultural area because it only rains an average of six or seven inches a year. So we pump and sprinkle. We're next to the Arroyo Seco, which isn't that dry, and we've drilled a couple of wells to irrigate to 25 inches—what it takes to bring a vine crop through. Here in Livermore we get about 15 inches. We used to be able to dry farm here because we had an alluvial high water table and the vine roots would get down to ground water, but when urbanization became entrenched here the water table was pumped down, so we have to pump to compete. In Livermore, an alluvial fan has washed out of the arroyos in the mountains in back of us. There is a very old, hard rock here which has broken down into an uneven gravelly soil, with clay particles mixed in. It's tough to work. The soil in Monterey is more friable, though there is a lot of big rock and soft chalk rock on our Monterey ranch.

Is the gravel limey, here in Livermore?

No, not lime here, there's a much higher lime content where we are on the west side of Monterey. There are some areas of lime on the east side too, particularly up around Chalone Vineyards.

What kind of a yield per acre do you get in both areas?

We get an average of three tons an acre. Our 10 or 12 year old vines in Monterey produce a little more because we were very careful to plant all virus-free stock and also they're in the prime of their productive life. The soil is better down there for production, but the temperature would be better here for productivity. So we run a little less than four tons down there, and about three tons here.

Are you planted on flat land in both places?

Yes, but benchland in Monterey.

How far apart are your vines planted?

Typically, 8 by 12 feet apart.

What kind of pruning do you follow? Do you try to limit the yield?

Sure, that's the name of the game. Although we find that the virus-free vines produce much more, and we must modify our old pruning systems somewhat. In some cases, when we're first training the young vines we thin them—green-drop the crop. Both here and down there. A lot of green-dropping. Helps quality.

Who picks the grapes?

We harvest practically all of the Monterey grapes and about a third of those here with a machine. The hand crew that picks the rest is mostly related to people working here steadily.

Do the machines harvest the immature grapes along with the ripe ones?

On the contrary, its discretion is better than most hand pickers'. Have you ever tried to pick a green peach? You pretty nearly have to pull the tree down to get it off, whereas the ripe one just falls into your hand. The same thing happens when the machine vibrates the vines. Some people complain of too many leaves and other junk in the machine, but the cause of that is just a poor harvesting operation. We carry a third man. One man drives the tractor, another the harvester, and the third man is strictly for quality control. He sees that no "MOG"—material other than grape—goes into the crusher. We crush in the field, and ship to the winery in 900 gallon tanks. We have found that if we remove the stems immediately, crush them immediately, there is practically no oxidation. There is always a little oxidation with hand harvesting because you always get a little breakage, the juice is running around, giving an almost infinite interface of juice to air with berries in a tank. When we harvest down there, we'll have three of these machines and they'll each pick a tank in an hour or less, and we can count on having a truckload of crushed grapes moved out every two hours and driven right up here to the winery.

How much wine do you produce each year?

About 350,000 cases. We intend to continue expanding to some extent. For years we had more winery capacity than we had grapes, so we planted vineyards, and now we have more grapes than capacity in the winery. The American economy and tax structure make some growth almost mandatory. We try to keep a very slow growth rate, but it's just one of the facts of life.

What size staff do you have?

About 25 in the winery, 45 in the vineyards, and then a few people in the tasting room.

Is the Wente family itself still active inside the winery?

Oh, yes. After my grandfather passed away, my father, Ernest, who's retired, and my late uncle Herman carried on. I'm the only one in this generation, but I have two sons, Eric and Phillip, active in the winery. Eric graduated from Stanford in chemistry, then got his Master's in oenology at Davis, and he's acting as winemaker now. Phillip is principally working in the vineyards; he just graduated from Davis, in viticulture and agricultural economics. I went to Stanford, and graduated in microbiology.

Is your fermentation all in stainless steel?

All in stainless steel, temperature controlled. We'll ferment a typical dry white at about 55 degrees, and for something like our *spätlese* we'll ferment around 42 to 45 degrees. The reds, 75 degrees.

On the sweeter wines, how do you stop fermentation to leave some sugar?

We centrifuge the yeast out, then run it through a membrane filter to sterilize it.

Do you use a mutė *for sweetness sometimes?*

No.

Do you start fermentation by yeast inoculation?

Yes, on all the whites. We like to use a Geisenheim 1949 variety yeast on them. We have fiddled around by letting the reds run on the natural yeast, but we haven't noticed a heck of a lot of difference and you run a good risk of messing things up with wild yeast. It really isn't worth it.

Do you have to adjust acid often?

I don't like to. We seldom adjust acid on anything except a wine that is going to be a "bulk out." In other words, we sell at least 25 percent of our production in bulk, in tank cars. I don't approve of adjusting acid. You never make as good a wine as one with sufficient natural acid. Sometimes we have too much acid from the Monterey grapes while Livermore tends to produce low acid. So it helps to have these two areas giving us the opportunity to blend.

When you do adjust acid, what kind would you use?

The only thing we would use in our bottle wines would be tartaric, but as I say we never add acid in our bottle wines. For bulk we use citric for an acid adjustment problem.

Do you ever use concentrate to adjust sweetness?

We used to add a little to our Rosé. But we don't use concentrate in the fermentation process.

What kind of fining and filtration do you give the wines?

Bentonite on the whites, then a tight filtration, and just prior to bottling they go through a millipore filter. And they've also been centrifuged after fermentation.

So you've centrifuged, fined and filtered. Wouldn't one or two of those procedures accomplish the same thing? Are you running any risk of losing some of the flavor constituents?

The principle of centrifuging is just to clean up the lees. It doesn't make the wine brilliant, unless you heavily bentonite it and recentrifuge. In the old days, we used to do four or five rackings to get the wine clear, and every time you do that you stir them up, oxidize them, and kick them around. We've found wine is in better shape if you take it off the fermenter fast with the centrifuge.

But isn't the wine picking up some character from the lees under the old method?

Not in the case of white wines. The darn thing starts breaking down and pretty soon you've got rotten egg smells. I think trying to get the flavor and aroma of the grape is much more important, so we get our whites real clean real quick.

Do you also cold stabilize them, to precipitate out tartrates?

Yes.

And how do you treat the reds?

We usually centrifuge coming out of the fermenter, and then we may or may not filter depending on how well they cleaned up. We typically filter before going into the bottle. If you're selling wines right out of the winery and people carry them straight home, you can forego fiddling around with bentonite fining, or any filtration on reds. If you're selling your wine out of state, as we do, you must have it well enough stabilized so it doesn't come unglued every time someone puts it in storage at over 70 degrees, or stores it in a refrigerator.

By "coming unglued," do you mean throwing a sediment?

Heavy sediment. Our Pinot Noir and Petite Sirah throw a light sediment. This doesn't bother me. I don't like to see a sediment in white wines, or a cloud—this you don't want, it affects the flavor as well. Most of the so-called "unfiltered" wines have been fined and then heavily centrifuged, and that is as tough on them as filtration. We could play around and rack them a half a dozen times, but I think one centrifuging is better on them.

How long in wood do you age your red wines?

We keep the reds six to eight months in several-thousand-gallon redwood tanks, and then they go into oak, either 50 to 60 gallon barrels or ovals. Our Pinot Noir goes into the 50 gallon barrels and 175 to 500 gallon puncheons, then we blend it upon bottling. It's in that smaller cooperage roughly two years. I think the use of oak is like the use of garlic in cooking. We're here to make wine that has the flavor of a grape, not a two-by-four. It's just a condiment. You want fruitiness and varietal character and aroma.

Which varieties do you consider your forte?

Well, our white wines have always been the largest part of our production. Our Grey Riesling is by far the most popular of our wines.

What is it that makes that wine popular, is it the name, or the flavor?

I think it's a combination of both. It's a very soft, very drinkable wine.

What percentage of the varietal grape is in your varietally labeled wines?

Generally 100 percent. Our Chardonnay, Sauvignon Blanc, Dry Sémillon, are all 100 percent. Pinot Noir sometimes has a little of something else in it, like Pinot St. George or Petite Sirah. I think even the Burgundians will agree that Pinot Noir needs a little monkeying around, blending here and there. So we aim for 100 percent, with minor exceptions.

Do you think the 51 percent legal requirement for varietal labeling is too low?

I think so. I'd like to see it go to 60 percent. I like the opportunity for a little blending with the Grey Riesling, Pinot Noir, sometimes the Petite Sirah.

What do you blend the Grey Riesling with?

Sylvaner and Johannisberg Riesling.

What would you think of the government requiring the percentage to be raised to, say, 60 percent, and also requiring disclosure of the other grape varieties so the consumer knows what he's getting in the other 40 percent?

So long as they don't require us to list the percentage. Our Blanc de Blanc, for example, is made of Chenin Blanc and Ugni Blanc grapes, and the federal government came along and said if we're going to use those varietal names on the label it has to be 60 percent Chenin Blanc and 40 percent of the other. So we said, the hell with you, you're telling us how to blend this? It varies on every blend, and it's none of your damn business what the percentages are, as long as we show it's those grapes alone.

Blanc de Blanc, your Rosé and your Chablis are your only generic wines. Have you ever contemplated getting rid of the name Chablis, which is the name of a geographical region in France?

We have, along with our navel and a lot of other things. We simply have decided to keep it for the time being. It has always been such a good seller, we haven't gotten up the gumption to call it "White Wine." It's made almost entirely from Chenin Blanc. It's essentially a dry Chenin Blanc.

Once that gets out the price will go up! Do you ever make separate lots of wine from individual vineyards and indicate on the labels that certain wines are from certain vineyards?

We don't, no. We do make special lots of *auslese* and *spätlese*, this sort of thing.

Yes, you've only been doing that in the last few years. How did that come about? Did you wake up one morning and find botrytis in the vineyard?

These wines have all been from Monterey County, and 1969 was the first year we made them. We suddenly found that year that the Johannisberg Riesling grapes were all getting rotten, so we had two alternatives: one was to stand around and wring our hands, and the other was to try to make something out of the rotten grapes. So we did, and it came out quite well.

You had to hand pick those grapes?

Yes, because as the berries start getting dry they lose their weight, and they don't vibrate off well by the machine.

Did you follow the German meanings of the terms auslese *and* spätlese?

Yes. Specifically. *Spätlese* means "late picked," with a certain amount of botrytis. *Auslese* is a picking of the grapes that were almost all botrytised. We have never gone into a *beerenauslese* or *trockenbeerenauslese* because of labor costs. *Beerenauslese* means you take each berry and pitch it in, and *trockenbeerenauslese* means you sort out the dry berries. I figure it would cost $250 a bottle to have a *trockenbeerenauslese* in the United States.

What are you going to call these wines in the future, now that the government prohibits the German terms on American labels?

We are still urging them to reconsider on the basis that these are generic words.

Do you see yourself as a modern, scientific winemaker because of your use of sophisticated equipment like the centrifuge and harvesting machines?

Probably so. We depend much upon modern technology in our winemaking. But as far as decisions as to what we're going to do, when we're going to pick our grapes, for example, that depends on the look of the vineyard. We test the sugar, of course, and may or may not test the acid—you sometimes confuse yourself with facts, you know—but we can tell a lot by the color of the leaves and so forth. And again, when we make our blends in the winery we do it by taste.

There are many in the industry today saying that the best wines will be made by small wineries specialized in only a few types of wine. Now yours is fairly large for a premium winery—350,000 cases you said—and you produce a wide range of wine types. How can you compete for quality with the small, specialized wineries?

We have a lot of technical knowhow, one of the best equipped wineries in California and our vineyards are some of the best in the state. With personal family dedication we feel that not only will we be able to produce nationally distributed varietals, but we feel we can make small lots of special wines that will stand with any. We do tend to specialize in white wines; 92 percent of our wines are white.

In your judgment are the best California wines equal to the best European wines?

I think the best of each come awfully close to each other. I think, for instance, we can make a *spätlese* that's comparable to the best Germans. In the case of red wines, I don't think we've made the classic Burgundy yet with our Pinot Noirs. I'd like to see it done during my lifetime; we're spending a lot of time fooling around with it. Some very fine Cabernets are made in California, not as many as will be made, and you have to look longer and harder for them than you do for great wines of the Medoc.

Monterey County:

THE NEW GIANT

The Salinas Valley in Monterey County has long been known to Steinbeck readers as East of Eden, and to farmers as the country's salad bowl because of its abundant vegetable crops. But the hundred mile long valley was not particularly known to wine drinkers until the 1960s when overnight it became one of California's largest fine winegrape regions. Today it grows nearly 40,000 acres of vines, more than Napa and Sonoma combined.

Years ago, professors Winkler and Amerine at the University of California classified much of the area as cool Region I, suitable for grape growing. But no grapes were planted there until recent urbanization in the north pushed Mirassou, Wente, Paul Masson, Almadén and other winèries south to Monterey in search of vineyard sites. Rainfall is short, so water is pumped from the enormous underground Salinas River. The vineyards are vast and flat, so this area has pioneered mechanical harvesting. Strong, cold, Pacific winds sweep down the valley from Monterey Bay every afternoon, making much of it even cooler than University calculations indicated. Because of this wind and cold, skeptics still maintain the Monterey plantings are folly. But the wineries there seem to be proving the skeptics wrong.

Tiny Chalone Vineyards is not part of the new giant plantings or the climate of the valley. It sits, as it has for scores of years, in a warmer micro-climate high in the Gavilan Mountains which form the valley's eastern edge.

Richard Graff

CHALONE VINEYARD

Even if you took grapes from Chalone, Mt. Eden, David Bruce, Stony Hill—if you were to mix them all together it'd be like gathering a group of people and taking the mean of all their personality traits, you'd just have a blah.

Up dirt roads traversed only by cattle, in a distant niche in the mountains, inside a rustic farmhouse whose living room is dominated by a harpsichord and a huge painting, sits Dick Graff, aesthete as winemaker. We drink tea and talk into the late afternoon.

For him, wine is a matter of art, nuances and excellence, and comparison of his wines with the finest wines of France. "The comparison is often favorable," states Graff. In the case of Chalone Chardonnay or Pinot Noir, his remark is not braggadocio, it's fact. The achievements of Graff and his two brothers seem to come from their depth of formal training, and a thorough knowledge of French winemaking practices matched by few California vintners. Some of the success may also be owed to the soil. Chalone is perched on a unique limestone deposit, similar to the soil of Burgundy. Like the French—and unlike most California vintners—the Graffs attribute much of their wine's character to the soil. Their winery is so remote, production so limited, and the wine so fine, that Chalone has been accused of having "cult appeal." Welcome to the cult.

Recommended wine to drink while reading this chapter:
CHALONE VINEYARD
PINOT NOIR

Do the wines produced from this remote corner of Monterey County have an individual character you can identify?

Very definitely. It's something which is impossible to convey in words really. I would say that after someone has been drinking Chalone wine for a year or two or three, he will soon come to recognize what we call the *goût de terroir* of Chalone vineyards. All the Chalone wines—whether Chenin Blanc, Pinot Blanc, Chardonnay, or Pinot Noir—all have this underlying character. Of course, the taste of our wine comes first from the varietal character of the different grapes. Then you have a character which comes from our winemaking practices, and then this quality which comes from the soil and—I started to say climate, but it's much more the soil than it is the climate.

Few winemakers I've spoken to have thought soil significantly affects the character of their grapes. They say climate is the overriding factor.

There's a very simple explanation for that. The whole idea of soil versus climate in California was decided in favor of climate many years ago by professors Amerine and Winkler for the simple reason that the factor of climate produces differences in grapes which are measurable in the laboratory. The differences in grapes which are the result of soil are *not* measureable in the laboratory. If you grow Chardonnay in Fresno where you have a fantastically hot summer you're going to get a poorer wine largely because you have a large production, with a lot of sugar but low acid—sets of qualities which can be measured in the laboratory. Whereas, if you grow Chardonnay in various places along the coast you have immense differences which are due only to the soil. I think the most striking differences in Chardonnay exist between our Chardonnay and the Chardonnays which are produced in the Santa Cruz Mountains: Martin Ray's and David Bruce's. Now, we made Chardonnay up there at Mt. Eden Vineyards for several years—actually I didn't make it myself, my brother Peter was the winemaker up there—but we used exactly the same methods we use here, harvested at exactly the same maturity, used the same barrels imported from Burgundy, and the areas are very closely equivalent in terms of temperature. The wines are as different as night from day. And that's attributable to the soil.

Now when you go to Europe and you're talking about factors that influence quality in the vineyards, naturally you will be interested in the climate, but it's universally agreed, from centuries of experience, that soil is very important. If you go to the wine museum in Beaune, you will see very elaborate models and maps of the soils. They know almost exactly what is where because the geology of the area is so much less turbulent. You can see this calcite crystal here, which is limestone in its pure form; we have a deposit of it here. These crystals are also found in the region of Beaune in France. Our soil is very poor for general farming but great soil for grapes. Grapes, you know, originally got started on such areas because they were sort of leftover after the valley floors were used for grains. We have a reddish, decomposed granite, volcanic soil underlain by limestone.

Is it a unique deposit of limestone for California?

The geology of California is very complex, because of the way the plates are moving at the edge of the continent. There are none of the serene sedimentary layers you find in the east coast, or in England and Europe. The result is that while there's quite a bit of limestone in the Gavilan range it's as though someone had stirred it up.

Like a marble cake?

Right. As a matter of fact, at the north end of the range near Salinas, between Salinas and Hollister, there's a rather large, multimillion dollar industry extracting lime from the soil. But ours is just about the only limestone deposit in a place that's arable and has the right climate. There are other little patches of limestone, but they're likely to be on the side of a cliff or something.

You mean, in this region?

In this Gavilan range. In fact, I don't know of any other patches of limestone in any California winegrowing region, but then I'm not sure California has been thoroughly searched.

Would you describe where Chalone is? It's really a remote spot.

We're about five miles east of Soledad as the crow flies, and about two miles from the Pinnacles National Monument. It's on the east side of Salinas Valley at 2,000 feet, in the Gavilan range.

What is the Pinnacles National Monument?

Well, I think it's an igneous intrusion which came almost to the surface and was subsequently exposed by erosion, leaving spires and large formations of rock that jet up very dramatically. It's quite a spectacular place, very popular among mountain climbers.

Who first put a vineyard up here?

The area was first discovered by a Frenchman by the name of Tamm who decided this soil was the closest he could find in California to the soil of Burgundy and Champagne.

When was that?

Toward the end of the 19th century. He planted some grapes, but I think died shortly thereafter and nothing was done with them. This vineyard was planted by a man by the name of Bill Silvaer.

Did he operate the winery as Chalone Vineyards?

No, he never made any wine here. He sold the grapes to various people. After Silvaer died in the 1950s, his widow sold the property to a couple of guys in San Francisco. One was a stockbroker, the other was a psychiatrist. They bought it sort of as a weekend retreat, and adopted the ingenious plan of one guy's paying the bills one year and the other's paying them the next. They eventually decided they wanted to make wine, and they hired Philip Togni in the summer of 1960. They adopted the name Chalone.

Where does the word come from?

It's a local place name, after an Indian tribe that used to live in these parts. There's a Chalone peak, a Chalone creek, and actually this is the Chalone bench of the Gavilan Mountains.

I have read that you studied music at Harvard. How did you wind up a winemaker after starting out in quite a different endeavor?

Music for me has never been anything but an avocation, and as you may know at Harvard you don't really major in anything, the idea is to get a liberal education. Music has always been something I've loved—I play the piano and organ, and have taken up the harpsichord—and while I was at college I'd get a job at a church as organist and choirmaster, for a little extra money on the side. When I graduated from college . . .

When was that?

Well I was class of '58, although I didn't graduate until '59, due to a misunderstanding with one of my musicology professors. Then I went to OCS and was commissioned in the Navy, stationed for three years on a destroyer based in San Diego. When I got out, I had no idea of what I wanted to do. So, lacking anything better, I got a job at a bank as a management trainee, and enrolled in graduate business school at USC. I just hated it—well, actually I had some interesting assignments—but I've never been cut out for sitting in an office all day, working in a bureaucracy. The whole thing was very stultifying.

My father and mother had a quarter interest in Windsor Vineyards, which at that time was an old winery up near Santa Rosa, which they bought as land speculation. The four partners in Windsor Farms thought it'd be fun to make wine, so they hired Rod Strong who at that time owned a wine shop in Tiburon and was teaching dance in San Francisco. Well, he had come to know the guy who then owned Chalone and who wanted to sell it. Rod arranged for Windsor to lease Chalone in 1963 and 1964. I went up one day to Windsor with my father to taste some Chalone wines. At that time, I knew nothing about winemaking, though I was getting interested in wine. I had taken Nate Chroman's course in winetasting at UCLA. One thing led to another and I finally came here to see the place, and just decided this was what I wanted to do.

This would have been in 1964. Finally I entered a partnership with the guy who then owned it. We sold the grapes in '65 and I went to Davis where I spent a year as a special student taking all the oenology and viticulture courses they had at the time, and I had time for a full year of French, for which I've always been very thankful. The second semester I even took a course in conducting which I had never been able to do at Harvard since it was taught in summer. Just as I got out, my partner had trouble with his other business dealings and sold his interest in the vineyard to some other people, sight unseen. Well, a protracted dispute ensued which finally resulted in a lawsuit against me and my mother, who had lent the winery some money.

In the end, we wound up with the property. We set up a new corporation in 1969 which we call Gavilan Vineyards, Inc., and sold shares through private offerings. We have something like 100 shareholders now, most of whom are very small, friends interested in wine. The three principal shareholders are myself, Phil Woodward and John McQuown. For the first few years I was here virtually by myself. Phil is now president, and my official position is chairman of the board. About three years ago my brother John came to work here; he had just finished his Ph.D. in chemistry at the University of Chicago, and he is actually now the winemaker. My brother Peter, who has a degree in viticulture from Davis, is now vineyard manager. I'm sort of general supervisor.

How big are you, how many cases a year?

From our own vineyards, about 2,000. We just built a new winery last year with a 10,000 case capacity, which is our goal. We have about 50 acres of vines that aren't producing yet, 25 that just started producing, and we have another 50 producing acres; so there are 125 all told. But we've bought some grapes from the Napa Valley and we're making a French Colombard which we sell for $2.95. This is so we can use our winery while our vines are coming into production. In the old vineyard up here, we have Chenin Blanc, Pinot Blanc, a couple of acres of Pinot Noir and maybe 15 or 20 of Chardonnay. Our new plantings are Pinot Noir, Chardonnay, and Pinot Blanc. Pinot Blanc is very popular; we like it ourselves very well, and I kind of like the idea of having a little more wine at a lower price. A lot of people can't afford nine dollars a bottle for white wine, and even though our Pinot Blanc is expensive, at six and a half dollars it can reach a lot more people.

You have no Cabernet?

No, this is strictly a Burgundy area.

That French Colombard was first put out under a secondary label, wasn't it?

Right. We've used the "Gavilan" label instead of our Chalone Vineyard label sometimes on wines from grapes not grown up here.

What tonnage do you get on these various vineyards?

Well, from the old vineyards we get about a ton per acre. The vines are very old. And we're expecting on our new vineyards to get a ton and a half to two tons maximum.

Why are the tonnages so dramatically low? Is it your pruning?

It has a lot to do with the soil, which is very poor, deficient in organic matter, and just doesn't produce vigorous growth. Also, it has to do with the lack of rainfall. And that's all we want. Two tons is actually more than we originally planned on.

In the Napa Valley they speak of three to four tons per acre as being low. Do you think that even going to three or four tons would give you grapes that are less intense in character?

There seem to be two different curves as a vine increases its production: the production of flavor curve doesn't go up as fast as the production of quantity curve. It's almost as though a given vine can produce only so much flavor regardless of whether the crop is increased. That's not strictly true, of course, but it's one of the reasons that in France they set limits on the yield per acre.

Can you tell me about the climate? You said you don't have much rain here.

No, this is what's known euphemistically as a low rainfall area, which means we only average 12 to 15 inches a year.

That means you have to irrigate, don't you?

Well, the vineyard was always dry farmed here. Grapes are very drought resistant plants, and can be successfully dry farmed here in normal years as long as the cultivation practices are done carefully.

I thought you needed 20 to 25 inches, and that you trucked in water here.

We started irrigating when we planted new vines. So for the last three or four years we've been trucking water up from Salinas Valley, and last year we built a reservoir which we hope to fill in winter with runoff.

Will your need for water diminish as these new vines become established?

We don't really know. It depends on how much rainfall we get. In 1972, we only had eight inches of rain, so in a year like that we would want to irrigate.

What about the heat. Is this a temperature Region I?

Soledad is Region I, but we're quite a bit warmer up here, we're a low Region II. In other words, we have the kind of climate that produces great vintages in France when they have them. You probably know that those regions were based on mean temperature data, but what is often overlooked is that in Champagne and Burgundy, and the Rhine and Moselle, the grapes seldom get ripe, and when they do it's not a Region I year. So our climate is comparable to that of Burgundy in a year when they don't have to add sugar to their wines. At 2,000 feet here we're above the cooling breezes that flow down the Salinas Valley every day from the Pacific. Soledad is like a wind tunnel. I mean it's absolutely abominable down there, a 25 knot wind every day. And of course, fog every morning, which we don't have up here.

How are the grapes picked?

We augment our regular crew by three or four people, and they use grape knives and put the grapes into lug boxes. They're brought to the winery in 40 pound boxes. We do *not* use gondolas, nor do we ever intend to.

What's the disadvantage of using small gondolas?

Have you ever seen a gondola dumped? It's quite different from dumping a box. When you dump a box of grapes, the grapes are all whole when they go into the crusher.

Do you have the usual stemmer-crusher?

Yes, but we don't stem our grapes. For the white varieties we simply crush everything right into the press, stems and all. Stems are terrific for pressing. Of course you don't press very hard, you don't extract juice from the stems. We have a Howard Rotapress, the large stainless drum with two cylinders that move in toward the center.

You get more tannin from the stems that way, by crushing and pressing with them on?

The reason we leave them in is because the grapes are very difficult to press without the stems. Other people use rice hulls. You have to have something in with the crushed grapes in order to make them press well. A bunch of crushed grapes without any stems is a gelatinous mass; it's likely to squeeze through the ends of the cylinders. Some varieties are worse than others.

Is that true of the pneumatic bladder type press? Would you have that problem?

Probably not. I've never used one of those, so I don't know.

Do you add sulphur as you crush, at about the standard 100 parts per million?

Oh, heavens no. We add about 25 to 30 parts per million, never more than that. We're concerned, of course, about oxidation, especially in our Pinot Blanc which of all the varieties in the world is the one which oxidizes most easily. But we try to do as little as possible to the grapes, and we add the amount of potassium meta-bisulfite we think is really needed. And we do it at the press. Now for the reds, we don't add any at all before fermentation. You don't need it, unless the grapes are in poor condition. The practices we use are those of France, not those of California, notwithstanding our having studied all the methods Davis teaches. I decided long ago that since we want to make the best wines we can, we want to use the practices of the regions where the best wines in the world are made.

Do you start fermentation with a yeast starter?

Yes, we do.

Do they use yeast starters in France?

No, they don't, but you see those vineyards have been there such a long time that the native yeast populations are just right. In California, there are certain wild yeasts that are likely to produce off flavors or volatile acidity.

And then you ferment in barrels, rather than stainless steel?

Yes, all our white wines are fermented in 60 gallon barrels, imported from Burgundy—the same ones they use there. We put the juice in through the bung, filled to about six inches from the top. And there's one other thing that's important in white winemaking, and that's the temperature of fermentation. You've probably heard that whites should be fermented at refrigerator temperatures. In fact, the white wines in Burgundy are fermented at about 20 degrees Centigrade, which is about 70 Fahrenheit. The heat is dissipated from the small barrels, with their large surface-to-volume ratio, and is self-regulated; can't get too hot, just about 70 or slightly above. And we consider this elevated temperature—elevated by California standards—very important.

Do the reds ferment at the same temperature?

No, we like the reds to get up to 30 degrees Centigrade, 80 or 85 Fahrenheit. Our Pinot Noir, you see, is fermented in stainless steel tanks and it gets up to that temperature by itself.

But why do you ferment red wine in stainless steel when you believe strongly in barrels for the whites?

Red wines cannot be fermented in barrels unless a head is removed. As I say, we're just following standard Burgundian practices. Wood, of course, is the traditional material for fermenters, but anyone who can afford it has stainless steel for the reds. For whites, it's not the oak flavor you're seeking because it's fermenting so briefly there is really very little oak flavor imparted. But there is a very marked, noticeable difference between white wines fermented in tanks and white wines fermented in barrels. Any type of white wine fermented in tanks always has the characteristics of white wines fermented in tanks. "Tanky," I call it. Our French Colombard, for example, from the Calistoga grapes I mentioned, is fermented in barrels; actually we use 55 gallon American oak barrels for that. And, to our great delight, it has created a sensation. Yet we used precisely the same grapes that everybody else in Napa Valley uses to make French Colombard. The difference is that it was fermented in barrels, I don't have any other secret.

But this doesn't carry over to red wines?

No, and I suppose that's mainly because there's so much flavor and body in the reds. Also, the reds are in barrel a year longer than the whites. Now, the whites take 7 to 14 days to ferment to dryness. The Pinot Noir we leave in the fermentation tank with the stems for two weeks, which is also standard practice in France, although it horrifies my colleagues in California. The fermentation is over in about a week, and we leave it in the fermenter, with the headspace covered with inert gas to protect against oxidation.

Do you punch down the cap or pump over it?

We do both, punch down while we're pumping over, about three or four times a day.

Do you fine or filter?

We fine the white wines lightly with bentonite, and filter them before bottling. The Pinot Noir we fine with egg white, about four to six egg whites to a barrel, and we rack it about once a quarter. The Pinot Noir is not filtered at all.

Do you always have a malo-lactic fermentation?

In the Pinot Noir, yes. The malo-lactic organism is, I think, the most idiosyncratic on the face of the planet, and it's very difficult to manage but usually takes care of itself.

Do you ever have to adjust acid?

We occasionally add tartaric acid, and in the case of Pinot Noir half tartaric and half pomalous—that's malic acid, the acid that is converted to lactic acid during the malo-lactic fermentation. The acid that disappears first, as grapes ripen, is the malic acid. Malic acid is the acid of apples and when you keep apples for any length of time they lose their hardness and freshness; well, the same thing happens with grapes. In the Pinot Noir we want a malo-lactic fermentation, so we add the natural form of malic acid that appears in the fruit anyway but is rapidly lost as the fruit matures.

What kind of aging do the wines receive?

White wines are normally bottled in April or May, about eight months after harvest, having spent that time in 50 to 60 gallon barrels, and having been topped every week and racked every few months. The Pinot Noir is bottled a year later, the spring of the following year. For our Pinot Noir and Chardonnay, I should mention, we use new oak barrels every year. For the Chardonnay, depending on how big the wine is we may use a portion of used barrels, but in principle we use new ones every year. Again, this is standard practice in Burgundy, for those who can afford to do it. The barrels are made by hand and dried in the open air, so they're made to be used new for wine. In all these things, you see we are simply following the traditional French practices, not unthinkingly, but when we have decided they are important to quality.

One of my criticisms of the University of California at Davis is that they do not require a foreign language for people who are taking winemaking. That's extraordinary, to say the least. It would seem to me a winemaking student should at least be able to read French fluently. Because, with due respect to Dr. Amerine's works, almost all the important books on winemaking are in French. So while I was studying at Davis, I spent a lot of time researching French methods, and then spent some time over there, and I subscribe to several French journals and so forth to keep up on what's going on.

You mentioned when I came in that you are writing a book yourself. Is it a book on winemaking?

No, it's a treatise on philosophy. It's an idea and a system which has a lot of new thinking, new approaches, basically a new concept in ethics. It's impossible to get across in less than a book.

In your view, can the larger wineries produce some of the best wines?

No, definitely not. And there are two reasons for that. One is that a large winery will not find it practical to use the traditional methods which seem essential to high quality. And the other is that if you produce a large quantity of wine, the grapes, of necessity, come from several vineyards, or even if it's one vineyard it'll be huge, covering hundreds of acres. Any individual characteristic of the particular vineyard location is lost.

In other words, even if you took grapes from Chalone, grapes from Mt. Eden, grapes from David Bruce, grapes from Stony Hill—all of those produce superior wine—but if you were to mix them all together it'd be like gathering a group of people and taking the mean of all their personality traits, you'd just have a blah.

In your opinion, are the best California wines equal to the best European wines?

Hah! Well, I know that's a loaded question. But I think the thing you have to start with is the inescapable fact that the great wines are, and have traditionally been, produced in France, in Burgundy and Bordeaux. Some people say we should not compare California and French wines because it's comparing apples and oranges. But I think the reason people say that is because they don't want to invite a comparison which may prove unfavorable to California wines. I look at the great French Burgundies as standards of excellence. It's difficult for me to imagine a great California Pinot Noir or Chardonnay which would not compare favorably with those of France. So I'm always very interested in comparing our wines with the French, and in our case the comparison is often favorable to us.

We've only produced a couple of barrels a year of Pinot Noir so far, but those we have produced have in fact been true Pinot Noirs, and what I mean by that is that they have the same characteristics which you associate with the red Burgundies of France. As a matter of fact, in a blind tasting the guy who's the head of Romanée-Conti was quite positive before the bottles were revealed that our '69 Pinot Noir was in fact the Burgundy, and that the Burgundy we had at the same tasting—which was made by a friend of his—was the California wine.

Now, this is not due to any brilliance on our part, it's simply the result of the soil we have here. Actually, we do produce Pinot Noir in an entirely different way than anybody else does in California. Most California Pinot Noirs, as anybody will tell you, are just ghosts. One of the important things is fermenting with the stems. This is another thing that slavishly following the university-set standards has done: people think that Pinot Noir is to be made just as other red wines are, but unless Pinot Noir is fermented with the stems it doesn't have any tannin or much body. And the other thing is that Pinot Noir is much more sensitive to the soil.

How many wineries would you say there are in California producing wines of a caliber comparable to the best French wines?

There are perhaps a dozen or so which produce reasonably comparable Chardonnay, but I don't think there are any besides ourselves which produce a Pinot Noir with its traditional Burgundy character. There are maybe two or three other wineries producing good Pinot Noir, but because of the soil they are grown on they are usually quite un-Burgundian.

Donald Alexander
MIRASSOU VINEYARDS

Mechanical harvesting has to be better than picking by hand. We capture the flavor by crushing right in the field.

The Mirassou winery sits amid the freeways and shopping plazas of San Jose, a relic of the serene farming days of the Santa Clara Valley. As orchards and vineyards were leveled for tract homes, the Mirassous acquired other vineyard areas and today, although the winery and a few vineyards remain in San Jose, Mirassou is most appropriately considered a Monterey County winery, for nearly all its grapes are grown there. Another relic is a quaint little house on the winery grounds, once home of the Mirassous' grandmother, now maintained—with all her fine knick-knacks—as a guest house. I talked to Don Alexander, Mirassou brother-in-law and winemaker, in the old living room. Although the Mirassous are noted for their flamboyance, Don Alexander was soft-spoken and modest as he talked about his delight in being a winemaker. The winery, which has grown prodigiously in the last decade, is currently best known for its dry white wines and sparkling wines—good, crisp wines, though consumers are still waiting for the truly exceptional wine from Mirassou.

Recommended wine to drink while reading this chapter:

MIRASSOU
PETITE ROSÉ

I understand you became a winemaker by marrying into the Mirassou family.

Right. I was married to Norb Mirassou's daughter. I'm one of the partners along with the four Mirassou brothers. Peter cares for the vineyards, Dan is in marketing, Steve is in sales, and Jim is the president and takes care of the financial end. I think the greatest thing that ever happened to me was becoming a winemaker. It kind of happened by accident. It's a romantic vocation. It's nice to say, "I'm a winemaker." I have to compliment my partners and Ed and Norb, they're winemakers too. Everything just clicked; a bunch of people got together, and it clicked. We're moving right along.

What were you doing before you came into the winery?

I was working in an electronics firm. In 1960, Ed asked if I wanted to come in and sell wine at the winery. Then in grape season they needed help, and

I started out helping Max Huebner, our winemaker at the time. He was getting on in years and needed some help. As he got older I gradually took over his job. He's about 75 now. He's from Germany originally, and has been with us over 30 years. He's still here, however, out at the scale house right now weighing trucks. He doesn't have to come to work at all; we pay him anyway.

Did you have any formal training, at Davis or anywhere else?

When I came here I didn't know which end of the bottle the wine came out. I wish I had formal training, but I didn't. On the other hand, it's all experience. I have taken the few short courses they have at Davis from time to time, but not heavy education. I spent a month in Germany and France last year. The wineries treated me well, taught me a lot. All the wineries are adequate; no matter how old the winery is it'll have all the equipment it needs. The German wineries are modern, clean, efficient. A centrifuge in almost every winery. During grape season you don't find any French winemakers over here trying to learn what we know, and you don't find any American winemakers over there. Yet grape season is the most important time to go! Their view of California wine is kind of interesting. In Burgundy they'll tell you, "Oh, yes, California makes really good wines, they taste just like they do in Bordeaux." And in Bordeaux they'll tell you, "Oh, yes, California wines taste just like those in Burgundy."

Is the winery owned by the so-called "Fifth Generation" of Mirassous?

No, the fifth generation owns the label and 600 acres in Soledad, Monterey County; and we own the cooperage and lease of the old Cribari winery. We call it Village Winery now. So Ed and Norb Mirassou own Mirassou vineyards and the winery here. That's the fourth generation. There are two separate partnerships.

Who came to California and started the winery in the old days?

Pierre Pellier was the original one. He came over from southern France in the 1850s and brought cuttings—brought the first French prune trees too. It's not known whether he came around the Horn or crossed the Isthmus of Panama, but fresh water began to run out, so he bought all the potatoes on the ship and stuck his grape cuttings in the potatoes to keep them from drying out. Charles Wetmore gave him credit for bringing the French Colombard and Folle Blanche grapes to California. Pellier settled right around where the winery is today, and his daughter married Pierre Mirassou who had a neighboring vineyard.

The first through fourth generations at the winery all sold bulk wine to other wineries only, is that right?

No, there was some bottled under the Mirassou label before that, certainly in the 1950s. In the early 60s, Mirassou Vineyards planted the Mission Ranch in Soledad, and a few years later we formed our partnership.

Actually, at that time we grew vegetables down there—carrots, sugar beets and things. Then we planted the vineyard in 1961. In 1966 we started selling under the Mirassou label. We sold only 3,000 cases that year, and this year we're pushing 200,000.

Are you going to level off at 200,000?

We haven't set a maximum figure, but we don't intend to grow as fast as we have in the past. We want to stay in the quality range.

How many acres of vineyards do you have right here around the winery?

Oh, I don't think we have more than a couple hundred. We're next to the urbanized eastern foothills in San Jose, no room for expansion. Down in Soledad we have 800 to 900 more. Jim and Daniel and Pete also have a little vineyard in Gilroy.

Do you buy grapes from other growers?

A few, but strictly for bulk wines to sell to other wineries.

What grape varieties do you grow?

Quite a few. Gewürztraminer, Johannisberg Riesling, Sylvaner, Chenin Blanc, Pinot Blanc, Sauvignon Blanc, Chardonnay, Pinot Noir, Cabernet, Zinfandel, Petite Sirah, Gamay Beaujolais. And we make Chablis, Burgundy, Champagnes and Rosé. Our Petite Rosé is an interesting one. It came about quite by accident. We were crushing grapes for Grenache Rosé when Petite Sirah grapes got into the crusher in an amount that was too much to call Grenache. So we called it Petite Rosé; the first time anyone ever made a Rosé here out of that grape. Our Grenache Rosé was a slow mover, but our Petite Rosé really sells! Another wine we've done well with is our Monterey Riesling. It's made mostly from the Sylvaner grape.

It's not made from Johannisberg Riesling?

Heavens no. Our Johannisberg is very good too. I think Johannisberg, Gewürztraminer and our Rosé are probably the best of the line, plus our Champagnes.

Which grapes do you use in your Champagnes?

Pinot Blanc, Chenin Blanc and a very little French Colombard. I heard that Moët & Hennessey's new winery in the Napa Valley bought grapes weeks ahead of time, green, before they were even ripe. It stands to reason, because I understand the grapes in Champagne, France, just don't get ripe; it's too cold. That's why they can take Pinot Noir and make Champagne out of it—it's green. And here, wineries take Pinot Noir, crush it and wonder why it's kind of pink.

Do you ferment all your Champagne in the bottle, and put it on riddling racks and turn it?

Yeah, all in the bottle. Macky turns them on the racks, he still does. We also have automatic racks that change position every six hours, for the same effect.

Which of your wines have been doing best in the tastings?

Our Gewürztraminer. People have put that against the Alsatian Gewürztraminers, and it does well. And our Chenin Blanc is just flying, people think it's just great. We also have a late harvest Zinfandel right now, made from that tiny vineyard in Gilroy that's really getting attention. Our reds fluctuate more in the wine tastings. Sometimes they'll be up at the top and sometimes way down there. Maybe that tells us something, maybe that's an interesting wine, something for conversation. You can make the greatest wine in the world, and it just may not sell. Cabernet is easy to sell, people just grab up Cabernet, Cabernet, Cabernet. I wish they'd grab the Johannisberg Riesling, for instance, because we make some great Johannisberg. I have the hardest time making Cabernet. I don't know why, maybe the grapes in particular years are better than others. We put the Cabernet in barrels, just like they do in Bordeaux. But whether you use barrels or a 50,000 gallon tank, it isn't going to make great wine unless you have good grapes.

Do you think that Cabernet just isn't going to do well in Monterey County?

I think it will, in time. For some reason these vines take more time before they produce the grapes you want.

Were you the first people to go down to Monterey County?

Ed and Norb found some land down there, and Paul Masson paid them to plant the vineyards. It depends on how you look at it. Masson could say they were first, but we feel we were first.

How did they get the idea to go down there, to a brand new and very cold area not known for wine grapes?

Ed and Norb went all over California, and even out of state. They took frost readings, looked at records on rain, temperature, everything. They weren't interested in a Region III, but in a I or II, the colder the better—providing you can get the grapes ripe. And they wound up down there in the carrot and lettuce fields in Monterey.

But it turned out to be cooler than they thought, didn't it?

You're never sure, you have to take a chance. We had to get out of Santa Clara Valley, there's subdivisionitis up here. They're moving right in on us. You'd pay for the land ten times every year in taxes, I'm sure. The winery will stay here, though.

Do you believe the Monterey soil makes much difference in the quality of the grapes?

Soil is apparently the least important. Temperature is the name of the game.

How many tons per acre do you get, on the average, in the Soledad vineyards?

It varies with the variety. Anywhere from one ton to four or five. People say quality is best when the yield is low, but I think your best quality comes when you have a normal yield. If you have a Cabernet that gives two and a half tons an acre and suddenly one year it gives five, something's wrong. Or if you only get a half ton an acre that vine is suffering, and it's going to suffer right to the bottle.

Mirassou was about the first winery to get into mechanical harvesting, wasn't it?

Yes, we helped develop a method of mechanical harvesting. There were problems with leaves in the crush and giving off flavors to the wine. But it has to be better than picking by hand. We capture the flavor by crushing right in the field, and you've got your SO_2 and CO_2 in there before they're shipped to the winery. You capture more flavor because there's no oxidation. Any oxidation and you lose some varietal character. A lot of people won't notice it, but we're concerned about that. We want Chenin Blanc to taste like Chenin Blanc, Johannisberg like Johannisberg. Of course, a step back from that is the maderized flavor, when the wine has really been oxidized. It's brought up here 30 tons at a time, about 6,000 gallons. It's 90 miles from here, takes an hour and a half to two hours. We can unload a truck in 15 minutes. So, we took a stand on mechanical harvesting.

What kind of a press do you have?

We have two Willmes bladder type presses, and another which is a continuous press but is not a good press at all. It must have been designed for apples or pears. We only get press wine from it anyway and sell it for distilling material. Or sometimes somebody from the San Joaquin Valley will want wine like that because it's got a lot of character. It's not the character *we* want, but maybe it's the character somebody else wants. We'll keep the press wine from the Willmes presses separate too and then put that, say, in our Burgundy.

How much pressure do you use in the press?

We start out at five pounds, almost as good as free run, and go up to 80 pounds which is pretty mean stuff.

You have all stainless steel fermenters for both the reds and whites. What temperatures do you maintain during fermentation?

That's a real variable. I don't want to give you a lot of baloney and say we invariably ferment our whites at 40 to 55 degrees and our reds at 70 to 85 degrees. The whites go through the juice separater to take the skins out, then the juice is centrifuged to take the undesirable solids away. Next it goes into fermentation, and we ferment it as cold as we can, sometimes as cold as 50 degrees, sometimes as high as 55 or 60.

Does the yeast have a hard time keeping the fermentation going at 50 degrees?

Very hard. It's very slow, and centrifuging the solids out of the juice before fermentation slows the fermentation too. Normally we ferment the wines dry, and then add a *muté* if we want sweetness. We've stuck some wines, stopped fermentation before all the sugar is gone. Say a half percent or one percent or three percent is still there.

How do you do that, by centrifuging out the yeast that's left?

By centrifuging, but then eventually we keep it cold and filter it. We learn by experience. When you stick the wine and add SO_2 it goes into what's called "total SO_2" rather than "free SO_2" which protects the wine from oxidation. When you bottle it, my God, your SO_2 is out of sight! So we learned that we should make a *muté*.

That's essentially adding sweet, unfermented grape juice to the wine?

Right. We ferment the wines dry, then bring in Chenin Blanc or a variety like that as ripe as we can get it, say 23 or 24 degrees Balling, centrifuge it, filter it, keep it cold, and add it to the dry wines for sweetness.

You don't use grape concentrate, though?

You always experiment, with both new and traditional things, even stomping them with your feet! You name it, we've done everything here to experiment. This year I'm going to experiment with the color and tannin in Cabernet: I'll draw off some at ten degrees Balling before it's through fermenting, and another batch is going to be left on the skins for several weeks, just to see what effect we get by skin contact with the juice. The University and the literature say that once a red grape is below eight degrees Balling you don't extract any color.

Another thing: a visiting French winemaker said that you lose color if you leave wine in contact with the skins too long, the skins draw it back in. He says you can prove it by adding pomace to red wine; it'll soak up the color. I forget what part of France he was from, but he was from one of the better wineries, and he was most knowledgeable. I learned a lot from that gentleman just in the hour he was here! He said there's no secret, all you'd have to do is to learn French and read their books!

Do you fine, filter and centrifuge, all three?

The most we do is centrifuge the wine twice, fine with bentonite, go through a pad filtration, and another filtration before bottling.

Do the reds go through a malo-lactic fermentation?

Yes, all except the Gamay. We especially need it because of our cold area, giving us high acid. One way to lower acid is malo-lactic fermentation.

What kind of cooperage then do the reds and whites go into?

With Cabernet or Pinot Noir, we like to get it into 50 gallon barrels. I'm talking about the special Harvest label wines. With the primary label—other than the Harvest wines—we put it in 50 gallon barrels and also 1,500 gallon tanks. For Zinfandel, we stick to larger oak casks.

By "larger," how large do you mean?

Oh, five, six, eight thousand gallons.

And what kind of oak is the various cooperage?

We're still experimenting. We made a White Burgundy, some in American oak and some in Yugoslavian oak, and let the public judge. We have a program where people buy wines when we come up with a new item. We sent two bottles to each person and followed up with questionnaires. In general they liked the Yugoslavian better. But we'll never stop experimenting.

What is that White Burgundy made of?

Pinot Blanc. It's a good grape. We used to bottle it as a varietal but I guess the name didn't catch on.

Explain to me the Harvest wine concept. What does that extra Harvest label above the regular one mean?

The difference between our Harvest wines and our primary label is the style of winemaking; Harvest wines—Pinot Noir, Pinot Chardonnay, Cabernet and sometimes Zinfandel—are stored in 50 gallon French oak barrels, the bottles are vintaged and bottled-dated. They also have a bottle number. Primary label wines are the same quality wines except that they are kept in larger cooperage and do not have bottle date nor number. Also, we ferment some Chardonnay in oak barrels, and that'll go into the Harvest label, and the other Chardonnay is fermented in stainless steel and that'll go into the regular label.

Are your varietals all 100 percent of the varietal grape?

Yes, as close to 100 percent as we can make them. You might have stray vines in the vineyard, for example. If you say 98 or 99 percent, it's better. Our Monterey Riesling is a blend of Sylvaner and French Colombard, but we don't call it a varietal, we call it Monterey Riesling.

Is there a "Mirassou style" of wine, a distinctive style identified with your label?

Not really, no. We do certain things a little differently, I suppose, but we have 15 varietal wines or so, and there is not really a certain Mirassou taste or something like that. Our grapes are mainly from a cool Region I, so we may have a little higher acid in our wines generally. That's good or bad, depending on how you look at it. I think the worst thing to have is a flat, low acid wine. You can't have a flowery nose and a lot of fruit without a good acid balance. The way I look at it, quality wines are interesting wines, something you can sit down and talk about.

Do you think the 15 or so wines you produce are too many to keep on top of? I remember Andre Tchelistcheff told me his ideal winery could produce no more than three wine types.

I agree on that; I would certainly like to get it down to very few. On the other hand, Andre and I are not out there trying to sell wine. We're winemakers, we've got purple feet, eh? Maybe we wouldn't last if we produced one wine. With only one bottle on the shelf, maybe nobody would pull it off.

Do you believe the best California wines are equal to the best European wines?

A Cabernet here is not the same as a Bordeaux over there. If we took a Cabernet and blended some Merlot and Malbec in the right proportions, I think we'd equal some of the great châteaux of France. But you couldn't legally call it Cabernet, nor Bordeaux, so why do it? Now take our Gewürztraminer, and those of other wineries. I don't think you can tell them from Alsatian wines. If we can do it on those, we can do it on other wines as well.

But we haven't done it yet on the others?

No, in general we haven't. Once in a while someone will have a wine you can't tell apart from the great French châteaux, so it can be done. But maybe we don't want to. We've got our own wines, our own markets.

Richard Peterson

THE MONTEREY VINEYARD

You know, if you leave the winemaking up to God, he'll make vinegar—not wine.

The Monterey Vineyard has mounted the biggest challenge to skeptics who say it is too cool in Monterey to grow fine wine grapes. It is the antithesis of the small, individually owned winery in the heart of a traditional winegrowing area, and because it is I pressed hard in questioning Dick Peterson about the winery's commitment, and ability, to make top quality wines. Peterson proved to be an articulate defender of The Monterey Vineyard concept.

One of the few Ph.D. winemakers in California, I found him directing crushing operations in the winery wearing rubber boots and work overalls with a name patch reading "Dr. P." He impressed me with his frank nature and experimental mind. As he took me through the winery he pointed out a group of barrels he had fitted with vacuum gauges, and commented that he was gathering evidence that oxygen does not enter barrels as wine ages, but rather a vacuum develops. If true, the finding would be revolutionary for it could mean that the prevalent practice of topping barrels in order to prevent oxidation is unnecessary or even harmful. Peterson, in short, is an experimenter and The Monterey Vineyard his giant laboratory.

Recommended wine to drink while reading this chapter:
THE MONTEREY VINEYARD JOHANNISBERG RIESLING

You followed Andre Tchelistcheff as winemaster at Beaulieu Vineyards, which has to be one of the most prestigious positions in the wine industry. Why did you leave there to come to a brand new winery?

Most people assumed there was some anti-Heublein motive in my leaving but that wasn't the case. Heublein bought up Beaulieu Vineyards while I was there, in 1969. Actually, I enjoyed many features that Heublein offered—especially the consulting trips to Portugal. It's true I didn't like a lot of their early approaches. Heublein is basically a sales organization, and I had trouble at first making some of them understand what true quality in wine really is. I remember once in the early days, just after the Beaulieu Vineyards takeover, one of the Heublein people asked me, "Why do you use Chenin Blanc in Beaulieu Vineyards Champagne?" And I said, "Because we don't have any excess Chardonnay." He said, "Oh, no, that's not what I mean. Don't you realize Thompson Seedless is only $50 a ton and, for Christ's sake, you're paying $900 a ton for Chardonnay?" I said, "If you think you can get me to use any Thompson Seedless in *any* Beaulieu

Vineyards wine, we'd better just talk about something else." He looked at me and kind of shook his head and said, "Dick, you'll never make a million dollars."

Now, on the other hand, we have to give Heublein credit. In the five years I worked for Heublein at Beaulieu Vineyards they *never* ordered me to do anything that lessened the quality of any Beaulieu Vineyards wine. The real reason I left Beaulieu Vineyards is because Myron McFarland came to Rutherford and showed me maps of his new, vast plantings in Monterey County; I said, "Do you mean to tell me there are 10,000 acres—all varietal grapes and all Region I climate?" He said, "Yup, that's right," and I told him "I think you're crazy, but I'd like to see what 10,000 acres of quality varietals look like." Eventually, the pioneer spirit in me took over, and I just had to go to Monterey.

Backing up a moment, what was your training before you joined Beaulieu in 1968?

To start at the beginning, I grew up on a farm in Iowa, and we raised a few Concord grapes for jelly. There were no wineries in Iowa of course, but my Dad had made wine occasionally when I was a kid. When I was a freshman in college I made my first wine. That was 1948. Read a couple of old books from the library and thought I knew all there was to know about winemaking. The grapes were Concord, which tells you something about the wine. But I thought it was the greatest wine in the world. I did this two or three years in a row.

After college at Iowa State I went into the Marine Corps and forgot about winemaking. Later I enrolled in graduate school at Berkeley and studied under Professor Maynard Joslyn. I studied food technology, actually, but one of the aspects was winemaking. I did some wine research; we published a paper on copper casse in wine in 1956, and I got interested in winemaking again. When I graduated in 1958 with a Ph.D. in agricultural chemistry, I interviewed several companies in the food business and one of them was Gallo. It just seemed natural to go to Gallo, and I stayed there ten years, from 1958 till 1968. I learned a lot at Gallo too, it's a terrific school. I started as research chemist for new products and processes and ended as assistant production manager for winemaking. But there were things at Beaulieu Vineyards that Andre Tchelistcheff knew and did that I had never heard of at Gallo. We got along very well and I learned so much from him. Even today he's one of my closest friends.

And ultimately it was the McFarlands who enticed you away from Beaulieu Vineyards by showing you these new vineyards in Monterey?

That's right. Myron and Jerry McFarland are brothers. They're farmers from the central valley. The town of McFarland over there is named for their grandfather. They've been farmers for a long time and have had this long term dream of being involved in a quality wine operation. So they looked all over for good vineyard land, even out of this country, and ended up in the Salinas Valley.

You had nothing to do with the planting of the vineyards or selection of varieties?

Not at all. The grapes were in the ground when they called me. They organized these vineyards as limited partnerships, with partners from all over the country, some corporations but primarily individuals. Now, the winery is separate from that; it was organized in '72 and today has about 40 shareholders. I'm a shareholder, and there are other individuals and some companies who own stock. No investor owns more than 15 percent. I answer to a board of directors, and that's how it's run. We aren't really connected to the vineyard ownership, although some of the investors are the same. We have 30 year contracts with the vineyards to buy the grapes, and part of the deal is that I determine when the grapes are to be picked.

What is the role of Gerald Asher, the Gourmet Magazine *wine critic?*

Gerald Asher was president of our marketing arm, which we called "Monterey Bay Co." The winery, The Monterey Vineyard, Inc., owned 50 percent and the Foremost-McKesson Company owned 50 percent. Foremost-McKesson never had any investment in either the vineyards or the winery, just in this joint venture company. The two partners in Monterey Bay Co. have just recently decided to dissolve the company. During our first year in 1974, Gerald did an excellent job of public relations. He knows wine, and probably more important, he knows most of the leading writers involved with wine. Gerald gave us credibility with these people very early.

I certainly agree that you established credibility virtually overnight. How did you deal with the criticisms leveled at you that you were starting a winery in the wrong place at the wrong time, that Monterey *was too cold and that the market for wine was glutted in the early 70s?*

We gave no answer at all, we just answered with the quality of the wine. And we had people like James Beard talking about the wines, or Andre Tchelistcheff who tasted the Merlot wine right out of the fermenter last year and told me, "This is absolutely the best Merlot I've tasted in my whole career."

How much wine are you putting out now, and what's your maximum goal?

Thirty thousand cases in '74 when we started, and by the early 1980s we plan to hit our final plateau at about 500,000 cases. To put that in perspective, Beaulieu Vineyards is close to 250,000, I'd guess Bob Mondavi is around 200,000, Paul Masson must be 3,000,000 cases, and Almadén has got to be bigger yet. My point is, we aren't as big as it sounds.

The operation you've described is that of a winery producing wines on a big scale, with aggressive marketing. Aren't you open to the criticism that you are too big and commercial to produce great wines?

I think we are open to that kind of criticism, but the only thing that answers it is the wine itself. Why is it that large wineries do not have the reputation for quality that small ones do? I agree that they don't, and that size is an apparent negative. Size is the only thing I had against coming down here, because people would say, "Oh, another Gallo." I think you've got to break winemaking into two parts: one is the technology of it and the other is the grape supply. Now I don't think anyone can criticize Gallo's winemaking ability. When I went from Gallo to Beaulieu Vineyards, for example, Andre will be the first one to tell you that he learned quite a bit from me also. So why aren't Gallo wines as good as Beaulieu Vineyards wines? I think it's the grapes. If Gallo had 25,000 acres of grapes similar to those from Beaulieu Vineyards' Madame de Pins Vineyard Number 1, Gallo would have the top Cabernet Sauvignon in the country just as Beaulieu Vineyards has had.

What do you do about other fundamental considerations, such as oak aging?

Okay. Let me tell you how I dealt with the size problem. I told our people if we could become another Beaulieu Vineyards on a scale that could pay the bills, fine. But I insisted on handling it my way. I insisted on the same ratio of barrels per gallon of wine that we had at Beaulieu Vineyards, for instance. I believe Beaulieu Vineyards could double or triple in size without hurting the wine quality provided they had enough barrels, tanks, and people to run it. I don't think there is a problem with Heublein's expansion—with one exception: there just aren't many vineyards like Madame de Pins Number 1. Expansion today in the Napa Valley means substandard grapes. Here in the Salinas Valley there are not so many wineries scrambling for good grapes and we have 9,600 acres from which to choose. I grew up on a farm and have grown grapes for a long time. If I can't pick the best grapes out of those vineyards, then they've got the wrong man here. I've already seen that out of those vineyard blocks some aren't any good at all, and others are absolutely terrific.

Can you afford to not use some of those grapes?

We can. We're only going to make and bottle under our label 25 percent of the wine we'll have. Three-quarters of it will be sold in bulk to other wineries, or under private labels. So if we get some wines that aren't up to snuff, that's part of the three-quarters. My job is simply to pick the best tank from every four. It's a good concept.

The 500,000 cases you plan to produce by the early 1980s will be only a quarter of your total production?

That's right, the other million and a half cases worth will be sold in bulk or under private labels. We're getting calls from nearly every one of the top wineries, including many Napa Valley wineries. Demand for Monterey bulk wine is just coming out of the woodwork.*

Why should you even be interested in producing bulk wine? Because it's a profitable venture?

Yes, it cuts down the capital requirements. I told Myron I could promise no profit for ten years, but there are only eight years left now and we have to show a profit at some point.

How are you going to be able to control the quality of your wines when you have such vast quantities flowing through, and so many different types?

Actually, it's much much easier than you're guessing it is. Beaulieu Vineyards has a surprising 22 different wine types. Most California wineries do not consider ten or more wine types too many to handle, and we'll eventually have 15.

Tchelistcheff told me his ideal was a winery which produced one, two or three different wines, no more.

Yes, Andre's a very European-oriented guy, and that's the European approach. Here it's a different market. My job as winemaker is to hire the assistants needed if I don't have time to get around and smell each tank every two weeks as I presently do. That's our job in building a company, to build the kind of organization that can handle what we have to do. Certainly wineries this size do put out quality wines.

When you say "quality wines" in that context, do you mean quality wines of very top caliber?

The quality of Bob Mondavi, Beaulieu Vineyards, Joe Heitz and others. I don't include most Inglenook wines in that category anymore although some are still quite good. So our concept is quality first. We have no intention of cheapening the wine in the interest of dollars. I've never gotten that message from the investors at all.

I've heard it said that the Amerine and Winkler classification of this area as Region I years ago was based on mean temperatures and failed to take into account the shorter day, so the number of hours of warmth per day is also short.

That's true. We have thermographs in ten locations throughout the

---

*Some months after the interview, Peterson was forced to change some of his thinking. He issued a statement to the public explaining: "The Monterey Vineyard was simply unable to continue buying all the grapes that the vineyards could produce in the hope of selling them in tank lots to other wineries profitably . . . . It was necessary to cut all ties between the Monterey Vineyard and the nearly 10,000 acres of vineyards controlled by the original founders. Instead, our grapes are supplied now by only three smaller, independent growers between Gonzales and Soledad whose bearing ranches total less than 900 acres. This size is more in line with the traditional fine wine producers of California's coastal counties, and is much more manageable from our strictly quality point of view."

vineyards and I see them often. They may hit their peak for only a few minutes and drop rapidly as the afternoon fog rolls in. The wind comes right down the valley from the Monterey Bay. The vineyards north of the winery are doing best. They're elevated 400 feet or so and protected from that afternoon breeze; we may get 2,100 degree days up there, and only 1,600 here near the winery. The vineyard area around Gonzales here in the Salinas Valley is the *coolest in California!* Some of the sections wouldn't even make Region I, if you use 2,000 to 2,500 for Region I. Actually, everything less than 2,500 is considered Region I.

Doesn't that spell disaster for some varieties?

Yes, for some varieties. Farmers planted the vineyards, and they fully expected that some would have to be grafted over to other varieties that do better. Out of the 10,000, we may well lose 2,000 acres. We're finding out a lot about the micro-climates of Monterey; it's so new, we don't know it all yet. But the coolness is also to our advantage, because it gives the wines a uniqueness of personality and style. We harvest latest every year; I won't even consider picking the Cabernet this year until after Thanksgiving. That long, cool growing season develops strong flavor and a crispness that no other wine region in California has been able to match, and it's really exciting.

Does the coolness also mean you have to raise the sugar level by adding grape concentrate sometimes?

I've not yet had to do that, and I don't expect to. You can often save a bad year by doing that, but it's never as great as if the grapes ripen naturally. Listen to some of the sugar levels this season from this print-out: Gamay Beaujolais 22.2, Sylvaner 19 (that one ranch is not so good), Chardonnay 22.6, Pinot Noir 23.8, White Riesling 21.7. We're getting sugar, because we leave the grapes on the vine a month or six weeks longer than they do elsewhere. It's a risk, because it may rain. Now when we make a slightly sweet white wine like Sylvaner or Johannisberg Riesling, we ferment the wine to dryness and then use grape juice concentrate as a sweetening agent, adding one to three percent just before bottling.

I thought you said you hadn't had to use concentrate.

Not in winemaking, no. But used for final sweetening just before bottling it's equivalent to using *muté* which we used at Beaulieu Vineyards. Most wineries use concentrate in this way.

Isn't another classic way to get that sweetness to stop fermentation before all the sugar is gone, by centrifuging or some other procedure?

I doubt if anyone in California does it that way as a general practice. They all use concentrate or *muté.* Some individual small lots are done in the way you suggest, but the amount is infinitesimal.

How do you think your soil affects character?

It's decomposed granite, very thin and sandy, won't hold moisture well at all. But once the grapes establish their root systems deep, it's good soil, known to produce intense flavors. The strongest flavored Beaulieu Vineyards Cabernet, for instance, was from the Madame de Pins Vineyard Number 1 and that's the sandiest of their vineyards. In Monterey, our yield on these young vines is only one to one and a half tons per acre. And even when they get older, I don't expect over three tons per acre. Sandy soil is the reason, and that low tonnage is another thing that gives us those intense flavors. The soil works for intense flavor, and the climate works for intense flavor, and in the case of virtually all white varietals that's a plus.

What is that intense flavor, how would you describe it?

It's just more of it; concentrated varietal flavor. As I said, the whites are all helped by it. In the reds, Zinfandel is improved by that intensity, but in Cabernet it's probably a negative. One hundred percent Cabernet in Monterey County will be rare; it has to be blended down because it's just too strong.

Why should that be, because Cabernet flavor is quite delightful even at 100 percent. I'm thinking of Heitz's Martha's Vineyard Cabernet or some of the Ridge Cabernets.

Martha's Vineyard Cabernet is not particularly intense in Cabernet flavor. It's a good, well balanced Cabernet, but if you doubled the flavor level I don't think it would be quite as enjoyable. Some of the Ridge Cabernets are quite heavy. Cabernet to me tastes like green peppers. Other people call it olives or asparagus. And true Cabernet *does* have all that, but when there is too much of a good thing you don't really like it.

Are all of your wines 100 percent of the variety?

They are now, but as we learn about the grapes here I'm sure we'll blend some. The 1974 Zinfandel, about to be released, is ten percent Pinot Noir because I thought it made the wine a little more complex and interesting.

Are the grapes all mechanically harvested?

No, they're all hand picked. In the long term we think we'll have to mechanically harvest because you can't handle that many acres by hand. This year we're harvesting 100 acres by machine and we'll keep that lot separate to see what it's like. There's still some controversy over mechanical harvesting, so I'm going to experiment and then decide.

How are the grapes brought to the crusher?

In gondolas of two or two and a half tons, which is really in small batches. Twenty of those gondolas fit on a flat-bed truck, so it's a way of doing it big but keeping it small. They're dumped into the hopper, sulphured at 50 parts per million, fed into the crusher and pumped through the must line. In the case of the whites, the must is immediately dragged across the dejuicing screen which is good in that it's fast but bad in that it generates finely divided solids, so we immediately centrifuge to remove them. It's all very fast; within minutes after crushing we have the clarified juice ready for fermenting. It's the cleanest and fastest separation of clear juice from varietal grapes that I've seen, and is a reason for the fresh character of our white wines. The centrifuge is a terrific piece of machinery, but it can be used wrong. You must be careful not to clean up the juice too much. We leave a lot of solids in the Sylvaner, for example, to develop the flavor, but Gewürztraminer has plenty of flavor anyway, so we clean the juice up more before we ferment it.

Are both your reds and whites fermented in stainless steel under controlled temperatures?

Right, we start fermentation with a Montrachet yeast, the same one we used at Beaulieu Vineyards, which is imported from the Pasteur Institute in Paris each year. Whites are fermented at 50 degrees, the reds mostly at 75 degrees although Pinot Noir and Gamay Beaujolais I like to ferment at 70 degrees.

Some vintners swear that Chardonnay should be fermented in new oak barrels. I guess you can't do that practically since you're so large. Is that one of the disadvantages of being large?

Possibly, possibly. We fermented Chardonnay in oak at Beaulieu Vineyards. But Andre and I did a test, split the '68 Chardonnay into two parts, one fermented in oak, one in stainless steel, and put both in barrels after fermentation. Three months later, neither one of us could tell which was which.

How heavily do you fine and filter?

We basically don't do much to our wines. Whites we fine with bentonite; on the reds we'll use a light gelatin right after the malo-lactic fermentation and after the barrel aging maybe use egg whites. That I got from Andre and I like the procedure. Average gelatin fining might be a quarter to a half pound per thousand gallons of wine, so you see it isn't much. Of course, it doesn't remain in the wine, it's filtered out.

Do you then filter both reds and whites?

Yes, and just before bottling we filter with a millipore filter.

Don't you use the centrifuge except prior to fermentation?

Oh yes, for whites it's very important to centrifuge the yeast out right after fermentation. I'll bet 90 percent of the problems you have later on with a wine can be traced to your failure to get rid of the lees promptly after fermentation. Wineries with centrifuges invariably have cleaner, fruitier white wines than those who don't. Germans have proven that for decades.

You say you don't do very much to the wines, yet you fine, filter and centrifuge. Some winemakers claim there is a risk of taking too much out of the wine.

Fining, filtration and centrifuging are *good*, not bad. They're gentle, not harsh. They remove elements from wine that would downgrade the wine if left in—and often would fall out on their own anyway if not removed. I think it's particularly dishonest for a winery to claim that any wine is better *because* it hasn't been filtered or fined. I guess I've tasted most of them, and there isn't one that doesn't have some defect. You know, if you leave the winemaking up to God, he'll make vinegar—not wine. It sometimes happens that a given lot of wine might not need fining. I've made lots of wine that never needed, and never got, any fining at all. But to claim special virtue in these cases, either for one's self or for the wine, would be ludicrous. Filtration, on the other hand, is virtually always necessary since wine, by definition, is a clear liquid. Somehow the claim "unfiltered" implies that filtration, per se, is bad—yet we know it to be as necessary and good in wine production as it is in apple juice, beer or drinking water. I don't believe the phony virtue of "unfiltered" wine ever emanates from a competent, experienced winemaker. It can only come from the sales department.

Doesn't the centrifuge take the place of filtration?

It can. Filtration removes solids from the liquid by passing the liquid through an inert matrix which physically retains the solid particles while allowing the clear liquid to pass. Centrifugation removes the solids by whirling the mass around and around so that the solid particles are thrown outwards, while the clear wine is removed through an outlet near the center. Wines marketed as "unfiltered" very often substitute the centrifuge for the filter. Maynard Amerine said it best when he addressed about 300 winemakers and technical people at Davis last spring, and really raised hell with people who accuse filtration of being bad. He said it's a good tool, and one shouldn't imply that filtration is bad by saying "unfiltered" on the label. And then he stood back from the microphone and yelled: "Why should it cost the consumer more for a wine that you didn't do anything to?" And the crowd just roared approval.

What kind of cooperage do you have, and how long are the wines aged?

Again, we're still experimenting, because of the strong flavors. We do put the Cabernet in 50 gallon American oak—something I learned from Andre. We'll use Limousin barrels for Chardonnay, we put Zinfandel and Pinot Noir in the Yugoslavian oak 5,000 gallon tanks and a little of it in the small American barrels. I was afraid that the new, small barrels would overwhelm it with oak, but we got a nice marriage I think. You do get some flavor out of these Yugoslavian oak tanks too, even though they're relatively large. As for length of aging, we're playing with it. The Cabernet has been in barrels for ten months, and my guess is it'll take another six.

What wine types do you have on the market right now?

We have Chardonnay, Chenin Blanc, a proprietary name called Del Mar Ranch, named for the vineyard where the grapes are grown—it's almost half-and-half Chenin Blanc and Pinot Blanc, with about seven percent Sylvaner. And we have Sylvaner, Johannisberg Riesling, Gamay Beaujolais, and early Zinfandel. Coming down the road are Merlot, Cabernet, "December Harvest" Zinfandel, Pinot Noir and Gewürztraminer. Eventually we'll add Sauvignon Blanc and Sémillon in a Sauternes style. We have plenty of botrytis every year for that. Again, that will give personality to the region. One thing we've got plenty of is flavor. If we use the advantage properly we'll develop a Monterey personality, which is what we want most. I believe Monterey's personality quality level ranks with the other top regions around the world: Napa Valley is one of them, Burgundy is one of them, and so is Monterey. The way our Monterey wines will differ will be their stronger, more intense flavors, their fruitiness and freshness due not only to the region but because of our procedures in keeping the air out during winemaking; they'll have lighter bodies and be lower in alcohol than Napa wines.

One of my pet peeves is to go into a wine shop and see a "Burgundy" section, a "Bordeaux" section and a "California" section. Instead of "California," there should be "Napa Valley," "Monterey," "Sonoma" sections and so on. If they really have different personalities they should be in different sections. There's no question Monterey has a different personality.

In your view, are the best California wines as good as the best European wines?

Yes, with the exception of Burgundies.

You mean with the exception of Pinot Noir and Chardonnay?

Yes, we tasted some good Montrachet against the Chardonnays of Joe Heitz, Chalone and Hanzell just two nights ago, and that Montrachet still was the best; not by much, but better. That is, I picked out the Montrachet. Andre thought the Hanzell was best, but only slightly.

I've never yet tasted a California Pinot Noir that I thought was really as good as a French Burgundy; even that Chalone Pinot Noir we had the other night I thought was not as good as the La Tache. For some reason Pinot Noir just doesn't do it here. In Clarets, California's are easily equal. We've had several tastings with Beaulieu Vineyards '45, '46, etc., with Lafite '45 and so on, and Beaulieu Vineyards Cabernet is right in there in the same category.

Napa Valley:
THE HEART OF TRADITION

A roadside sign welcomes you to Napa Valley by quoting Robert Louis Stevenson's remark, "and the wine is bottled poetry." This is wild literary license, for Stevenson actually pronounced the wine "merely good," and wrote, "Bit by bit, they grope about for their Clos de Vougeot and Lafite. Those lodes and pockets of earth, more precious than the precious ores . . . where the soil has sublimated under sun and stars to something finer, and the wine is bottled poetry: these still lie undiscovered." But history has caught up with the quotation; we may assume Stevenson would agree that many precious pockets of Napa earth have now been discovered and much of the wine *is* bottled poetry.

If Napa lacked great wine at Stevenson's visit in 1880, it already possessed traditions of a great winemaking region and vintners who played their roles in grand style. Charles Krug was known in those days as "wine king" of the valley, Jacob Schram had dug his underground cellars (today, Schramsberg Champagne Cellars) and the Beringer brothers were building their spectacular Rhine House. If you travel in the valley today you will be regaled with tours of old mansions and stories of the colorful characters who have made Napa wine in the last hundred years. Napa, more than any other region, has long been the heart of California's wine tradition.

Only thirty-five miles long and one to five miles wide, this valley hosts over fifty wineries, the most intense concentration of winemaking activity in the country. Napa Valley owes its fame to this intense concentration, rather than to any identifiable Napa style or exclusive possession of California's greatest vineyards. Not all its vineyards produce superb grapes, but many do. Some vineyards run along the flat valley floor—here in deep, loamy soils, there in thin, volcanic soils. Other vineyards climb onto rolling benchlands and up into steep mountains which bound the valley east and west. Unique microclimates surround the vineyards tucked away in niches and those at high elevations, while breezes from San Pablo Bay adjoining San Francisco determine the general valley climate. Cool salt air is strongest at Carneros next to the Bay, weakest at Calistoga in the valley's hot northern end.

Unlike Burgundy and Bordeaux where wine is the product of a long settled *ménage à trois* of climate, soil and grape variety, Napa wines come from all possible combinations of these. But winegrowers are developing sophistication in matching variety to climate and quickly discovering those "precious pockets of earth." This, along with infusion of a new generation of colorful characters, carries the Napa tradition not only onward but upward.

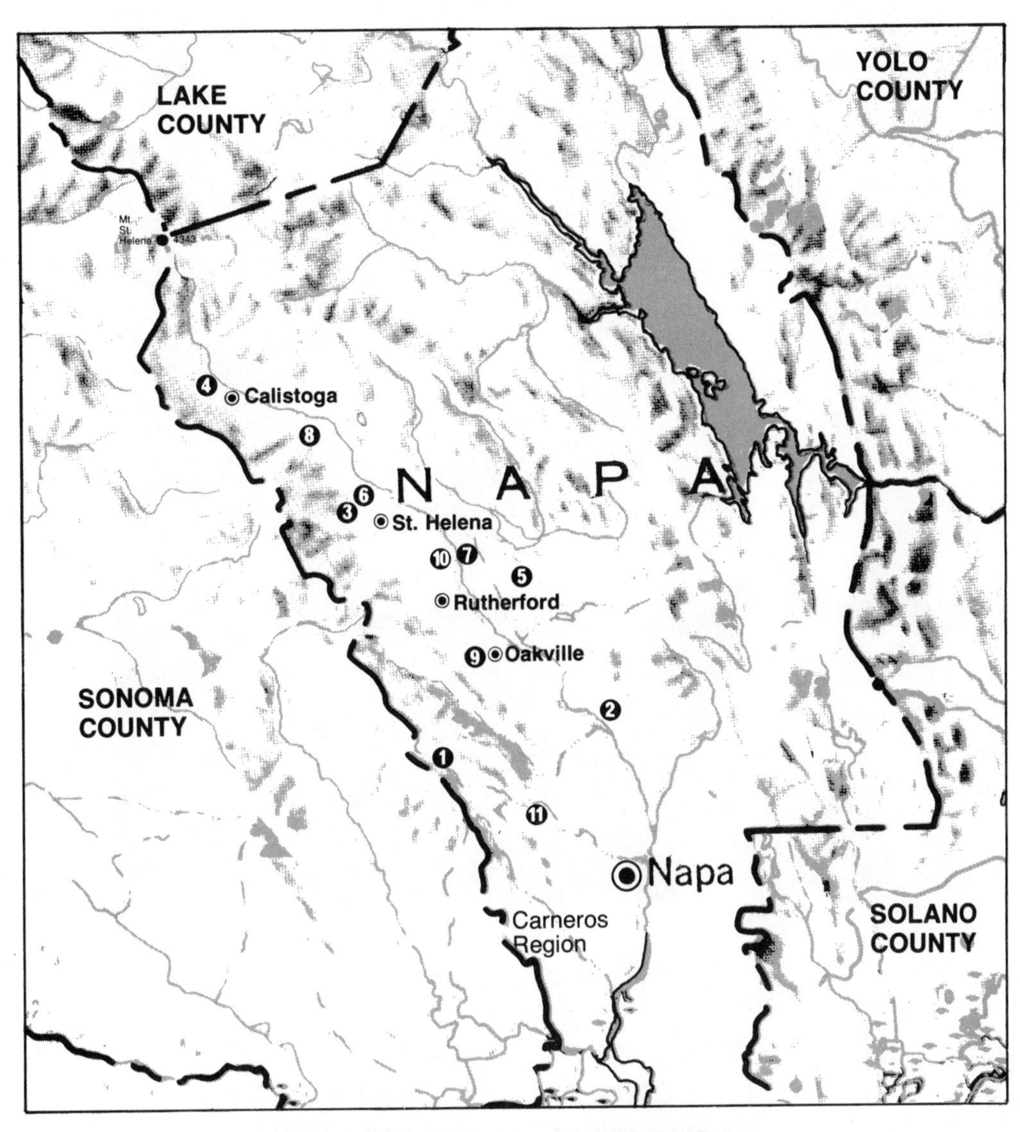

1 Mayacamas Vineyards
2 Stag's Leap Wine Cellars
3 Spring Mountain Vineyards
4 Chateau Montelena
5 Chappellet Vineyard
6 Freemark Abbey Winery
7 Heitz Wine Cellars
8 Sterling Vineyards
9 Robert Mondavi Winery
10 Louis M. Martini Winery
11 The Christian Brothers

North of San Francisco Bay
NAPA VALLEY: The Heart of Tradition

Andre Tchelistcheff

It is very false for us to steal the appellations of Europe. I accepted it with the bleeding of my heart, but it was a necessity, a compromise I accepted with tears.

He has been called "the winemaker's winemaker," "the unquestioned master of Cabernet Sauvignon," "wise," and "pixyish." Other winemakers covet his praise. Though diminutive in height, he is surely the vintner of greatest stature in America today. Andre

Tchelistcheff, expatriate Russian with Czechoslovakian and French training, has been an American winemaker for four decades. He is now in his late seventies and retired from his long career as winemaster at Beaulieu Vineyards, but he is rushing into his fifth winemaking decade as a consultant to wineries all over California and out of the state. Over the years, he has challenged his colleagues, above all by his triumphs of Cabernet Sauvignon and Pinot Noir produced at Beaulieu Vineyards, as well as by his theories of fermentation, by his crusade to match the right grape varieties with the right micro-climates, and by his emphasis on soil as a critical quality factor. In this interview, calling himself extravagant and aggressive, he again seemed anxious to throw down the gauntlet to his colleagues. As we talked in his pleasant Napa home and I watched him sit on the edge of the sofa and gesticulate in the grand European manner, I was amazed, and grateful, that his career is only now reaching its apogee.

Recommended wine to drink while reading this chapter:

1968 BEAULIEU VINEYARDS
CABERNET SAUVIGNON
GEORGES DE LATOUR PRIVATE RESERVE

I understand you were born in Russia, the son of a law professor?

My father was a professor of criminal law and also a chief justice of the Russian Imperial Court of Appeal in Moscow. A man of high intellectual caliber, he published a tremendous amount of historical research dealing with legal reforms in Russia. He changed his career to Secretary of Justice in the south of Russia, when Russia was divided during the civil war into two entirely different political territories. Then he emigrated to Yugoslavia, became a consultant jurist for the Yugoslavian government. After the Second World War, he emigrated from Paris to California and spent a few happy years at the end of his life with me and my brother and sister in California.

Were you a young boy during the period when your father was in Yugoslavia?

I was then already a college student. My educational career was interrupted by the civil war, because I was also active in the civil war. I graduated from the military academy of Kiev and so therefore participated in the civil war in Russia. I migrated to Yugoslavia, and from there I started my steps toward future education, and was admitted to the Institute of Agricultural Technology in Brno in Czechoslovakia. That's my first graduation. And then life brought me to France, and in France I was reeducated in the Institute of National Agronomy, went to work in the industry of France, came back to the Experimental Station of Paris, and then in early 1938 signed a contract with the founder of Beaulieu Vineyards in California, Georges de Latour.

What induced you to come to California?

My California career, I would say, was accidental. Because in Paris, as an assistant at the Oenological and Viticultural Station, I was exposed to several temptations. The first was to stay with the Institute Pasteur where I took the course of Alcoholic Fermentation and began my experimentation in microbiology with some outstanding authorities of the Institute Pasteur, in the Champagne region, in Moët & Chandon's vineyards. And then it happened to be I had two colleagues in the Experimental Station in Paris, one Chilean who eventually became a professor of viticulture in Santiago de Chile, and the other a future Secretary of Agriculture in Red China. So I had the opportunity to go to Chile, to stay in France, or to go to the Chi Foo region of Manchuria to make Chinese wines. But instead . . .

Mr. Latour found you!

Mr. Latour found me. As a matter of fact, the California challenge was a little stronger to my ears, because I was already introduced to the research work of Professors Bioletti, Winkler and Amerine at the University of California. My acquaintance with California wines actually started in 1937, at the International Exposition in Paris, where I had the opportunity to taste two California wines. The first one was Valle de Oro Sémillon of Wente. And the second was a Gewürztraminer of Inglenook.

And did they appeal to you?

Well, it was something very extravagant.

You were about 37 years old then, in 1938 when you came here to work for Beaulieu, and you stayed at Beaulieu until 1973?

Right, and when I retired from Beaulieu in 1973 I decided to go to free lance consulting. I thought the challenges, new, individual aspects and efforts in entirely different ecological regions of California, Washington and Oregon would give me far more constructive energy to end out my professional career. I am active now in three states, in Washington State with Ste. Michelle, and in Oregon with two young wineries, Erath Vineyards and Wynquist which is in the process of building up. I took the Buena Vista winery here, the little winery of Stag's Leap plus the Hoffman Mountain Ranch in Paso Robles. Then in Los Olivos, the Firestone

Vineyard in Santa Barbara County. So you see my scope of operation. Recently I touched another project on the Jordan property in Alexander Valley. And then, of course, there is the Simi winery where I am spending a great amount of time, working with the winemaker, Mary Ann Graf. She is my last industrial training exhibit. Of course, I have younger people than Mary Ann Graf in the new projects I'm starting, but she is a challenge to me because I had been acquainted with working for women superiors, such as Madame de Latour and Madame La Marquise de Pins at Beaulieu, but I had never been acquainted with the idea that someday in my life I would work parallel in a team of plowing horses with a young lady on the side of me.

You were actually consulting even during your Beaulieu years, weren't you?

In 1947, I opened my oenological experiment laboratory in St. Helena, and founded a professional organization which I called Oenological Research Center of Napa Valley. This became a nucleus for the Napa Valley Technical Group, which today covers 70 or 80 members. All these wineries remained within my consulting scope, because I consulted then, with all of them, giving a great amount of time to Beaulieu of course, but also working for Charles Krug, Inglenook, Louis Martini, Sebastiani, Buena Vista, and so on. That's the way this thing mushroomed—my activities continuously expanding, expanding, expanding.

Now you've been working in Washington State and all over California, substantially in the Napa region, have you come to any conclusions about which areas are most conducive to specific varietals?

Well, actually you are touching the most sensitive part of me by asking such a question. Being a man of European education, and carrying a great amount of European philosophy about viticulture and oenology, I have always faced in my long winemaking career a very critical division of my own personality.

Ecology is very up-to-date in the California wine industry today, as it was forty years ago, regarding two basic factors: micro-climate and grape variety. I grant these are two factors of great importance, but I've always fought for my own philosophical principles in winemaking. I believe there are third and fourth factors which correlate to the general ecology. The third factor is soil—physical and chemical structure, profile of exposure, depth, humidity and richness of the soil; the fourth factor is the human being as ecological manager. We divide the ecology into the ecology which is given us by Mother Nature or the Great Lord, and we can't change that ecology, and then managerial ecology, which is full of the possibilities of man. Man uses the raw materials given by the Great Lord—soil, varieties and climate—and manages them in the best way, according to his own dream, image, or ideals.

Now, the reason I mention this fourth factor, management, is because in modern viticulture we can do great things positively and we can do great things very negatively. To start with we must plant the proper rootstock corresponding to the individual vinifera varieties that will be grafted on the particular rootstock. We must select according to the soil, according to the climate, according to topographical position, all the vineyards and the varieties. We must have a proper orientation, proper management in bringing up the individual vine within the known number of vines per acre, and proper pruning assigned within all these complexities to a maximum quality of production.

May I ask you specifically about the Napa Valley? Do you believe there's a great difference in quality between grapes grown on the valley floor and grapes grown in the hill regions?

This again corresponds to my general philosophy. Even the valley floor should be divided into different zones, because it directly correlates to and is managed by micro-climatic regions. As I see it today, I divide Napa Valley into three belts: I start from Carneros in the south which is my "North Pole" because it's cooler, and I go to Calistoga in the north which is my "Southern Pole," because it's much warmer. The first region starts at Carneros near San Pablo Bay, because the exposures there almost touch the bay, and north to Yountville I draw the first red line on the map. And I assign this section for the varietals of early maturity, because the late maturing varieties have always been a complete fiasco in this region. Unfortunately, several growers will not listen to this and are still planting late maturing varieties in this subregion of Napa Valley.

You were one of the first to urge that Pinot Noir be grown in the Carneros region.

That's right. Louis Martini and I.

And what other varieties are suited to that subregion?

Chardonnay. I divide the whole area into two sections, Chardonnay and Pinot Noir. Louis Martini also: Chardonnay and Pinot Noir. Moët & Hennessey are coming now and planting even lower toward the Bay, and planting Chardonnay and Pinot Noir. There is a possibility of growing in this region a Gewürztraminer, *maybe* a Johannisberg Riesling which is not a bad idea at all, and several growers are trying it. There is a possibility for certain acreage of Merlot, specifically, for those vintners already planting Cabernet in this critical region. To counterbalance the weakness and retarded maturity of Cabernet here, I definitely recommend planting 30 percent to 40 percent of Merlot. You can add Gamay Beaujolais to the area if you want to.

Is most of the quality difference in this region explained by the temperature? What about your soil factor?

Soil is of great importance even there, because as soon as we touch deeper soils the quality goes down; but we do not have in this region the soils I would love to have there. I have a beautiful micro-climate, and this is not only summation of temperatures, but also the humidity and air movement and fog, all these are very important. So this region gives us the privilege to preserve the organic acidity of the fruit. It is very important in whites and Pinot Noir to preserve the malic acid. We are interested in producing a maximum amount of lactic acid in the Pinot Noir in the malo-lactic fermentation.

And the middle region?

We went to Yountville and we are almost touching Oakville. Now, we are starting from Oakville and we are going to Zinfandel Lane. I divide this area into two subsections, starting from Oakville and going to Zinfandel Lane on the left side of Highway 29. In other words, your eastern boundary is Highway 29 and your western boundary is Mountain Ridge, Mount St. John, which dominates that section. This is the greatest region for production of Cabernet Sauvignon in California. That's where the greatest wines are produced, and the greatest are produced by Heitz in Martha's Vineyard, by Bob Mondavi who has Cabernet right in front of his winery, the greatest Private Reserves of Beaulieu are produced from there and the greatest Inglenook wines come more or less from the same section.

What act of God made that piece of land so great?

This is volcanic soil, and volcanic erosion. There is a great amount of gravel moved into that section and the soils there are basically not too rich and of rather medium depth, or even shallow. The region prohibits a production of Cabernet Sauvignon above three and a half to four tons per acre, and that's it. Mother Nature, the ecological regime, does not permit you to produce more than three and a half or four tons. Once you try to produce more, the vineyard complains. Therefore, in this particular region, we have the Cabernet, Merlot, château types from Highway 29 going west to Mt. St. John, and going north to Zinfandel Lane.

Between Oakville and Zinfandel Lane going east towards the Silverado Trail, they are heavy, heavy soils, sometimes 12, 14, even 15 feet of heavy, rich soil. And again, Bordeaux type grapes, including Sauvignon Blanc, do beautifully in this particular situation, as do Cabernet Sauvignon and Merlot; and you can also grow decent Chenin Blanc. But I definitely do not recommend planting any other varieties. And you can grow Muscat Canelli, you know, as an exceptional thing—early maturing. It's a very exotic variety with a tremendous personality; even in this soil where the production is between four and five and a half tons, Muscat Canelli can do well, as an exception. This is the original ground where Georges de Latour created his high reputation for Muscat de Frontignan. Zinfandel is not suitable for either region, west or east of Highway 29, although much is planted there.

What about in the hills just east of the Silverado Trail? Is that Zinfandel territory?

Zinfandel, up, up, up we go! Zinfandel needs to be in the poorest soil, gravelly and reddish, *terra rosa;* that's the ideal situation for Zinfandel in the Napa Valley. Eastern slopes—even going way up. Zinfandel. Never put Zinfandel in the lower sections, except some very warm situations in the Calistoga region where Zinfandel is doing very well, even in deep soil, but there is sufficient heat to really concentrate the Zinfandeliness. You can really make an excellent Zinfandel, not gravelly Zinfandel, but a very robust Zinfandel, in the heavy soils of Calistoga.

Within your middle region, would the grapes you suggest for that region be even better grown in the hills?

I think they would be much better in this particular region, as in all regions of the Napa Valley, where we have more gravel. And there are more gravelly soils in the upper slopes—not exceedingly steep slopes, but 15 degree slopes.

Why do gravelly soils produce better quality?

In gravelly soils you've got two basic factors, which relate to the international prestige of soils. Gravelly, stony soils with a generous amount of calcium oxide, iron oxide—in other words the white cycle of soils, or the *terra rosa,* pink-red soils—are known as the quality producers with a greater or lesser amount of stones, gravel, I mean even boulders. The physiology of the vine doesn't change, because, you know, as a human we must have a certain amount of calories regardless of where we live. And in a hot soil under the hot sun of southern France, or a cold soil of the Champagne region, or in South Africa, or in Argentina, or in Russia, we still need the same elements of life. Vines are reacting exactly as we are reacting. Therefore, there are minimum, maximum and optimum prerequisites. The optimum response to these prerequisites of ecological complexity gives you the great wine. You see there is always this question: what is your image? Average quality? Good standard quality? Or excelsior? You know, *non plus ultra,* greatness. I am looking always for the great wines!

What about the third zone, up near Calistoga?

Several people are sitting in that third belt with Cabernet and Merlot and Pinot Noir and Chardonnay and Riesling and Gewürztraminer. It's wrong but that's their own decision. I am not accusing them, I present you this excuse: when the pioneers such as Krug, such as Schram, such as de Latour, moved into the Napa Valley, they moved as they moved into the Sonoma region or Mendocino region, with the idea that this is God's country. We have beautiful summers, little summer rain, beautiful rains during the winter which supply enough moisture, mild temperatures in the spring, and late falls which permit late maturity for the late varietals, so in this climate we can combine any varieties.

This view was inherited, and the marketing spine of the industry was very weak, because the original immigrant from Europe consuming this wine was asking for the same damn thing he drank in Europe. He was asking for Burgundy, he was asking for Sauternes, for Chablis, for Rhine. He was asking for Port, Sherry, Tokay, and Muscat; he was asking for all this. And the distributor, with a weak exposure to the consumer market, refused to deal with selected vintners with two, three, or four varieties. He said, "The hell, what am I going to do with you? I'm selling so many bottles of wine and I need so many classes of wine to succeed with our marketing."

But some people are still, I would say without thinking, following the same philosophy, and they still like to have 12, 14, 15 labels. This is a tremendous error. This will never be corrected by anybody but the consumer. The consumer is the great master of today in the production activities in the back office of the winery, and in the front office in marketing. The consumer is going to force the marketing offices to adjust their philosophy towards the road to limitation. And I'm happy to tell you that several newcomers are coming up with a very limited selection of wines. That's why I am so crazy about preaching this philosophy because I can hear already ears are listening, and thinking parallel with me about the importance of tomorrow. Because what we are building today, we are building for the existence of the industry and for the prosperity of the industry for the next 30, 40, 50, 100 years.

I'd like to ask you about certain varietals. What about the Johannisberg Riesling? Is the potential for that grape in the state of Washington greater than it is for California?

This is, you know, a delicate question. I would say all the Johannisberg Rieslings produced in Napa, Sonoma, Mendocino, Monterey, Salinas, Santa Maria, are very acceptable, very good California Rhine types. But they are not the stars yet. There may be starlets with the radiation of light in a very dark night. In some classes such as botrytis, with a great amount of artistic finishing by the winemaker, they are producing the starlets. But they do not have the ecological complex to create great Rieslings. Now Washington State—in their sandy, light soils, I'll give the class of Rieslings a little more bright light in the starlet structure. It is a far more shiny starlet maybe than our north coast counties and Monterey Rieslings. But they are still not great stars, not great stars.

Where to look for great stars of tomorrow? Where to go? I've got my hopes. As a matter of fact, I've even got proof that the greatest Rieslings will be produced in the very cold regions of Santa Barbara County and in Temecula in Riverside County! There are two reasons: Riesling matures there very late, as it matures very late in the upper Rhine. And they are grown in gravelly, light, granitic soils which are only available there.

What about the Rieslings of the Monterey region?

They are very good, very elegant, fragrant, with a little excess of the varietal greenery in the nose, and I would say shallowness of complexity in their structure. Again, they are starlets, and very promising starlets. But all these Rieslings are lacking the final finesse, a finesse that's only successfully produced in the gravelly terrace vineyards of the upper Rhine, with exposure to the same moisture they have in Monterey without gravel. They are very interesting wines, no question about it, very amusing wines, tolerating all kinds of compliments without any question. But they do not have the finesse I would like in great Rieslings. I think I will be able to locate this finesse in these two regions, because I have the soil and proper climate. Very cold climate, and very cold nights because a breeze from the ocean goes right there, and then I have a natural botrytis.

I wanted to ask you next about Pinot Noir. Why is it so difficult to make in California?

Because we have the variety, the climate, but not the soil. Accidentally, we occasionally get good Pinot Noirs as a result of the other ecological factors: tonnage, seasonal climate or submicro-climate, humidity, early maturity. These factors give us, without the gravel, *accidentally,* this great complexity. That happened to me in 1946 in the Pinot Noir of Beaulieu, and partially in the 1947 and in the 1968. But you see I spent 35 years working there and if I count three vintages of a high standard that's all I accomplished with it in my life. So I am looking to new regions—to Paso Robles, and partially to a subregion of Dry Creek of Sonoma, in gravelly, not productive soil. And partially in the Forestville region of Sonoma, again in poor, gravelly slopes.

In Paso Robles I have a very limey soil, to the extreme of gravelly lime. There I can make an individual Pinot Noir, different from Santa Ynez, which has another individuality. And the limey soil of Chalone Vineyards, where Dick Graff makes such a beautiful Pinot Noir. I am going to tell you, honestly, as a winemaker of certain prestige, not greatness, but of a certain prestige, that I tasted recently, in the company of Dick Graff and my wife, a 1969 Pinot Noir of his, and I put myself on my knees. It was a great, great Pinot Noir.

So I have these sections. And there is another section in the Napa Valley for instance, the Schramsberg section with limey gravel, where Chardonnay and Pinot Noir are planted for Champagne production. They can produce great still wines there too. But, again, this Pinot Noir will give far superior quality in Champagne than any other Pinot Noir grown in the Napa Valley. You see how spotty it is. This is appellation of origin!

Would you like to see these specific subregions delimited with their own appellations of origin, and restricted as to vineyard practices and the kinds of varietals that can be grown there?

By all means! How soon can it be accomplished? Right now, we are very *liberally,* with you, and even with the grape growers and the vintners, *gently,* in let's say a very smooth, very elegant form of conversation, *generally* discussing this philosophical principle of quality production. But we have never touched this strongly, as strongly as I'm touching. It's already acceptable for such a thing, for intellectual maceration.

But it's going to take years of experimentation, isn't it?

Years of experimentation or . . . the dramatic energy of a Martin Ray. The fighting energy of Martin Ray, who decided to build—with success or maybe even with defeat—his own appellation of origin. Individual people within the industry are talking about and sponsoring this idea. Beaulieu, for instance, has continuously promoted my idea that Pinot Noirs and Chardonnays should be produced in Carneros. Beaulieu has pressed already the appellation of "Private Reserve" in the Napa Valley. Several people are doing the same thing, so therefore we are in the process. Now, how to organize and how to jump from voluntarily sponsored appellations of origin, which practice has very little value to the consumer as long as it's not controlled by the county, state or federal authorities?

As the first step, I see individual, self-sponsored, self-promoted appellations of origin, with individual *clos*—three types of Zinfandel, two types of Cabernet, coming from entirely different vineyards. Gradually, more people in the industry are starting to think similarly, not in such an aggressive, extravagant form as I am preaching. I am very aggressive by nature and extravagant. I like to believe in principles as someone who believes in them, not artificially. I like to explore the principles because I believe in them.

Would you like to see generic names such as Burgundy, Chablis, Sauternes, given up?

Temporarily they will be with us, and people buy them primarily because they are good wines, and far more reasonably priced than varietals, and still a good type for everyday use. I understand it is very false for us to steal the appellations of Europe. I never accepted this. I accepted it with the bleeding of my heart, but it was a necessity. This is one of the compromises I accepted with tears, but it's a *modus vivendi,* a way of living; you've got to have a piece of bread and glass of wine and a little butter or cheese at least. This is a conflict between my own dreams and reality.

May I ask you some questions about winemaking techniques? I recently read a column where you were quoted as saying you believed in "classic, open fermenters." Could you elaborate?

Classic, open fermenters, in California, have almost completely disappeared, outside of Beaulieu; outside of Beaulieu, a few small growers still use open fermenters where they punch the cap, and Simi is still using open fermenters for their red wine production. There is a tremendous amount of pro and con. In the closed fermenter you have to pump over the must far more often because in the closed fermenter you've got a center belt of refrigeration, or you have two belts of refrigeration, and despite the rotation of the wine must during the fermentation, you've got different average temperatures of the must. In other words, you have a cap temperature, a middle band of low temperature due to the belt of refrigeration and an inbetween section. So actually, in the biology of fermentation you have three or four stages going independently. To homogenize we pump over, and in pumping we spread this must over the dry cap. In the open fermenter, since you have a great surface of caloric migration, heat loss, you have only one single belt in a 10,000 or 12,000 gallon fermenter. Therefore, the closed fermenter forces you to do this *remontage,* as the French say, or pumping over more frequently, say twice a day. Some people, even in the open fermenter, are pumping over twice a day. I do not recommend such a thing, but some people lean to this philosophy that the more they circulate to the cap the more extraction they will have. I do not agree with either. I still believe the open fermenter with punching down, and only one pumping over, will control everything much better.

We have to reconsider the amount of pumping over. Because during the pumping over—with the CO_2 escaping and heat escaping and the aromatic substances we call "aroma of fermentation"—the tank starts to smell delightfully with this beautiful aroma. We should do everything possible to preserve in red wines that aroma of fermentation.

What about the submerged cap idea?

It's not going too well, because you don't have elegance in the wine. The wines are very robust. It's not my idea. Neither is continuous circulation, the Christian Brothers' method. Some small producers still punch down, and some in Bordeaux still punch, and that's good. So I limit the pumping over, and I readjust my temperature of fermentation to an entirely new scale. I would like to create 85 degrees but go very rapidly out of 85 degrees and leave red Bordeaux or Burgundies an additional two to four days in fermentation at lower temperatures.

And what about Chardonnay, do you believe in fermenting that in small oak?

Very much so. But cautiously! Some people overdo it. Oak, Limousin oak and American oak, any oak in the bottle is nothing else but seasoning. Just as a great chef uses seasoning in creating great *plats du jour.* Oak is connected with the final taste like pepper and salt is to your dish.

You've been the principal sponsor of the idea of malo-lactic fermentations, haven't you?

Yes, that's my child. Since 1961 I have been working on this regime in all cellars I dominate. And I am very proud: in cooperation with the oenologists of Ste. Michelle, I even promoted it in Washington State, the induced malo-lactic fermentation. All the firms where I am consulting accept this as a prerequisite.

You believe in inducing even if it may well happen naturally?

Well, you see, natural malo-lactic fermentations are questionable because they have a great complexity of off flavors. The induced fermentation has off flavors too, but I am able to control them much easier. The lactic nose, and behind the lactic nose, spontaneous fermentation, sometimes gives you H_2S—rotten egg flavor—or some piggy, dirty flavor that's very hard to remove. Do you know, my dear sir, that when I came to California nobody in the industry believed malo-lactic fermentation, as a phenomenon, even existed? In my first research in my own laboratory, with the cooperation of my assistant, Mr. Suverkrop, we sponsored this idea. We started research on malo-lactic fermentation with wines of the North Coast and showed that in all red California wines, regardless whether they are in Mendocino, Napa, Sonoma, there is a malo-lactic fermentation as a phenomenon. They were always talking then about lactic spoilage—an entirely different microbiological phenomenon—but they never considered malo-lactic fermentation. The first report that was published, in 1947, was my report on malo-lactic fermentation on red wines in California.

Do you believe the very best wines will come from the small wineries in California? Does size have anything to do with quality?

The best wines will come from the small wineries specialized selectively in one or two types, four types at the most. On a big industrial scale the best wines can be achieved in large volume production from 50,000 to 75,000 cases a year, but with one single class of wine, uncompromisingly. If you have a single instrument to play, you know everything about it. All capricious, emotional reactions of the wine will be known to the winemaker. This, by the way, is a very old question.

I ask you to accept my explanation of this because I've dealt in the wine industry of California with 16 or 18 types, and I have only one head, a pair of eyes, a pair of ears, one nose with two nostrils, one mouth with a single tongue, and that's my perception. Beyond my perception, I have only a small amount of grey substance to concentrate with—my brains. When I am dealing with a complexity of 18 products, with entirely different genetic and generic, microbiological, physical, technological structures and management, I have to divide all this among 18 different types. Then I multiply them by the number of vintages I have in the winery—a quality winery has usually three vintages in the process of aging, plus wines graduating from grammar school to high school, and youngsters coming to me in the process of fermentation. It is impossible to achieve! But if I deal only with one type, then I will have sufficient intellectual capacity to enable me to live in constant physical contact and understanding with the wine I am making and nursing. The successful winemaker establishes this contact—every part your own, every vintage your own, every tank your own, every barrel your own.

Bob Mondavi is counteracting my philosophy. Bob Mondavi says "No! Andre Tchelistcheff is wrong! I do not agree with Andre Tchelistcheff! Instead of one head, I am presenting in front of Andre Tchelistcheff a team of winemakers and I have eight heads that are producing!" But it is not so. Only if he divides the responsibilities—specialist in Chardonnay, specialist in Pinot, specialist in Cabernet, specialist in Riesling—and does not let these men taste or manage any other wine, will I agree with him. But he is not doing that. All these eight men taste this unlimited selection.

Let me press you on that one point, because you yourself have produced some of the best Cabernets in California and some of the best Pinot Noirs, yet at the same time you were producing them you were putting out a line of 12 or 15 wines.

But I never claimed my greatness except with Cabernet Private Reserve. And Beaulieu accepted this. In the stable of Arabian horses, I have a sire: Cabernet Private Reserve. Then I have a Cabernet: well, a stallion, a very good stallion. And I have a number of mares, some of them promising mares, some of them common horses. But I always concentrated my attention. Why was my success at Beaulieu limited to the Private Reserve, Cabernet, and accidentally Pinot Noir and some Chardonnay maybe? Because my basic attention, devotion, my effort, was always guiding me to far more love, far more energy toward this selected line of Beaulieu, and the secondary line was just good, average quality. That's my answer.

My last question is, in your view, are the best California wines equal to the best European wines?

Well, I must answer you exactly as Dr. Amerine has answered. I never willingly compare European wines against California wines. Because I would do great harm to the image of them both. I apply the same philosophy not only to European and California wines, but Australian and South American wines as well. There were great wines of Chile, of Argentina, great wines of South Africa, Australia, California and Europe. Every one of them should be classified individually, and never be compared. Genetically, we tend to compare since they come from the same genetic variety, but under absolutely different ecological regimes. As my son is a genetic type of Andre Tchelistcheff, I am a genetic type of Victor Tchelistcheff, Sr., but I am entirely different from my father, as my son is from me. So inherited genetic character is visible, but does not represent my personality. Physically, yes, but not spiritually or in the complex of my individuality. That's the whole damn thing! In every tasting they compare the Bordeaux and California wines! They are ruining their reputation in Bordeaux and ruining their reputation in California. This may be attractive to the public, very good food for commercial advertising, but not for me.

Robert Travers
MAYACAMAS VINEYARDS

There certainly was a large gap between the best of Europe and California and that gap has been closing . . . but it will take a while for the word to get around.

Bob Travers was riding high on his tractor, pursued by great billows of dust, when I drove in. He dismounted and led me into his office within the cool walls of the winery. A novice when he bought Mayacamas Vineyards and moved his family to the 2,000 foot top of the dense mountain range that separates the Napa and Sonoma Valleys, he nevertheless produced wines in a very short time that captured the imagination of wine enthusiasts. He keeps it very small, devotes himself to only three wines, and produces some of the biggest, most characterful wines made in California. Some of the Cabernets may not begin to display their full personalities for many years, and predictions are that when they do they will richly reward those who save and savor them.

Recommended wine to drink while reading this chapter:
MAYACAMAS
Late Harvest ZINFANDEL

Do your wines have a characteristic Mayacamas style?

Yes, that's changed and is just becoming evident in the wines we're starting to sell now. When we first bought the place we used the grape sources they had previously and we didn't have much vineyard here. Almost all those purchased grapes came from valley floor vineyards, which gives a different style, so the wines were much lighter in character than those we've been making recently from our own vineyards and the other mountain vineyards. Starting with the 1970 vintage I would characterize our wines as big, slow aging wines. Our Chardonnays, for example, are five or six years old before they're at their best. Our 1970 Cabernet will probably be 15 or 20 years old before it's ready.

Who originally founded a winery here, and when?

John Henry Fischer was his name, and the winery was completed in 1889. A few of the original vines are still alive. Jack Taylor, an Englishman, owned the winery from 1941 until 1968 when I bought it. They had 17 wines on the market, and it took several years to lop them off, and get down to three. It was my intent from the outset just to make those few I liked best. I thought I could probably do the best job with those wines I was interested in. Some of the wines they produced were good sellers and we didn't want to slit our throats the first day in the door, so the ones that weren't selling well went out right away and we were down to about ten wines the first year, and then it was only a couple of wines a year for several more years until we got down to three wines: Cabernet, Chardonnay and Zinfandel.

What did you do before you became a winemaker?

I was a research analyst in San Francisco for an investment bank. But I guess I had some country in my blood—both my parents were from agricultural families, although neither grew grapes or made wine, and I worked on various ranches for relatives in summers while I was going to school. After living in the city for a few years, I decided I really wanted the country, and a hobby was studying grape growing and winemaking. I had no real practical experience, but had studied the field. I took night courses and short courses from the University of California at Davis, read all their textbooks. Then in late 1963 I started looking for property with the idea of starting a vineyard, selling the grapes, working it on weekends: some way to get started. After a good two years of looking I came to the slow but sure conclusion that I didn't really know what I was looking at and didn't know what to do with it if I did find something. So in 1967 I went to work for Joe Heitz at the Heitz Cellars winery. I worked there for a year and then bought this place in 1968.

Are all your wines 100 percent varietals?

The Chardonnay and Zinfandel are. In three of the last four years we experimented with the Cabernet by adding a small amount of Merlot, between two and eight percent. I'm just looking for a little more complexity in the character of the wine.

Of the three varietals you make, two of them are so-called "noble" varieties, but Zinfandel is not. Is it your view that Zinfandel is as noble as Cabernet, Pinot Noir, Chardonnay and Riesling?

I certainly think in California it makes better wine than Pinot Noir, a "noble" variety. I don't know if I'd put it quite in the same class as Cabernet and Chardonnay in California.

Were you the first winemaker in California to produce a Zinfandel labeled "late harvest?"

Right. And it got us a wildly wonderful amount of free publicity; it was great. I did that in 1968, the first year I came here.

How did you get the idea, especially as a new winemaker?

I stumbled across it completely; 1968 was a year when things ripened early, the weather was warm during the ripening period, and we knew those grapes were ready to pick but told the grower to hold off for two or three days because we were busy with other grapes. We probably misjudged the sugar in our field tests, which is easy to do anyway. It was very warm in those intervening days and they got a lot riper. Zinfandel also is a grape which tends to raisin. You get dehydrated berries, partially raisined, and they go into the fermenting tank with their concentrated sugar. They don't break down right away so you don't get an accurate sugar reading at any one point. But obviously, the sugar had to be in the mid-30s since the alcohol turned out to be 17 percent.

Where do you buy the Zinfandel grapes?

In the last three years they've come from Amador County, over in the Sierra foothills. We don't grow any Zinfandel in our own vineyards. We have 12 acres of Cabernet, some of it young and partially bearing, and 32 acres of Chardonnay, about ten of which are young and not bearing yet. Those vineyards produce about half our grape requirements and we buy the other half from vineyards on this mountain, and in Amador.

How cool is it up here?

We don't have enough records to be sure. We're probably close to the borderline between Region I and Region II on a heat summation basis. That doesn't tell the whole story, because you do get a different ripening pattern in the hills and a different heat distribution pattern at this altitude. We get less variation in temperature extremes during the growing season. We get more variation in winter, due to our altitude and the snow. We get more rain here in the hills, about twice as much as the city of Napa which averages 30 inches to our 60. There are other differences too. Our soil types are quite different from those in the Valley. We don't have any loams, any deep, rich soils at all. Most of our soils vary from 18 inches to three feet deep, are very rocky and gravelly. And of course there's not a single bit of flat land, it's all sloping, some quite steeply. That causes differences in radiation, depending on how the land slopes. Also our soils drain rapidly.

Do all those factors of climate and soil combined, in your opinion, impart a distinctive character to your wines?

I think they do. While grapes do well in a broad range of soils, they do react differently. You can have good quality fruit grown in soils with different balances of mineral nutrients, but they all taste different. Also, when you have shallow soils that are rocky, steep and well drained, you get lower productivity. Our production ranges from less than a ton to two and a half tons, maximum. That's less than half what valley growers expect. Of course, it varies with variety and many other factors, like what shape the vineyard is in. If we left enough wood out there we could increase our productivity a little—I've never even considered the possibility. I'm sure it still wouldn't be as high as the valley's. But we do prune very severely so the crop won't be large. You know, in the Napa Valley, it's common to put three or four, maybe even five or six canes out on cane pruned vines, but we never put out more than two canes. That's our maximum, and our average is closer to one cane. On some we don't leave any, depending on the size and vigor of the vine.

That very low productivity makes the difference in quality?

It's a factor. Other factors influence quality too. Temperature, as I mentioned earlier, is one. Extremes of heat are detrimental to good quality wine grapes. We don't get the extreme high temperatures the valleys do and this has a measurable effect on our grapes because they always come in at a higher acidity and the same sugar.

Are you able to describe the character of your grapes, their flavor?

No, I'm not very good at that. The grapes up here seem to have a fairly intense, concentrated flavor—varietal character is very pronounced.

Who does the picking of your own grapes?

The five of us who are with the winery full time, plus sometimes as many as 15 others. I have used some migrant laborers, but in the last few years I've used mostly local people who live up here on the mountain and want to pick up extra money, a housewife or college kids.

What do they pick the grapes with?

A knife.

Do you do any selected picking of bunches?

No, but of course we're very strict about avoiding picking the immature "second crop" grapes.

Is any of the Zinfandel you buy mechanically harvested?

No, they're from two different vineyards that are 80 and 90 years old and head pruned only, and by no means can you use a mechanical harvester on them!

Would you ever accept mechanically harvested grapes?

No, not here. As a matter of fact, I don't even accept grapes in gondolas. They must be picked into boxes; we do not have a gondola receiving station here. We use only the old fashioned method of boxes, and as you just found out, we have a long, rough road coming up here. We accepted a couple of loads of grapes in gondolas in 1969, and they arrived in very poor condition. They had been exposed to considerable bacterial and oxidative spoilage. The iron content, from riding that long in a gondola with grapes at the bottom already squashed and in solution, was six times normal just from being in contact with that big iron machine. And it didn't look like it had that much paint chipped off. That can cause serious problems and depreciates the quality of wine. But it's primarily the bacterial and oxidative exposure I'm worried about.

Do you operate the winery by yourself?

I have four full time employees, plus a number of part time and temporary people. It's small: we produce 4,000 to 5,000 cases a year. That's about double the size they were operating at when we bought it and is as big as we plan to get.

Do you think a large winery can produce wines as fine as those from small wineries?

Boy, I don't know. I'm amazed how good a job some of the big places do sometimes. They do seem to let wines get away from them and have unattractive wines on the market, but sometimes they do a surprisingly good job. I really don't see how they do it. Yet, I don't know any big winery that consistently makes wines as good as those from many of the small wineries.

How do you crush your grapes?

We have a regular electro-mechanical crusher-stemmer we use on all our grapes, and a Willmes bladder press. We get about 140 gallons per ton for whites and 160 for reds on the initial yield. That's light pressing compared to some makers, and heavier than others.

How much sulphur do you add at the crush?

We add it in the tank just after crushing, and depending on the condition and variety of the grapes it ranges from 60 to 100 parts per million.

Do you ferment in stainless steel?

No, we have concrete block fermenting tanks lined with an epoxy. We ferment both reds and whites in those. We hang heat exchanger plates in the middle of these tanks to control the temperature. The Chardonnay is fermented in the high 50s, 57 to 58 degrees, and the reds ferment in the low 70s. We leave the reds on the skins until they're completely dry, or within a percent or two of being dry, and we use the press wine in the free run which adds even further to the character.

So your Chardonnay ferments a little higher than those of many winemakers who keep them just below 50 degrees, but not as high as the Chardonnays fermented in small oak barrels like those in Burgundy. How did you decide on 57 degrees?

As a matter of fact, I thought most Chardonnays were fermented around 60 degrees Fahrenheit, but you have undoubtedly asked that question of more winemakers than I have. In any case, the high 50s gives us the flavor balance we seek.

Have you given any thought to going over to stainless steel?

No, if I were starting over I think used stainless steel might be cheaper than building concrete tanks into this hillside, but the ones I have are very satisfactory.

What about fermenting Chardonnay in oak? There's a school of thought that says that's the thing to do.

Right, there is. I think I'd have a hard time controlling the temperature that way since I don't have a cold room. And also, some of those wines come out too woody for my taste. I like a detectable amount of wood flavor, but I don't like it to dominate the wine as it does in some white Burgundies and California Chardonnays.

Have you ever experimented with starting fermentation with the natural wine yeast on the grapes?

No, I've always used a cultured yeast, usually the Montrachet. Depending on the type of indigenous yeast, and its population level, there is a good possibility it will affect the flavor of the wine. But it can be affected in either direction, it can get better or it can get worse. So, you're always taking a chance by using wild yeast because you're never sure which of the several wild species on the grape will dominate in fermentation. If you can be reasonably sure which will dominate and you like the flavors it produces, the only disadvantage is it always takes much longer to begin fermentation, increasing the chances of bacterial and oxidative spoilage the longer it sits. If you have a wild yeast culture that produces a flavor you like, I think you might see if you can culture what's on your grapes and inoculate with it so you don't have the risk of the long start time.

Do your red wines go through a malo-lactic fermentation?

The Cabernet always does. The Zinfandels we've made in the last few years have been 15 percent alcohol or higher, and none of those has undergone malo-lactic; I don't expect them to with that high an alcohol content.

In fermentation, do you punch down the cap or pump over?

We pump over, generally; we have punched down the cap for a few small lots.

Do you ever have to adjust acid levels?

Often, but not always. Sometimes a fairly minor adjustment with tartaric acid.

How extensively do you fine and filter?

Since the 1967 Zinfandel and 1969 Cabernet, we haven't fined the red wines at all. They are very lightly filtered just before bottling. Chardonnay, I fine with bentonite and then filter with a medium porosity filter.

How often do you rack the red wines?

When they're within a percent or two of dryness we rack them out of the fermenting tank and then again in a week, then a month after that, and annually after that. The Chardonnay is racked when it's fined, then racked off the fining lees, then a few months after we rack it into small barrels.

How long do the wines spend in cooperage?

Zinfandel, only large American oak tanks—500 to 1,000 gallons—for a year and a half to two years, then it's bottled. Cabernet spends two years in large American oak tanks, and a third year in small oak barrels. I have about half Nevers oak and half Saône oak, 60 gallon cooperage. The Chardonnay is aged only in Saône, except for a few barrels of Limousin. With new barrels, the Chardonnay spends about three months in the barrels, and that's increased about a month each time I use the barrels, up to a year. I haven't gotten that far yet.

In your judgment are the finest wines of California equal to the best European wines?

I'm glad you stated the question that way. No, they're certainly not equal. They're different wines.

I didn't mean "the same." I mean equal in quality.

Now you've got me. I don't even know, but my judgment is they are not *yet,* anyway. It's an old saw but many wine comparisons are like preferring apples to oranges. Some of their and our wines are at least comparable, if not equal, but so many factors such as environment, experience, etc., can influence judgments of equality or preference. Most wines are not comparable, and it is impossible to say anything meaningful about equality. Among those that are comparable, there certainly was a large gap between the best of Europe and California and that gap unquestionably has been closing in recent years. Whether or not it has disappeared depends on a myriad of who, what, when, where and how variables. And even if that happens, or has happened, it will take a while for the word to get around.

Warren Winiarski

STAG'S LEAP WINE CELLARS

These people are in it because they love it, and love heightens their powers of observation, intensifies their interest, intimacy and knowledge.

Stag's Leap Wine Cellars took an historic leap and landed in first place in the 1976 Paris tasting. Its 1973 Cabernet Sauvignon nosed out a Château Mouton-Rothschild 1970 and a Château Haut-Brion 1970, and placed ahead of two other great Bordeauxs and five other

California Cabernet Sauvignons. The triumph of Stag's Leap, an infant winery barely half a dozen years old, may have been nearly as painful for the older California wineries as it was for the French. The wine was made by Warren Winiarski, an idealist who once stated he was out to do "the noblest kind of farming and to make the most superb wine," although Andre Tchelistcheff, as consultant to Winiarski, was an acknowledged influence behind the wine.

The winery's seemingly whimsical name is derived from a craggy bluff called Stag's Leap that protrudes from the eastern foothills of the Napa Valley. One of the many legends surrounding the bluff tells of an Indian maiden waking from a dream to see a stag leaping across the chasm that divides it. The bluff crowns vineyards which now sprawl below and the Winiarski family gazes down upon these vineyards from a spacious home on a hilltop across from the Leap. The other side of the hill rolls west to meet the Silverado Trail, and at precisely that point the Winiarskis have placed their winery. A simple, attractive barrel-aging building sits on the shady slope next to the trail; the crushing equipment, press and fermenting tanks stand directly outside. Warren Winiarski and I sat among these cool, stainless steel giants and chatted one morning shortly after the Paris tasting.

Recommended wine to drink while reading this chapter:

STAG'S LEAP WINE CELLARS
CABERNET SAUVIGNON

Do you actually perform the winemaking operations yourself, or do you have assistants?

I do it. I have one or two assistants who are key people, and I don't perform every single manipulation from beginning to end, but I have. My training was primarily in the cellar: I scrubbed the pots. A great part of winemaking is cleanliness, meticulousness in each of the steps. Nature never put wine into a barrel, never topped a wine, never determined how you ought to top. Do you open all the bungs beforehand or open them one by one? All these little things have an effect, depending upon what you do in each of the steps and whether you have observed the differences, or thought out what the differences might be if you did things differently.

Where did you get experience in the cellar?

I worked at the old Souverain Cellars with Lee Stewart, and I worked two years with Robert Mondavi. We came out to California in 1964 and I wanted an apprenticeship, in the old sense, to learn from someone whose wines I respected. I learned a lot between Lee Stewart's very small operation and my exposure to the whole sequence of steps from grapes to bottled wine, and the experience at Mondavi which was primarily winemaking and at a different order of magnitude.

What had you been doing before you came to California?

Nothing related to winemaking. I was teaching at the University of Chicago in a general education program.

That's unusual, isn't it, for someone outside of California to move here to become a winemaker?

Not necessarily. Many people today have chosen deliberately to pursue this as a second career and have infused a great degree of enthusiasm and dedication in the industry. These people are in it because they love it, and the love heightens their powers of observation, intensifies their interest, intimacy and knowledge. I think that has done something for the California wine industry. I think this kind of dedication in California brings it closer to the European tradition. In Europe, it's not necessarily by choice, but there is often the tradition of many generations following the same occupation. Take the families working on the great cathedrals for a century or more. European winemaking has that kind of tradition, that long term devotion where observations, techniques, judgment and art are all passed on. And that has happened in California, not over generations, but in an abbreviated span with this wave of interest in fine California winemaking. The potential was there, the technology was there; but the technology itself would not have done it.

In Andre Tchelistcheff, incidentally, I feel you have the combination of technology and love, because he combines the spirit and the science in himself. He has been a great influence, as a consultant here. I was thinking that the common bond between the two wines that placed first in the Paris tasting is that the people who made them, Mike Grgich and myself, you might say were trained by the same people. Mike was at Souverain, then went to Beaulieu where Tchelistcheff was, then to Mondavi before going to Château Montelena. Of course, all Mondavi's great enthusiasm does not trace back to Tchelistcheff but Robert Mondavi and Lee Stewart both owe a lot to Andre. I'm not saying that Tchelistcheff was *the* factor, but he's certainly been an influence.

Why did this quality breakthrough come so suddenly in the last five or ten years? Tchelistcheff and Stewart and the others were all here before then. Why didn't their spark catch on until so recently?

Probably because you didn't have enough economic interest. Recently there was so much capital infused by people riding the wave of economic forecasts. Capital was infused in vineyards and in small operations which could give the continuity of attention to detail that's necessary to produce really outstanding wines. The stage was set, the potential was there, but economic underpinning was necessary to actualize the potential. We did this at Stag's Leap with the same kind of economic support, of course. We have partners in this enterprise.

Who are your partners; who owns the winery?

The winery is a limited partnership which overlaps a little with the vineyard partnership; some of the owners are identical. I'm the general partner of both. The winery partners are individuals from the San Francisco Bay area and from New York and Germany.

How many cases do you produce a year?

We made about 8,000 cases this year, and we'll ultimately increase to about 15,000 cases. That's all the room we have, and that's all I can keep my eye on.

Do you think larger wineries can produce wines as good as those from the small wineries like your own?

I think they can, but it's more difficult in principle. If you have to watch over a hundred children, you can't spend the time with them you could if you had three children. You can't watch their development, nuances and small things going on. It's just not possible for the human organism to exceed its limitations.

You limit yourself to five wines?

Yes. Cabernet, Merlot, Gamay Beaujolais, Riesling and this year, '76, we'll make a Chardonnay for the first time. We made a Merlot in 1974 because the grapes were so fantastic, and probably '75, but not every year.

Are your wines 100 percent varietals?

We don't believe in simple, dogmatic principles like "It has to be 100 percent," because that may not make the best wine. The '74 Merlot is about 15 percent Cabernet. Merlot has to be true to type of course, but if it's better with some Cabernet we'll blend it that way. The Gamay Beaujolais is a blend of Pinot Noir, Gamay Beaujolais and Napa Gamay. We get different things from these different varieties; we get a fruitier, rounder, deeper, smoother, more flowery wine if we blend—a wine worth making.

Was the '73 Cabernet Sauvignon 100 percent of that variety?

It was about three percent Merlot. We haven't blended the Riesling, but there again, people wonder where that specific character comes from in some of the great German wines; they would be amazed to discover that some extraordinarily subtle vineyard blends are responsible. So long as the overall purpose of blending is clear, and the blend strengthens the wine and makes it more elegant, more beautiful, with a more complex personality, still typifying the original variety, then it's a good thing.

Do you grow all your own grapes?

No, only the Cabernet and the Merlot. We buy the others. We have a number of practices in our vineyards that would be difficult for me to suggest to some of our growers, though I have recommended some of them; for example, cluster thinning to control the crop size. Also, we don't "average harvest," we harvest in blocks as each section is ready.

Your vineyard is right behind the hills of the winery here at the edge of the Silverado Trail, just a half a dozen miles north of the town of Napa. How many acres are up there?

Forty-four acres; about four are Merlot. All planted mostly in 1970.

You mean the '73 Cabernet came from three-year old vines?

Right. I know people are astounded by that. People say you can't get good Cabernet out of young vines, but that's because they want all the grapes. If they get a big crop, that's true, the grapes won't produce the quality. It's hard to tell what our yield was in 1973. We obtained about 35 tons from the vineyard that year.

What climate region is the vineyard in?

Probably a low Region II or high I, one of the cooler areas of the valley. It's a little different micro-climate, doesn't cool off quite as much at night and is somewhat cooler during the day.

Is it the climate that gives you the good quality grapes?

It's a combination of many things. The soil is fairly good, a bale loam with about 15 percent gravel, and it's on a slight slope coming down from the foothills to the Silverado Trail. But probably the most critical thing is our thinning and the selective harvesting. Normally, a grower will walk through a vineyard and test for sugar and say "Well, we have 21 sugar in this section, and 23 in that other block, so I would say we've got 22 on the average." Now you're never going to make outstanding wine that way, because if 22 is what you want you've got half unripe grapes and half overripe grapes. So we start and stop the harvest, section by section. And we make arrangements with our pickers: pick all season with us, this stop-start program, and we'll pay you so much extra per ton.

What do they pick the grapes with?

Knives.

And do they pick into gondolas? What size?

Into two to four ton gondolas brought into the winery immediately. We do no field crushing.

Where do you buy your grapes?

Birkmeyer Vineyard is in Wild Horse Valley. That I think *does* contribute to the character of that Riesling. It's on rocky, red mountainside soil, and has an extremely low yield, less than a ton per acre. The Chardonnay we will make this year comes from southeast of Napa in the Coombsville Road area.

How do you crush the grapes?

We have a variable speed crusher, because the grapes do have different crushing characteristics and we want to take advantage of technology as far as we can to reflect that. On the white grapes we get a gentle bruising action, whereas on the red grapes we really rupture that skin and almost turn it inside out. We do that to expose the interior of the skins to the action of the fermentation.

Are all the grapes stemmed before crushing?

Yes, but sometimes it depends on the year. Being small, we can make these fine adjustments that can't be made on a large scale. In a year we think it's necessary, we might tune our crusher to allow some stems into our must, as on the Cabernet.

Was the '73 crushed and fermented with some stems?

Yes, it was. But the big thing is judgment: how long do you leave the stems, do you do anything differently to the must *because* you leave the stems? The repercussions of every step, accounted for at each of the further steps, is what makes a wine what it is. My answers that we do leave stems in, or do this or that, don't tell the full story.

You have all stainless steel fermenters. How long and at what temperature would the Cabernet, for example, ferment?

Every year is different. Every year the grapes have different characteristics, and it's the business of the winemaker to determine on the spot at what temperatures he wants to ferment and that also varies with the amount of pumping over he's doing. Pumping over is probably the most important factor in red winemaking. In the old days there was a direct response of the wine to the winemaker's physical personality, when they punched the cap down. A strong, vigorous man punching it down, and macerating it and pushing the skins underneath the liquid would make a stronger wine. And a man who was more gentle would make a more gentle wine; to exaggerate for purpose of illustration: each stroke makes a bigger wine.

Since fermentation temperature varies, necessarily, then, let me ask about the '73 Cabernet as an example.

As opposed to '74 when we had a lot of sugar, '73 was somewhat lighter. The classical French technique when they don't have a lot of alcohol is to moderate the degree of pumping over, because pumping over by entrainment carries with it some of the volatile characteristics, but it also removes some of the alcohol. Seventy-three was a cooler year, with some warmth at the end; the Cabernet grapes came in at about 23.5 sugar. They fermented for about six days.

About 75 degrees Fahrenheit?

Someplace between 75 and 80, even a little higher in some years.

How often would you pump over?

Normally twice a day.

Is that a bladder type press you have?

It's a Willmes but not the bladder type, it's the ram type. We feel it gives us better control. A lot of whirling takes place in the bladder type, and as the ram comes forward in ours we can see better the precise time when we want to separate our press wine from the free run. As you know, the material that constitutes the character of the wine is in the skins, for the most part. If you get too much your wine will be coarse, not enough and your wine will be bland. You know, press is press, but where do you call it press wine, at 120 gallons or 110 per ton, or what? This year it'll be a different set of figures from a year when the grapes are heavy and turgid. This year, 1976 vintage, the grapes will lack that fullness, because of the dryness of the soil. So as that ram comes forward, the operator is standing there and watching the color of the juice and at a certain point he decides that's it, the rest is press wine. We'll generally sell the press wine in bulk, or put it into our secondary label, the Hawkcrest label. And that's good wine. The public has a funny idea about press wine, people turn up their noses at it, even at two and a half or three dollars a bottle, and that's entirely unjustified. I believe that in Bordeaux, in some years, every single drop of the grapes is put into the bottles. It depends on how you handle it.

Will you ferment your Chardonnay in stainless steel too, or in oak?

In stainless steel. Oak is easy to abuse and I don't find oak all that attractive in white wines.

But you don't get much oak from the short fermentation period in oak barrels do you?

You get it more rapidly, because each of those little CO_2 bubbles is attacking the wood; it's mechanical agitation against the wood. If you ferment in oak, you'd better watch how long you age in oak.

Your red wines go through malo-lactic fermentation, don't they?

Yes, we see to it that they do.

Do you inoculate all the wines with a yeast starter to begin fermentation?

Yes, with a Champagne yeast.

You don't have a centrifuge, do you?

No, I don't know I'd use one either. I'm not sufficiently impressed that it improves white wines.

Do you think it damages white wines?

Before fermentation, I think so. The process appears to take too much out of the grapes.

There are people who say it only takes out the solids you don't want fermenting anyway.

I know. And I know they use them in Germany. I haven't been to Germany, but the literature reports sufficiently diverse opinions about the effect of centrifuging before fermentation. Fortunately, it's a matter I don't have to go into, because we've been able to make our wines without one. We settle our Riesling before fermentation, we give it minimum amounts of bentonite and gelatin fining, and it's filtered pretty tightly before bottling.

How do you obtain the residual sweetness in the Riesling?

We've done it both ways. We've used a sweet reserve, a *muté,* and we've stopped fermentation before dryness was reached. You chill the wine to stun the yeast and then filter them out.

Which of those two methods did you like the best in terms of the final character?

I don't prefer one over the other. There are more dangers in trying to stop fermentation; it has to be filtered more times. The sweet reserve method is certainly easier.

How frequently do you rack the Cabernet?

Often, at first. Especially, after the malo-lactic.

Don't you run a danger of oxidizing the wine?

That's what I want. I want to change the wine over. We rack over this screen several times, and finally we give it a light gelatin fining, light filtration and then put it into thousand gallon Yugoslavian tanks for a month or two for repose. Then we put it into small barrels. It stays in the small Nevers oak barrels for about 14 months, without racking, then returns to the tanks for another period of repose before bottling.

How long do the other wines spend in wood?

We'll make the Chardonnay this year and I imagine it will spend from five to nine months in the moderate sized Yugoslavian cooperage, about 1,000 gallon tanks. I doubt we'll put it in small barrels at all. Now the Riesling also goes into those Yugoslavian tanks, for a few months, maybe even one month. Then when we're ready to bottle a wine, we'll make the final blend from all the barrels. Winemaking is actually wine*making*. You create, you build the wine, you put your hands on it and put it together in a certain way. So my wife and I, and Dorothy Tchelistcheff and Andre, and others, will sit around and taste different combinations of blends from the different barrels, because you know they're all minutely different. That way, we get not just my own blend. I want response. The painter paints the portrait, but then he stands back and looks at it as though somebody else were looking at it, and I want that kind of perspective.

I assume you agree with the tasters in the Paris tasting that some California wines, such as your Cabernet, are equal to or even better than the best European wines.

I think we are going to see many more tastings comparing California and European wines. I've attended some and my impression was California wines had a greater appeal from a certain point of view in a systematic way. They were fleshier, had more texture. I'm talking about Cabernet, in particular. It's like the difference between milk and cream. This is true even when the wines are almost identical in alcoholic content. In some of the older French wines the contribution of the fruit is already so diminished by the presence of the wood and wood tannin, that I find they have an austerity and dryness and lack this fleshy character of some California wines.

But in the Paris tasting, the French wines being compared were all '70s and one '71.

That's right, they were. I've not tasted all those wines together, and I'm waiting for a similar tasting to be arranged by someone.

Will your '73 Cabernet be even greater 20 years from now?

Why do you think 20 years is the time to drink a wine? That was my objection to the article Frank Prial wrote in the *New York Times* on the Paris tasting. He said, where will this wine be when the other wines will be approaching their peak? Well, I don't know what those wines will be like in 20 years and he doesn't either. In 20 years it will be a different tasting. We're tasting the wines for what they are now. So I look forward to more tastings of that kind. I think they will be instructive and will help California to make better wines. It's all for the good.

Michael Robbins

SPRING MOUNTAIN VINEYARDS

The amateurs in our area have turned winemaking into a competitive sport . . . and the track gets faster every year.

We enjoyed Mrs. Robbins's cold zucchini soup accompanied by Spring Mountain Chardonnay on the veranda, then Mike Robbins and I retired to the living room to talk about wine. His home is the finely restored Victorian that can be seen sitting on a slope at the edge of Napa Valley's main highway just north of St. Helena. Robbins remodeled that home and started his winery in the 1960s, but continued his career in real estate until just recently. Now comfortably retired from real estate, he is at last spending full time making wine.

Robbins is an amateur only in the original sense of that word: a lover, one who does something for its pleasure alone. He loves not only wine but the tradition and life associated with it. He is currently renovating "Miravalle," the nineteenth century mansion built on Spring Mountain by Tiburcio Parrott as a counterpart to the Beringers' Rhine House down the road, and soon will move his family, winery and vineyards to that grand estate. I think Robbins demonstrates clearly why the "amateurs," with their sporting enthusiasm, and analytical abilities developed in other professions, may be largely responsible for the quality breakthrough in California wines. His Chardonnay and Cabernet are proof that Robbins is among the fastest on the track.

Recommended wine to drink while reading this chapter:
SPRING MOUNTAIN CHARDONNAY

You left another profession to become a winemaker. Why did you do it?

This all started when I came to San Francisco out of the service in '54. I really discovered wine for the first time. I don't recall ever having had wine prior to that. And it grew slowly. I was penniless in those days and I used to drive up with a date to the Napa Valley in my VW with the sun roof back because we could have a ball up here for virtually no money. Following the night law school bit, I went to Europe for three months and traveled around with some letters of introduction. And I guess really what captured me was the incredible life style. I just envied the life style of the vintners here and in Europe so much that it redirected my whole approach to life.

And yet you went on to another career first rather than plunging into winemaking right away.

Right, I graduated from the Naval Academy with a degree in engineering but I'm not an engineer; and I went to the University of San Francisco Law School at night, but I never took the bar; and I also picked up a real estate credential at night school from the University of California, and went back to night school at University of San Francisco for graduate business school. I worked for Coldwell-Banker doing commercial and industrial real estate, and later on went on my own and took on big projects—the Alcoa Building in San Francisco, and just recently I finished six years of commuting to Los Angeles to do a project for Alcoa in Century City, the Century Plaza Towers. And now, at last, I'm a full-time winemaker. I founded Spring Mountain in 1968, but my first brush with the wine industry was in 1960 when I had a small interest in, and was a vice president and director of, Mayacamas Vineyards. I was not doing any winemaking, I was merely the peddler—the marketing vice president.

How did you decide where to locate your winery?

I really did it all backwards. I should have located a prime piece of land and planted a vineyard, and then when the vineyards were bearing started a winery. After all this was very liquid I could have built the château. Being an old-house freak I drove up the valley in 1962 and saw this old Victorian wreck sitting on the hillside. It was irresistible. Therefore, I did it all backwards: I bought the château first. It's on Highway 29, right off the road. I figured I'd pour a few dollars into the house and start the winery in a couple years. I really got into a swamp with the expenses for the house, hence the winery was delayed until mid-'68. Then I started the winery, and later in '68 I purchased 21 acres of beautiful vineyard land, east of Rutherford. It runs from the Silverado Trail to Conn Creek.

I subsequently purchased the adjoining acres and now have a 105-acre block there, called our Wildwood Ranch. In '73 I purchased 21 acres which we call our Soda Creek Ranch, way down the valley running from the Silverado Country Club. I purchased that not only for the great soil, but because it gives us a micro-climate for fine Chardonnay of a little lighter style, and for Pinot Noir. I planted 12 acres of the great French clone of Pinot Noiren Petit.

Where did you get the vines?

A friend attempted to bring 10,000 cuttings from France and they all died. Then Darryl Corti from Sacramento called me and said, "Mike, I saw a picture in the paper Paul Masson puts out and right in the foreground is Pinot Noiren Petit." Now you can distinguish this from Pinot Noir because the vine grows a little more laterally instead of upright. Instead of triangulated, heavy-shouldered bunches it has pine cone shoulders and cylindrical bunches.

So I called Martin Ray, who used to own Paul Masson, and I asked him if it was indeed the Pinot Noiren Petit, and he answered, "Yes, and when I sold Paul Masson I took the budwood from there and within an hour and a half it was budded up here on Mt. Eden." He said, "You may have the budwood, but I can save you a trip because in 1952 I gave some to Keith Bowers at the University of California station in the Napa Valley."

Going back, this clone was given by Louis Latour—the present Louis Latour is about 75 years old, but it was his father—to Paul Masson in 1898, reputedly either from Romanée-Conti or from Louis Latour's vineyard in Beaune. I called Keith Bowers and he had ripped out this clone after experimenting with it, but he had given some to Joe Swann, who had planted it in the Sierras. I checked with Joe and he had transplanted it to Forestville at his Swann Vineyards, so Joe let me come over and prune his vineyard and that's how we got it.

What a detective story!

This whole crazy business is a matter of detail, and you have to be a fanatic if you're going to make fine wine.

How many cases a year does the winery produce?

We hope to build it up to around 18,000 cases a year, but right now we produce around 10,000. By the time we reach that 18,000 case level, it will be all our own grapes—a story in itself. We make three varieties now: Cabernet, Chardonnay and Sauvignon Blanc. Eventually, when the eight acres of old Sauvignon Blanc vines are ripped out we'll drop Sauvignon Blanc altogether because you can't justify planting Sauvignon Blanc on that kind of land. We'll replant with Chardonnay. We'll pick Pinot Noir this year so we'll still be making three types. We'll continue to make Pinot Noir if it proves as I hope; if not, we'll re-bud all that to Chardonnay. The new property we're moving to is the old Parrott estate called Miravalle, a 265-acre piece I bought in '74. It's on Spring Mountain, roughly a half mile wide and a mile and a quarter long. Of that 265 acres, from aerial photographs and tramping around, we think we have about 110 plantable acres. So someday all our wines will be from that property, or that property together with the Soda Creek piece. The Wildwood piece near Rutherford will be spun off as a separate winery in five or seven years.

Is Soda Creek a Region I?

As you know, I consider that system to be nothing more than a rough guide. That is to say, it uses the median temperatures instead of the mean (average) temperatures, and then makes comparisons with ten year averages in Europe which, for my purposes, is irrelevant. That system is just not up to UC Davis's usual high standards.

Is your Soda Creek Ranch as cool as the Carneros region?

No. Again, I can't give you any facts but I suspect Carneros is a lot more like Champagne. And I think Moët & Hennessey were very smart to put their Champagne vineyards in Carneros. You pick Champagne grapes at 18.5 or 19 Balling, which is underripe for fine still Chardonnay.

Would you like to see subregions like these within the Napa Valley delimited and carry their own appellations of origin?

Certainly. The Napa Valley is small, only 25 miles long and from a half mile to two miles wide, but you have climate differences ranging from those of Alsace to those of Italy. The further north you go the warmer it gets. This sounds crazy until you remember that the Bay to the south and the ocean to the west keep our temperatures moderate. As you go north you get farther from the Bay influence and it gets warmer. In Calistoga you're almost into a warm Italian climate. So "Napa Valley" is climatically more or less a meaningless term by itself.

I've modified all my preconceptions of a few years ago. When Mike Stone and Peter Newton bought 400 or 500 acres near Calistoga for Sterling Vineyards, I thought, "They must know something I don't." I would not have taken such a gamble in that area at that time. But two things have happened. For one, right from the beginning they've made some exceedingly fine wines out of those vineyards, even out of varieties like Chardonnay. Second, we've gone through a climatic change since their purchase. From what I've read, the whole northern hemisphere has undergone a drastic climatic change; we've progressed almost a fifth of the way toward an ice age since 1945. Africa has suffered terrible droughts year after year, and it's not a temporary thing. Apparently we have gathered agricultural dust and pollution in the North Pole area. This has moved our jet stream 200 miles south.

California is getting weather we never experienced before. I've reversed my plantings on the Wildwood property. I originally planted Chardonnay on the mountain soil near the Silverado Trail, and Cabernet near the creek. But if we get earlier and earlier rains, I'm switching. They'll mature earlier and I'll get them off the vineyard before it rains.

Do you think the soil and topography play as important roles as the climate does?

They have important roles, obviously. First is the question of how many tons you get. The heavier bearing soils give you more tons, but in general they will not give you the quality of the sparsely bearing soils. Second is drainage. The clay soils will not produce the same quality, generally, as well drained, gravelly soils. Aside from that, I go with the old French concept that you pick up mineral content and flavor components from more complex soils—chalky soils and gravelly soils. Many people disagree, including some people at Davis, but I feel that I can discern the differences in my own vineyards from one patch to another.

Exposure is another important variable. They talk about heat, but nobody talks about sunshine, whether the same temperature in the shade gives you the same quality as direct sun. Nobody talks about solar radiation. France is much further north and gets distinctly different solar radiation from California. I don't have any of the answers, but we are assembling most of the questions. I'm always looking for the edge. The amateurs in our area have turned winemaking into a competitive sport—a very American trait. When it becomes a competitive sport you're dealing in little edges of difference. It isn't a breakthrough by one winery, by Spring Mountain, or Robert Mondavi or Heitz, but a breakthrough across the board in some varieties.

Ten years ago, in a Chardonnay tasting we probably wouldn't have placed more than one in the top ten. Today, *the French* are lucky to get more than one in the top ten. All of a sudden there's been a major breakthrough in California Chardonnays. And the track gets faster every year, and just to stay even you must run faster.

What did make that breakthrough?

I feel that Joe Heitz had a lot to do with it, and maybe Brad Webb, and his mentor Tchelistcheff. First, somehow we got ahold of a couple of good clones. Second, we've gone to cold, 45 degree, fermentations. Long fermentations for three weeks. That seems to have given us the edge. In Burgundy these wines are made somewhat haphazardly. Every grower who owns an acre in Burgundy makes his wine in his basement. Then it's bought by the *negociants* who blend and bottle it. In California, we've borrowed all the great traditions of the past and supplemented them with new technology. We've had an open mind and still do. Our own cellar practice at Spring Mountain is loose-leaf, because as we learn a better technique we just pop the new one in. We will never have all the answers.

Do you get a low yield from your vineyards?

Yes, we prune for a very modest crop. On the Wildwood piece we're getting two to two and a half tons per acre on the Chardonnay. On our Cabernet last year we got only two and a quarter tons, because we had some shatter. We don't irrigate. We thin out the second crop before we pick because no matter how you talk to pickers about leaving the immature grapes on the vine, they often don't stop to differentiate. Picking is a frantic endeavor and they are paid by the ton; they don't consistently sort the first and second crops.

Do you harvest any grapes mechanically?

No. The grapes are trained so that I could do it in case we're ever driven to the wall, but I'd hate to do it. I don't think I'd get the quality I'm looking for, especially on the Chardonnay. I'm not sure you can successfully mechanically harvest 24 degrees Brix Chardonnay, though I know it's been done at lower sugars. Cabernet is tough as a weed, and it could be harvested mechanically without seriously damaging the grape or the vine. We're going the opposite way. This year we're going to in-field crushing. They'll be picked by the basket, dumped into a small crusher-stemmer, put into a tank with a CO_2 blanket and brought to the winery for fermentation. We'll have instant crushing to avoid oxidation. A ripe Chardonnay grape is wildly susceptible to oxidation. If you have a six ton gondola, the first grapes may be put in at seven or eight in the morning and the last at four in the afternoon. All that juice and all those broken grapes. Occasionally after they arrive at a winery at five in the evening, they sit until the next morning.

Do you think of your wines as having a distinct character from other Napa Valley wines?

No, not in those words. Like all other fine producers in the valley, we're trying to make the greatest wine in the world. We make better wines as we go along because we're using more and more of our own grapes, over which we have control, and now we have all of our own facilities. Until now, we've crushed and fermented at other people's facilities. We've done the work but used their facilities. Now that we have our own facilities and more of our own grapes, our wine should be much better as we'll be making fewer compromises such as hauling our wines around the valley in a tanker. We buy the best grapes we can get, at huge prices, but go through our cellars and compare them with grapes from our own vineyards. In most cases it's hands down that our own grapes make better wine. If we ever get them all together, maybe we can prove this point. It all starts in the vineyard. A fine winemaker with the right philosophy can make a difference, but you must have a silk purse coming out of the vineyard to make a silk purse.

California growers and vintners are still matching varieties and locations in this state. Fortunately we aren't burdened with the French legal rigidity that prevents them, for instance, from planting Chardonnay in Bordeaux where I think they might make one hell of a wine. The Graves whites are an accident of history. Tallyrand owned Château Haut-Brion and had lunch with the owner of Château Yquem and laid it on heavily about how much he admired d'Yquem. So the man sent over cuttings of Sauvignon Blanc and Sémillon. Tallyrand's winemaker didn't know a thing about botrytis or sweet wines, so he made a dry wine from it and that's why they're still making them in Graves. But I think they could make great Chardonnay if somebody would plant it, and perhaps risk losing his appellation.

There seem to be two schools of thought on winemaking. One says nature makes the wine and man should interfere as little as possible and the other says nature needs to be controlled by technology. Do you belong to either school?

I suppose I'm down the middle. Nature can be pretty cruel. You don't want to bend nature to your will, but you must find an accommodation with nature, take nature's best and overcome the handicaps. We like to interfere with nature as little as possible, but we don't hesitate to interfere to prevent something from going wrong. For example, we don't make wine on its own yeast, because in California all kinds of wild yeasts grow on the skins. An uncontrolled fermentation may occasionally yield an exceedingly fine wine, but we prefer to kill the wild yeast. We use 90 or 100 parts per million of sulphur dioxide at the crusher, and use Montrachet yeast to start fermentation.

You have an oenologist to help you full time, don't you?

Yes. Chuck Ortman is a former amateur like myself. He was a commercial artist, not an oenologist, by training but after three years of doing this by myself I hired Chuck. He's been with me over five years now and has become an outstanding professional winemaker.

Do you ferment all the wines in stainless steel?

Yes. The whites ferment at 45 to 50 degrees. We used to ferment Cabernet under 70, but I read about the French and the older California vintners and we now ferment as high as 85 degrees. We like to get the color extraction from the reds, and there are two schools of thought on that. Heitz, I understand, feels you get it by longer association with the skins, at a cooler temperature. We tend now to go along with Peter Mondavi and the French, who believe you may get more color by getting it up to 85 or 90 degrees. Ask me in five years, but presently I think that the warmer fermentation for reds is a better procedure.

Does the Cabernet always go through a malo-lactic fermentation?

Sometimes yes and sometimes no. In California, the malo-lactic is a very mild thing, because we have very low malic acid left when we pick the grapes. We have warmer temperatures than France. Our malo-lactic fermentation might reduce the acidity by five-hundredths of a percent, whereas in France it can make a major reduction. Sometimes we inoculate to induce the malo-lactic fermentation and it still won't start. Some of our fine Cabernets have never gone through it, and we're worried it may start up in the bottle.

How do you treat the cap, do you pump over?

We punch down a little but we basically pump over. We're going to a larger hose, to get a larger volume pumping over and, we hope, better color extraction. I'd like to try the submerged cap like Ridge. Ridge wou
appear to believe in the total extraction of the grape. We believe, lik

French, that the art of winemaking is the fractional extraction of the grape. Don't ask me what that fraction is yet, because we're too new. We're moving toward greater extraction, climbing toward the Ridge concept, but we're probably not going to go as far.

What kind of a press do you have?

At the moment we have a Willmes bladder press here, but we used to have a small basket press at the other property. We always use a comparatively light pressing, but it's not strictly free run.

Do you ever adjust acid levels?

We adjust acid sometimes at the crush with tartaric acid. We do it then because later on tartaric drops out, and you must use citric acid for later adjustments. Bob Mondavi tried something brilliant one year: he added malic acid at the crush. I want to go down and taste those wines and go over his experience because that may have made it more like a French grape by replacing the malic acid lost through respiration in the sun.

Do you fine and filter both the reds and whites?

We do not cold stabilize the whites, that's why you'll find tartaric crystals in our wine. We do use bentonite fining for heat stability. We use as little as possible. We try not to filter or fine the Cabernet, though that's not true of the '68, '69 or the '70. We did sterile filtration on those wines. But '72 and '73 are unfined, and unfiltered, and not centrifuged either, which is kind of a form of filtration. On the whites, we have generally sterile filtered them to avoid problems later on in the bottle.

What kind of racking and aging will the Cabernet go through?

Maybe a half dozen rackings. The Cabernet will spend most of its first year in Yugoslavian 1,000-gallon tanks we had coopered in Italy. We have tasted wine from these versus wine from château model Nevers oak barrels, and find little difference except surface-to-volume ratios. We buy château model barrels because we feel the French use their best wood in barrels for their own châteaux and will sell us whatever they have left over. The first year, I could tell the difference between our château model and the export model barrels. That was only one trial, but since then I've purchased nothing but the Nevers oak château models.

The first year I used half Limousin and half Nevers for Cabernet. I wanted to find out if the French were right in using Nevers, or just chauvinistic. What I found out was that they were setting the standards, and if I was doing something else I was making a different and uncharacteristic wine. If we're going to play the game, we have to get a place in the starting blocks. So, after a year in Yugoslavian tanks, our Cabernet goes into these Nevers oak 60-gallon barrels for the second year and then they're bottled. We give it just a few months' bottle age to recover from the trauma of bottling. All our wine merchants have been advised to tell customers that this is a fine Cabernet for laying down; if you want something for tonight buy something else.

And how long does the Chardonnay spend in oak?

Depending on cellar temperature and the age of the oak, it spends anywhere from six to ten months in Limousin 60-gallon barrels.

Do you keep the grapes from different vineyards separate and make separate wines from them?

No, we ride with our label. We don't make five Cabernets from different vineyards, nor do we make several Chardonnays.

You don't make any generic wines, but do you approve of the California practice of putting out "Burgundy" and "Chablis"?

Not under those labels. I love a good vin ordinaire but I do not feel we should call our wine "Burgundy," "Chablis" or "Rhine." I have more trouble with "Port," "Sherry," or maybe "Champagne," because those describe a type of wine. We shouldn't unilaterally renounce the practice, but use it as a trade-off with the French who will not allow us to export Cabernet Sauvignon and Chardonnay to France, saying those are also French terms. That's a lot of hooey, because those are varietal names. We inaugurated that practice, which they are now copying. Somebody in our government should negotiate with the Europeans, so we could export our varietal wines in exchange for dropping their generic terms.

Do you think the best California wines can be made only by small wineries like Spring Mountain?

My natural predilection is to say the best wines come from small vintners, but how do you explain Robert Mondavi who has been producing surprising wines on a large scale? By our standards, even Sterling is a large winery, and they've also produced some phenomenal wines. It's simply that small vintners tend to have the edge in quality control commencing in the vineyards, but there's no denying you can make fine wines on a larger scale than I thought possible.

Do you think the best California wines are as good as the best European wines?

Depends on the variety. In Chardonnay, we made a breakthrough and I feel we dominate Chardonnays. That's not to say some of the great Meursaults are not as good, but you have to look hard now to find a white Burgundy to match our best Chardonnay. With Bordeauxs, we're just about even with their best wines from their best years. Year after year we'll beat their brains out, but their best wines in their best years still have more breed than ours do. In red Burgundies, we're not fundamentally in the game yet. A few have been really excellent in California. Pinot Noir is a crap shoot anyplace, but it's been more of a success in France than it has here. For quality, the end is a long way from being in sight, and California vintners will still be improving long after all of us are gone because we haven't really found our way yet.

Miljenko Mike Grgich

CHÂTEAU MONTELENA

I consider winemaking to be a combination lock. You have to know every number in order to unlock it. There are many people who know about winemaking, but they miss one number.

This genial European who, as he explains, has been a winemaker since he was old enough to stomp grapes, was suddenly thrust into the limelight when the Paris tasting of 1976 ranked his 1973 Château Montelena Chardonnay first, ahead of four great white Burgundies and five other California Chardonnays. The Château sits next to a locally famous geyser in the old spa town of Calistoga at the northern tip of Napa Valley. Mount St. Helena, from which the winery takes its name, rises in the background. Grgich is part of a new partnership which took over the old Château Montelena winery a few years ago. The winery, the closest thing to a real château in the Napa Valley, is blessed with a lake laced with bright red bridges built by a former Chinese owner. My conversation with Grgich was ambulatory. We talked as we inspected the winery, strolled out to the vineyards, and then crossed over one of the Chinese bridges to sit by the lake and finish our discussion.

Recommended wine to drink while reading this chapter:

CHATEAU MONTELENA CHARDONNAY

Yours is a very young winery—you've only been making wine here since 1972.

Yes, but I've been a winemaker all my life. My family owned a vineyard and winery in Yugoslavia—I am Croatian by nationality, I want to make that clear, though the government calls us Yugoslavian—and I stomped grapes even before I can remember. That's the way my father made wine, by stomping grapes. He had 11 children to stomp grapes, so no need to buy a crusher. I went to the University of Zagreb and majored in viticulture and oenology, and in 1958 I moved to California. I am now a partner here. The other partners are Mr. Paschich, Mr. Barrett who is a lawyer in Los Angeles and is our general manager, and Mr. Hahn who is in the construction business in Los Angeles.

Were you able to work at a California winery when you first came?

Yes, my first place was with Lee Stewart at Souverain, he was my first professor here. And then I worked at Christian Brothers in Champagne production for a year until an opening came at Beaulieu Vineyards, and I worked under Tchelistcheff for nine years. Next, I heard that Robert

Mondavi needed somebody, and I worked there for four years, from '68 to '72, when I came here. So those are my years in California. All fine places, and I'm happy I have been at each of them because it enabled me to develop my own style, which is not Andre Tchelistcheff's style, nor Robert Mondavi's nor Lee Stewart's, but my own completely different style. My idea is still European. I spent most of my life in Europe, and I still give more attention to the art of winemaking than to the science. Though I graduated in oenology at Zagreb, attended many courses at Davis and read many books about wine, I still naturally tend to be a wine-sitter rather than a wine-maker. In other words, make it right, and then leave it alone. Many other winemakers are proud of having a centrifuge, having all the filters and machinery, and I'm proud to say that I am making wine with a minimum of machinery. I know how to be a wine chemist, a wine microbiologist, a wine doctor, but I don't want to be a wine doctor; I consider myself a wine-sitter.

I'm quite interested in how you carry out that view in each of the winemaking steps. To start with crushing, do you have the usual stemmer-crusher?

The stems are removed, just as in other wineries. If I had to I would stomp the grapes. I wouldn't think that would be any worse than crushing them.

Do you ferment any of the Cabernet or Chardonnay with some of the stems?

No. And everything is fermented in stainless steel, but every wine under different temperatures and for different lengths of time. I make each wine in a different way, according to the vintage. My major job is to establish communication between me and the grapes and the wines, to learn about them and be a wine-sitter by meeting their needs. If you do so, and you have started with good grapes, there is no question but that the wine will be super.

Take the '73 Chardonnay, as an example. How was it fermented?

Between 47 and 50 degrees. But I don't go by temperature alone, I go by the speed of fermentation. I want to ferment at least a half degree Balling of the sugar every day. I am not one of those guys who chills the wine so the fermentation starts and stops all the time; I like to keep it going. If it's sluggish, I warm it up a little bit so it moves. I'm looking for a moderate fermenting action, not temperature.

And how long will it take to ferment the Chardonnay?

About a month. I ferment with a special yeast, developed by the Pasteur Institute in Paris. I have worked with that yeast for 15 years. It is very slow but does a good job. It creates lots of glycerol in the wine.

Is the yeast responsible for the glycerol?

The yeast converts sugar into either ethyl alcohol or glycerol which is high alcohol. It's the yeast's job to do that, nobody else can do it. And every yeast produces different by-products. Many things play a role in my winemaking. I consider winemaking to be a combination lock. You have to know every number in order to unlock it. There are many people who know about winemaking, but they miss one number.

The Burgundians ferment their Chardonnay in new oak, instead of stainless steel. Don't you think that's important?

They don't have stainless steel, temperature controlled tanks, so that's the best they can do. It's better to ferment in barrels than in large containers which heat the wine. Wine fermented in barrels doesn't heat itself because there is not much volume, so this is a natural way to cut the temperature. But when you ferment in the barrel, every barrel is an individual fermenter, and you have so many different batches. You might not be able to cool it enough. With a cold building it's all right, but if the building warms up you might have trouble because it might ferment in one week. You will feel that hotness later in the wine.

If you ferment in temperature controlled stainless steel and then put the Chardonnay in new Limousin barrels, there will be a slight difference, but not much. One year it might be better, another year worse. I think it's superior to control fermentation with technology. I am not against technology; I use only the best of the technology that's available.

Do you hold Chardonnay on the skins for any length of time?

No, but I pick my grapes late. So the skins are already full and soft, and much flavor is already entering the whole berry. It macerates on the vine, so I get plenty of varietal flavor without maceration in the tank. I do want strong varietal character, and you get that by leaving grapes on the vine.

Is the Chardonnay filtered and fined?

We usually rack the wine after fermentation and chill it for a short time. If it is clear enough we don't filter but put it directly into barrels. If it is not clear, we do a rough filtration so sediment doesn't go into the barrels. We might fine with bentonite and filter it prior to bottling.

How long did the '73 Chardonnay spend in oak?

About six months in Limousin barrels. Part was new and part was one year old. We try every year to have some new barrels. If you use only new, you wind up with too much oak.

How long does the Cabernet ferment?

Depending on the year and the grapes, from 7 to 15 days. I ferment Cabernet as the French fermented before: one week to get it dry, then fermentation is over and the skins sink into the wine and macerate for a week. You get the benefit of all the aroma and flavors and everything from the skins. We ferment it about 75 to 85 degrees.

Is the Cabernet fined and filtered?

If we have to fine, we do. We don't have a rule. We do filter it before bottling. The Cabernet will be two years in small barrels, Nevers, Yugoslavian and American. I have different batches from the same vintage in different types of barrels, and then I make a master blend before bottling, so they have a little character of each oak.

Do you blend varietals or are they all 100 percent of the grape variety?

I don't blend. When I produce varietal character, I can't have the same character with 80 percent as I do with 100 percent.

Do you have to adjust the acid levels on any of your wines, and if so do you use tartaric acid?

I prefer to have enough natural acid in grapes but sometimes if there is not enough acid to produce well balanced wine we correct with tartaric acid.

Do you have the bladder type press?

Yes. I use free run plus the light press in most cases. The heavy press I keep separate, and if I need to, I add some back in to get more body. If I don't need it, I may sell it.

Your Johannisberg Riesling has come out on top in some important tastings too. How do you get residual sweetness in the Riesling?

We chill the wine when the sugar drops to one and two-tenths percent sugar. That stops fermentation; then I rack or filter out the yeast.

Have you ever used a sweet reserve of unfermented juice, a mute*?*

Not here. All that sugar comes from the Johannisberg Riesling itself.

Is there a difference in quality between the two methods?

This is the better way. When you stop fermentation at one and two-tenths percent sugar, you get much more varietal character and fruitiness than when you go to zero and add sweet reserve. That one percent of sugar takes sometimes two weeks to ferment dry and a lot of character is lost during that two weeks. Your *muté* is unfermented juice, and juice tastes different from the wine itself. You can do it that way, but it's not the best way, it's the worst way.

How big is the winery right now, and how big do you plan to grow?

We make now about 20,000 cases a year. There is no plan nor room in the château for larger production. When we came here in '72 we decided to match the quality of the wine to the label, to produce château quality wine. We decided to make one wine, to specialize in Cabernet Sauvignon. We lived in dreams for about two months before we got the figures on what it would cost to produce that one wine in the first to the fifth year, compared with how much money would come in during those five years. We saw a lot of money going out, but not a penny coming in for five years, because it takes at least five years to make Cabernet the way we make it. So we added Zinfandel, Chardonnay and Johannisberg Riesling, to put some wine on the market in one or two years. Now Chardonnay is our leader.

We thought to become the house of Cabernet, but we've become the house of Chardonnay. We may be able to cut down to Chardonnay and Cabernet, and make other wines in years when we have something "extraordinaire."

Couldn't you make more wine by hiring a half dozen assistant winemakers?

You can do it, but you replace your nose with somebody else's nose and the results are different.

Can wineries of a much larger size make really fine wines?

Sure they can, but it is much harder.

You said that when you came here you decided to match the quality of the wines to the château label. That label, and this winery, have been around for a long time, haven't they?

Yes. Mr. Alfred Tubbs, a senator in Sacramento, traveled in Europe and fell in love with French wines. So he brought cuttings from France and brought a French winemaker by the name of Jerome Bardot, in 1882. They built this château in a typically French style; it's built mostly underground. They had no refrigeration in those days, but they used common sense and Mother Nature to create a good cool environment for wines. Temperature year round is between 50 and 60 degrees, and water seeps through the walls to create relative humidity.

Who built the lake on the grounds here?

Mr. Yort Franks purchased this place in 1958; he wanted to create the atmosphere of the way he lived in China, so he built the lake and zigzag bridges. The Chinese believed spirits travel only in straight directions, so they built zigzag bridges so even spirits won't bother them while they're meditating. We have inherited that, and it helps to have it for tastings and picnics.

Are all your grapes from your own vineyards here next to the winery?

No, we own 35 acres of Zinfandel and 65 of Cabernet. We buy the Johannisberg Riesling and Chardonnay.

Your own vineyards here in Calistoga are a warm Region III, aren't they?

No, mostly it is a Region II, depending on the year.

People further down in the Napa Valley routinely say it's too hot in Calistoga for good quality grapes.

People do say that, but we didn't find it so. We made Zinfandel from here, and there is no better Zinfandel in the district. We haven't produced a Cabernet from here yet, but I was judging last year that those are very nice Cabernet grapes about to come. One year it might be better down in the valley, another year better up here. We buy Riesling and Chardonnay from a cool section of the valley between Napa and Yountville, a climatic Region I. What you *say* is not important, wines are the best proof if you're right or wrong.

Is that on the valley floor or on the slopes?

Mostly on the floor, some on the slopes but not big slopes. We get some Chardonnay, Riesling and Cabernet from the Alexander Valley, which is on the slopes at the beginning of the valley. Those vineyards are as good as any in the Napa Valley. Beautiful grapes. The '73 Chardonnay was a blend of Napa and Alexander Valley grapes. The sugar on the '73 Chardonnay was between 23 and 24 and the acid between .8 and 1—mature grapes!

How many tons to the acre do those Chardonnay vineyards yield?

Between one and three tons; Chardonnay is a low yielding variety. Some of the vineyards are on the slopes, where it's dry and they just can't produce more than one or two tons. Now, the vineyards on the valley floor are pruned with the purpose of a low yield and high quality.

None of those vineyards is mechanically harvested?

Only one. A few others are talking about it. Mr. Wallace Johnson and I wrote a paper on that for the American Society of Enologists' conference a year ago, and mechanical harvesting produces good quality if it is well supervised. But it has to be done properly—everybody cannot do it. It's harder to do it properly mechanically than to pick by hand. When you pick by hand the juice is protected by the skin, but in mechanical harvesting the grapes come off the stems, the skin is broken and the juice is exposed to the air. It all depends on what you do then. It's best to crush in the field on a cool morning or day, cover with a blanket of CO_2 and deliver immediately to the winery.

Do the machines also pick the grapes that are not ripe?

They don't have eyes, they pick everything. But if the grapes are properly pruned and are mature you get a very small percentage of the second crop and we didn't find it affected quality at all.

What size gondolas do the grapes go into when they are picked?

From two to five tons.

Many winemakers have told me of the extreme efforts they make to use small gondolas and get the grapes to the winery for crushing within an hour or so, or of crushing them in the field to prevent oxidation.

It's usually between one and two hours before we crush them. Sooner is better, of course. But if the grapes are picked carefully by hand and not smashed, they'll be better too. Temperature of grapes is very important—the cooler the better.

Do you have any control over that kind of thing?

Yes. I spend half of my time in summer and during crushing in the vineyards. I watch the grapes since they start blooming in spring. And they are not picked before I give the sign. So when they come to my winery they are not strangers to me. I know what these grapes promise me, I already have some vision of what I'm going to try to develop from them.

To what do you attribute the greatness of those Chardonnay grapes—the soil, the climate, the vineyard practices?

Each of those plays a role. And it's not the grape only that makes great wine, but the cooperage and the winemaker too. There are so many factors, as I mentioned before, in the combination to the lock.

Since your Chardonnay has just been judged better than its rivals in that Paris tasting, it may amuse you when I ask if you think the best California wines are as good as the best European wines. So let me ask, why do you think your '73 Chardonnay placed first, what made it better than the other wines in competition?

All these factors came together. The grapes, yeast, cooperage, bottle aging, winemaker. If I had missed on one of those it wouldn't have come out that way. But the '73 is no better than our '74, and our '75 is better than either, so vintage plays a big role too.

Did that Paris tasting finally establish California as a great wine region?

California has been for long time a great wine region. This is only one more proof of it. Before Prohibition, California was making mostly ordinary wine. Once in a while some good wine would come along. And then about 40 years ago, after Prohibition, they started talking about varietal and premium wines, and quality began to be identified. That process has been continuing, and I've seen improvements in grapes and cooperage and methods of making wines. And I saw it coming when I left Robert Mondavi: I noted we had outgrown the premium quality image and we had the ability to make château quality wines, because the grapes were there, the cooperage was there, the knowledge was there—somebody just had to start.

People usually don't say it, but there are many Europeans involved in the California wine industry. And I think that European blood has contributed to the desire for quality, the pushing toward quality, carrying on the European care and love for winemaking. Californians are not yet equal to the French in the *art* of winemaking but will be soon. There are many budding young wine artists in California with the enthusiasm and time. They could pretty soon be equal to or better than the French. The French know they are better wine artists now, but they lack the technology we have. So our technology is helping us, but technology and knowledge are not enough. I know many winemakers who know everything there is to know, but they don't give their knowledge and their love to the wine. The local newspaper here wrote an article about wine. The headline read: "In beer it's the water, in wine it's the people that count." And that's true. So when I came to this place I had the château label and I said, "That's it! We are going to start the third level quality wines, not ordinary wines, not premium wines, but château quality wines." And this is not temporary. This is here to stay.

Donn Chappellet

CHAPPELLET VINEYARD

I did not want to be just another winemaker producing pretty good wines from the valley floor. I wanted to produce the very best possible, so I went to the hills.

The Chappellet winery is a visual gem, a pyramid hidden in woods high in the eastern hills of Napa Valley. The label and capsule of each bottle of Chappellet wine are embossed with a pyramid. This subtle representation of the winery seems also to define the style of wines: "elegant" is the word Donn Chappellet uses; "subtle" would also fit. Chappellet himself, a former amateur who escaped from business in Los Angeles to become a winemaker, is a big man with an imposing presence, but he is somewhat reticent, allowing the wines to speak for themselves. We climbed to a room at the peak of the pyramid to view the surrounding vineyards and blue, shimmering Lake Hennessey in the distance. Then we climbed down, opened a bottle of Chardonnay, and talked at his desk inside the quiet, cool winery.

Recommended wine to drink while reading this chapter:

CHAPPELLET
CABERNET SAUVIGNON

You are one of those who abandoned another vocation to become a winemaker. What were you doing before you founded your winery in 1967?

For two years I had been searching for the right property for a winery. I grew up in Los Angeles and I was working there with an industrial food service company. But I was disenchanted, I wanted to get out, and so I turned to my hobby, which was wine. This was in 1965 before the great wine boom really had begun, but looking into the wine field I became excited about the potential. It was already obvious at that time, from sales trends, that the wine field was going up.

Did you take any winemaking courses at Davis to train yourself, or did you more or less plunge in?

I plunged in.

How big is the winery?

We produce about 15,000 cases a year and have the capacity and the plans to increase to around 25,000 cases a year. We will do this gradually, over perhaps the next ten years. We won't go beyond 25,000.

One wine writer has called your winery the best looking winery built in this century. Who was the architect?

We didn't have an architect. We started with a design, and a structural engineer, Richard Keith of Santa Rosa, built it. He's well known. He's built several of the new wineries.

Are you the sole owner, or do you have partners?

I'm the sole owner.

What kind of a staff do you have?

Between the winery and the vineyards we have ten full time people, including our oenologist Joe Cafaro who has his degree in oenology from Fresno State.

Does your family help?

I have six children, but they're all in school. One of my sons is helping on the bottling line this afternoon, for instance, but generally they're not fully available.

How would you characterize the style of your wines?

I'm not certain. I suppose you might use the word elegant. Our Cabernet, for instance, has considerably more finesse than the big, heavy Cabernets of California. Our soil just won't produce the heavy style, yet it brings out subtle flavors, you might say aristocratic. Our 1969 Cabernet, by the way, was just ranked number one in a "taste-off" by the Vintners' Club of San Francisco against 11 other California Cabernets.

Would you say the same about your Chardonnay's style?

Yes. Again, it's lighter and more delicate than some others, and has less oak. It results from the grapes grown in this location. We could give the Chardonnay more wood, but I don't prefer the oaky style.

You've achieved wide acclaim for your Chenin Blanc, a grape usually considered secondary.

I considered it secondary too, but it was planted here when we arrived. So we made it, fermented it dry because I don't care for any residual sweetness in my table wines, and we gained quite a reputation for it. Most of the California Chenin Blancs tend to be on the sweet side. We don't pretend it's in the same league as Chardonnay: it sells for about half the price of the Chardonnay.

The three varietals you've mentioned plus your Johannisberg Riesling are the only wines you produce. Have you thought of expanding the line?

No, my chances of making the finest quality wines possible are much better if I specialize in four varietals rather than trying to make 10 or 15 and frequently miss. I'm interested in sticking to what I can do well.

How did you decide to locate your winery in the Napa Valley, and more particularly in these hills in the eastern part of the valley?

Napa was a proven area. I wasn't interested in taking a chance on some new area. I also wanted to be in the hills and not on the floor of the valley. I spent about six months just quizzing people on the merits of the hills versus the valley floor, trying to learn whether it was a myth that better wines can be made in the hill areas. I had noticed that hill areas around the world were noted for producing the finest wines. I talked to wine people about it. When I talked to Andre Tchelistcheff he told me he would prefer hill grapes if he could get them. I guess that was quite persuasive to me. I didn't want to be just another winemaker producing pretty good wine from the valley floor area, I wanted to produce the very best possible so I went to the hills.

So you put your winery on Pritchard Hill. Where is that exactly?

We're in the hills on the eastern edge of the Napa Valley, due east of Rutherford by some eight miles. The elevation is about 1,500 feet, though some of our upper vineyards go to 1,700 feet.

Has your preference for the hills been confirmed? Are the grapes different here?

Definitely. I think most winemakers in the Napa region would identify our wines in a blind tasting precisely because they're different. They may not agree that they're best, but they'd be able to pick them out. Much of that difference comes from our unique conditions: soil, basically a volcanic, sandy loam; the steep slopes which provide good drainage; and the weather. We have none of the deep fertile loam you find on the valley floor, so the vines have to struggle. We don't get nearly the tonnage per acre you get down in the valley, but we do get a greater intensity of flavor, and, at the same time, a certain elegance and subtlety.

You're of the school that believes the vines love adversity?

I don't think they love it, but they have to face it and I think they produce better fruit as a result.

What about temperature? Is this classified as Region I?

It's Region II. I would guess about a middle Region II. We average 35 inches of rainfall annually, but of course that varies. Rainfall, temperature, soil and topography all play their parts, but there is latitude in each; their presence as quality factors varies from year to year.

Would you like to see subregions such as, for instance, the Napa Valley eastern hill region, have their own appellations of origin?

I'm not persuaded there's good reason for that. I *would* like to see the laws changed so that 100 percent of the grapes in a wine with a Napa Valley appellation actually come from the Napa region. Ninety-eight percent might do, but certainly more than the 75 percent permitted now on non-vintage wines. I also think people ought not to be allowed to buy Napa grapes and set up a winery in the desert or Los Angeles and make a wine labeled "Napa" wine. The laws were changed to allow that a few years ago, and I thought at the time it was wrong.

What types of grapes and how many acres of each do you have up here?

We have 94 acres total. Twenty-five of Chenin Blanc, 13 of Johannisberg Riesling, 11 of Chardonnay, 10 of Merlot and 35 of Cabernet. Then there are the three neighboring vineyards from which we get grapes. We care for two of those, one with seven acres of Johannisberg Riesling and Chardonnay, and another of 20 acres of Cabernet and Chardonnay. The third vineyard was just planted and it has 30 acres in Cabernet and Chardonnay, and the owner may put in some Napa Gamay.

Were there vineyards here before you arrived?

There were vineyards here on Pritchard Hill in the 1880's. But three years before we came in 1967, the previous owner here had planted a new vineyard. That's where we got the Chenin Blanc. I probably wouldn't have planted it had I been the first to establish the vineyard, but we've been extremely successful with our Chenin Blanc. There was also some Napa Gamay here, which we've grafted over to Chardonnay.

How far apart are your vines planted?

We've planted them 8 by 12 feet apart, what the University of California says is optimum spacing. The new, neighboring vineyard is planted 6 by 11, and I'm inclined to think that's better for the hills because our vines never get as big as valley vines and the 8 by 12 spacing tends to waste space.

How heavily do your vines produce?

We average just under three tons per acre. On this new vineyard of our neighbor, I expect to see a little over three tons.

Is your pruning heavy, medium or light?

We prune quite severely. The most canes we'd leave on a Cabernet vine, for instance is four.

Who picks the grapes, and how is the picking done?

Our regular crew, plus some seasonal help, picks the grapes. It's all done by hand.

Is it too steep here for mechanical picking?

Yes, it certainly is for the machines they have now. If some machine were to become available in the future, I don't automatically rule out the possibility of mechanical picking. Right now, though, we pick by hand, and put the grapes into boxes. We may eventually go to using small gondolas.

Do you do any selected bunch picking? Do you pick more than once?

No, once you turn 15 pickers loose on the fields the chances are slim they could or would discriminate between bunches, except that we don't want them to pick the second crop, the grapes that are not mature.

How do you crush and stem?

We have the classic crusher-stemmer, which crushes the grapes in rollers and then works them through a stainless steel drum with paddles inside; the paddles slap the grapes and skins through the holes in the drum while the stems are left behind.

Do you ferment in stainless steel?

Right, all stainless steel both for reds and whites. They're jacketed with temperature control devices, so we can ferment the whites quite cool, about 40 degrees.

It must take a long time at that temperature.

Yeah, about 30 to 90 days, say 45 days on the average to complete their fermentation. And the reds ferment at 75 to 80 degrees.

Do you pump over the cap or punch it down?

We pump over.

Do you get a malo-lactic fermentation of the reds?

Yes, they all go through it. With whites we don't want it so we watch the sulphur level pretty closely to prevent it.

Do you start fermentation by yeast inoculation, or do you allow spontaneous fermentation from the wine yeast on the grapes?

Nobody has ever seriously suggested to me that spontaneous fermentation is a better method. We always inoculate. I know it's customary in certain parts of France to allow spontaneous fermentation, but I don't know whether anything is gained by it. It's risky.

What kind of a press do you have?

We use the Willmes bladder type press. But we only use a light pressing normally. For example, the heavier press of the Chardonnay and Riesling goes into our Chenin Blanc, which is about 60 percent Chenin Blanc and 40 percent these other two grapes. The Chenin Blanc grapes are lightly pressed, and the moment the color or taste start to change as the pressing gets heavier we change the hose to another tank to put it in our Pritchard Hill label wines.

Why do you use the Pritchard Hill label?

To begin with, we only use it on our secondary quality Chenin Blanc. We developed it to protect the quality connotation of our Chappellet label. At the same time a secondary quality label guards us against risks in the marketplace. So if the bottom suddenly drops out of the high priced wine market, we have the cheaper Pritchard Hill line that can compete.

Are your Riesling, Chardonnay and Cabernet 100 percent varietals?

The first two are. The Cabernet is about 25 percent Merlot. When the neighboring vineyards come into production and we get those additional Cabernet grapes, we may lower the Merlot to 12 or 15 percent.

Do you have to adjust acid?

Very seldom. In the last two years not at all. When we have adjusted the acid, we've used tartaric acid.

Do you ever use concentrate to adjust sugar?

Never.

Do you fine or filter or centrifuge?

We give the Cabernet one or two egg whites per barrel, but no filtration. We rack it every few weeks at first, then every few months, a total of six or seven times. We put it directly into 60 gallon Nevers oak after fermentation, where it spends almost two years. And we try to give it a year of bottle age before releasing it.

With the whites, we use bentonite and then two filtrations, one rough, right after the bentoniting, and a finer one right before bottling, using pad filters. We give the Chardonnay five to six months in 60 gallon used oak barrels. Some of that is Limousin oak. The Riesling and Chenin Blanc spend only a very short time in oak. And then not all of it is aged in oak—only a portion, which is then blended back into the wine which did not receive any oak aging. We don't centrifuge.

In your view, will the best wines in California in the future come from the smaller wineries?

Yes, I really can't see the larger people producing the very best wines. They might come out with a good wine, excellent wine, from time to time, but it would be hard for them to do it consistently. Bigness and consistent quality just don't go together.

Do you find the best California wines to be as good as the best European wines?

That's a tough question. I think there may be a half a dozen or perhaps ten California wineries which produce wines equal to the best of Europe, but they don't do it every year. They've proven themselves in isolated cases to be as fine as the finest of Europe, though.

Jerry Luper, left, and Charles Carpy.

Jerry Luper

FREEMARK ABBEY WINERY

I started at Gallo as a lab technician. I was eighteen and a teetotaler, but all this wine kept coming across the desk to analyze, and I began to decide it wasn't such bad stuff.

Napa Valley travelers know one of the most pleasant places for lunch is the restaurant in the old stone building of Freemark Abbey north of St. Helena. The restaurant and candle-making shop sit atop some of the finest wines in the valley, kept by the Freemark Abbey

Winery in the building's cellar level. An additional winery structure, in back of the old stone building, blends so subtly into the shade of California oaks it is possible to miss the small sign indicating it as the winery. This winery has Napa roots in more ways than one; the owners have long personal connections with winegrowing in the valley. Managing partner Charles Carpy probably claims the deepest roots, for he is the namesake of his grandfather who was born in Bordeaux and made Napa Valley wine in the nineteenth century. I spoke with Jerry Luper in his laboratory inside the winery and Chuck Carpy stopped by at the beginning of our conversation to answer a few questions about the genesis of the Freemark partnership.

As this book was going to press, Freemark Abbey entered a transition period. Jerry Luper resigned, leaving for an extended stay in European wine regions, though he is expected eventually to return to California and continue making fine wines. In addition, some of the Freemark Abbey partners purchased the small, well equipped winery formerly known as "Souverain of Rutherford" which had been owned by the Pillsbury Company. This change may mean only that there will be more wine produced at the Freemark Abbey level of excellence.

Recommended wine to drink while reading this chapter:

FREEMARK ABBEY
CHARDONNAY

You've had remarkable success in producing wines at the top of the quality spectrum in a fairly short period of time. How did you do it?

CHARLES CARPY:

It was primarily the influence of Brad Webb, one of our partners, in the winemaking style we developed here. Also, the varieties we make were chosen because they are the top four premium varieties. Our initial intent was to limit it to some number, and we chose four. We had those varieties in our vineyards—and we wanted varieties that mature at different times too, otherwise all your grapes have to be picked and all the wine has to be made at the same time and you need a huge plant to produce the same amount of product. We've picked up one more, Petite Sirah, and that was accidental. My partner Lawry Wood is a professional ranch manager and one of the places he manages is York Creek vineyard up on Spring Mountain. They have a little patch of rather old Petite Sirah vines which we made one fermenter of, and it turned out to be something quite exceptional so we're continuing to make a little of it.

How long have you and your partners owned Freemark Abbey?

We organized in 1967. There were originally five of us and two others joined soon after. Two of us were grape growers, one is in real estate, one was at that time overseas in India with the Asia Foundation, another is an attorney and he has since developed vineyards, another is in the venture capital business in San Francisco, and Brad Webb is a consulting oenologist. Lawry Wood was a grape grower neighbor of mine, and we had been looking in the mid-60s for opportunities to get into the wine business.

Who first built a winery here?

The first one was built around 1885, and a second owner then built this stone building over four phases starting in 1895 and completing it around 1905. That family sold it during Prohibition, and it was sold again around 1939 to the Ahern family who changed the name to Freemark Abbey.

Was it ever an actual abbey?

Oh, no! It was a combination of the names of three people: Charles Freeman, Mark Foster and Ahern (nicknamed Abbey), so it came out Freemark Abbey. They marketed wine into the 50s quite successfully.

You don't operate the restaurant and candle shop on the upper portion of the old stone building, do you?

No, that's completely separate, we only own the lower floor in a condominium sense, in addition to the new building we built here. It's turned out to be a happy accumulation of enterprises, though, because it gives a small winery like this the advantage of the tourist flow to the restaurant and shops, and gives the people coming here other things to look at in addition to the winery.

Jerry, did you come here as winemaker directly out of college?

JERRY LUPER:

Yes, I finished my oenology degree at Fresno State, and spent a few months in the fermenting room at Louis Martini winery in '69 before coming here. I shoveled pomace.

What made you decide to study oenology?

That's a long story. I started at Gallo in '59 as a lab technician. I was 18 years old and a teetotaler, but all this wine kept coming across the desk to analyze, and I began to decide it wasn't such bad stuff. Gallo, being so competitive, analyzed everybody else's wines too. My friend and I there would use a little for analysis, and save the rest for tasting. Over a two year period I got to know the wines of the Napa Valley, and in fact the wines of the world.

Gallo was analyzing imported wines as well?

Oh yes. So that's how I got interested. Then I went into the Army and went to Europe and really got exposed to German wines—they were so cheap and so good.

Do you believe your wines have a distinct style which differs from other Napa Valley wines?

I think so. We believe the ripest grapes have the most character, so we wait until the last possible moment to pick them. We try to pick Chardonnay, for instance, at 23.5 Balling; Cabernet, Pinot Noir and Riesling all at about 23, or above. And, of course, we watch the acid too, so we don't lose it. So I'd say our style is bigness of wine from very ripe fruit.

Would other Napa Valley vintners be able to pick out the Freemark Abbey wines in a blind tasting?

Oh yes. Maybe they would be picking them out because they've tasted them so many times and just know the wines. That may have more to do with it than a distinctive style standing alone, but it is our style they are recognizing.

Your Pinot Noir has been pretty successful among some wine critics. To what do you attribute that success?

A great deal of Freemark Abbey's success has been due to a scaling up of some techniques Brad Webb developed in his earlier days in winemaking. His first experiments were with Chardonnay and Pinot Noir, and because of that we know how to make those two wines very well.

How big is the winery in terms of cases per year?

We're crushing the equivalent of about 23,000 cases a year now, and that's the maximum we'll go.

Do most of your grapes come from vineyards the winery owns?

The original idea was to use only our own grapes, and the partnership owns several hundred acres which would more than supply this winery. But we've found some grapes outside the partnership we think are better, so we purchase between 30 and 40 percent of the grapes from other growers.

Where are the vineyards the partners own?

Mostly around Rutherford, and east toward Conn Dam. And Bill Jaeger, one of the partners, owns quite a bit of land to the south toward Napa.

Are any of those vineyards in the hills or on the slopes?

No, they're all on the valley floor. And they're predominantly planted to the "noble four": Riesling, Chardonnay, Cabernet Sauvignon and Pinot Noir. There are small amounts of Merlot, and a few other things.

Are most of those vineyards in Region II climatically?

I'd consider Rutherford a Region II, but down toward Napa you move into a high Region I.

You said you purchase about 30 to 40 percent of your grapes. Are those usually from the same vineyards each year?

Yes, we have two vineyards under contract. John Bosché's vineyard is west of Rutherford and slightly north, on the valley floor up against the hills.

That's close to Beaulieu's Madame de Pins Vineyard Number 1, and close to Martha's Vineyard of Joe Heitz, isn't it?

Near the de Pins Vineyard, but about three miles north of Martha's Vineyard on the same side of the valley. And our other contract vineyard is near the Stag's Leap area on the Silverado Trail. Both that vineyard and the Bosché vineyard are planted solely to Cabernet Sauvignon. Also, we buy a small amount of Merlot from down around Oakville.

What factors, in your opinion, make all those vineyards, which seem to be in some of the best locations in the valley, so good? The climate, the soil, what is it?

They are just lucky combinations of all three factors that are important: the climate, the soil and the vine itself. Now the area around Stag's Leap is a well known area for very fine Cabernet. The soil is light, so the vines don't really grow too heavily, and they produce two to three tons to the acre. It's right at the edge of the slope, back in from the actual flat valley floor.

What tonnage do you typically get from the vineyards in the Rutherford area?

It varies. There are probably ten different soil types—heavy clay soils where you might get six tons to the acre, and light gravelly places where you'll get one and a half to one ton. It averages out to three or four tons an acre.

And what is the yield on the Bosché vineyard?

It has varied from three tons to sometimes five tons to the acre. It's a very unusual vineyard. Though it's a light, well drained soil, the vines are quite healthy, they throw a good crop. And in spite of that the wine comes out very dark, very acid, very tannic. So these formulas about tonnage per acre don't hold all the answers. Here's a vineyard that produced five tons to the acre last year and yet made one of the best wines in its history. I've heard a lot about the best vineyards in Bordeaux being well drained, and this vineyard happens to be right next to a major drainage creek for the spring rain runoff. Maybe that has an influence.

Do you prune to limit the crop on your own vineyards?

We don't prune too severely, because if you try to limit the number of buds severely the vine grows heavy vegetatively, throws long canes and is hard to control.

Do you try to limit the crop by bunch thinning?

We've experimented on small lots. It can make a difference in quality but it's very expensive, probably not economical.

Who picks the grapes for you?

Predominantly migrant labor, although we have a fairly extensive year-round crew of ranch hands who usually act as supervisors during harvest. They use knives and pick into plastic boxes which are dumped into four ton gondolas.

Do you ever send the pickers through the vineyard to pick more than once, as the fruit matures?

No, grapes don't lend themselves to that. Normally, except for what we call the second crop, there will be a fairly uniform ripeness in the vine.

Are any of your vineyards mechanically harvested?

No. And at this point I personally don't think the quality of mechanically harvested fruit would be good enough. There is too much "MOG," material other than grapes.

What kind of a crusher-stemmer do you use, and what kind of press?

We use a Healdsburg stemmer-crusher, in that order. The grapes are stemmed first and then crushed. We have the Willmes bladder type press. I believe it's the best for making high quality wine. It's good for breaking up the cake between press cycles, it has a gentle squeezing action: very good efficiency with low pressure.

Do you make any free run wines?

In the whites all the free run and press juice are combined; we don't separate the two. The juice is chilled to 45 degrees and settled for two days and then racked off the lees of that settling for fermentation. For the reds, we keep the free run and press juice separate all through aging, and so far we've been able to blend our press wine back into the free run. It's not a very heavy press wine. We crush the Chardonnay directly into a tank, not into the press, and we allow the juice to stay in contact with the skins for several hours. We think this extracts more phenolics from the pulp and skins, where a great deal of the flavor of any grape is located. I think we get more Chardonnay character and a heavier, more tannic wine. With Cabernet, we again try to get the ripest grapes and leave them on the skins as long as possible. We actually do a strong pumping over that physically breaks up the cap, we don't just let it trickle down through the skins the way some others do it.

Do you start fermenting by inoculating with yeast starter?

Yes, we haven't as yet used spontaneous fermentation; we use a cultured Burgundy strain yeast for the reds and a Montrachet for the whites.

You said you haven't used spontaneous fermentation "as yet." Are you planning to do it in the future?

As a matter of fact I'm planning on doing one fermenter this year with spontaneous fermentation of the Chardonnay. But I don't know that it will be all that spontaneous. This valley has 40 wineries in it, and for 100 years the pomace from the wine has gone back into the vineyards, so I think the micro-flora of yeast is predominantly wine yeast. It's the European way, though, and, after all, most of the winemaking techniques in this country originated in Europe, so we're experimenting with it to do whatever we can to make better wine.

Do you ferment all the wines in stainless steel?

Yes, we ferment and clarify in stainless steel, and age in wood. The whites ferment between 50 degrees and 55 degrees, and the reds at about 75 degrees.

How extensively do you fine and filter?

We're of the basic belief that filtration, properly done, doesn't subtract any character from the wine. Filtration takes out matter you don't taste—a yeast cell or bacteria cell, super-large molecular particles. All the things you taste in wine are soluble components in the alcohol-water mixture, and they pass through the filter. With Chardonnay, we basically ferment, settle, filter if necessary, fine with bentonite and age. With reds, the Cabernet clarifies itself fairly well by settling, and then we do a rough filtration and it goes to the barrel for aging. For the past few years, I haven't had to fine any Cabernet. And that same treatment applies to the Merlot and Petite Sirah, but Pinot Noir has so much malic acid it undergoes a horrendous malo-lactic fermentation, really a catastrophic thing. And so many bacteria are grown in the wine that it won't settle out and we do have to fine it with a small amount of gelatin.

Do all the reds go through the malo-lactic fermentation?

Yes, we induce it by heat. We don't inoculate because the organism is present in the winery.

Do you adjust the acid of any of your wines?

Occasionally, in a warm year when we have low acid we have made acid adjustments with tartaric acid.

Have you ever used concentrate to adjust sugar levels?

No. It is possible to sweeten the Riesling with concentrate before bottling, but the best way to do it is to arrest fermentation.

Do you own a centrifuge?

No.

What kind of cooperage do you have?

We have 60 gallon French Nevers oak, exclusively, except for three American white oak 2,300 gallon tanks that we use for Riesling and Chardonnay. We usually hold one lot of the Riesling in stainless steel, put two lots in the 2,300 gallon tanks and then blend them. Chardonnay is complicated. About half of it goes to small barrels, a sixth will go in the big tank, and the balance remains in stainless steel; then it's all blended together. We just don't have enough room to put it all in barrels, because of space limitations in the winery. The half of the Chardonnay which goes into barrels will stay in about six to eight months. The reds go directly to wood after their coarse filtration, all of them to the 60 gallon Nevers oak. The Pinot Noir stays in for no more than a year and a half, the Cabernet will stay closer to two years.

How often do you rack it?

We don't rack after it's in the barrel; it stays in the same barrel the whole time. A barrel is a really fine clarification device, it's the best there is because it's small and the yeast and bacteria settle out very readily. But to break down those stacks of 1,100 barrels every six months is terribly labor intensive, and we just can't afford it. That coarse filtration before going into wood does pretty much the same thing for it, as far as clarification is concerned. After aging, we bring the wines back together to get a uniform wine, and then before bottling we run it through a bottling pad filtration.

What is your opinion of California wines in comparison with European wines? Are our best ones as good as the best of Europe?

Yes, absolutely. Without comparing styles, just on a strict quality basis, I think the wines we make in the four noble varieties, except possibly in the case of Riesling, are as good as those of Europe. The exception may apply also to Pinot Noir, but certainly in Cabernet and Chardonnay we're their equals.

Joseph Heitz

HEITZ WINE CELLARS

Basically, Mother Nature is a mean old lady, and mankind has to help make wine.

We sat, confronted each other really, across an oak table in the winery's tasting kitchen late one summer afternoon. Joe Heitz has probably inspired more discussion among wine buffs than any other winemaker, and I soon discovered why. He's a tough individualist, does things *his* way, and doesn't mince words. Yet I have seen him charm an audience of winetasters like a Tallyrand. Certainly his *wines* have charmed winetasters. He has achieved quite a reputation for being a skillful blender of wines made by others, but indubitably his greatest fame rests upon his Chardonnays and Cabernet Sauvignons, particularly the Martha's Vineyard Cabernet Sauvignon which is considered to be one of the very finest in the state today. It is priced accordingly. The winery, an attractive modern structure, sits in a quiet corner of Napa Valley next to the Heitz home and an old stone winery building of a former era. Our conversation that day was graced by samplings of a selection of Heitz wines arrayed on the table between us.

Recommended wine to drink while reading this chapter:

HEITZ CELLAR
MARTHA'S VINEYARD
CABERNET SAUVIGNON

Do you characterize your wines as having a distinctive style?

I did not in the beginning. But other people, other wine writers, have done it for me. Nathan Chroman says my wines have a particular style, and perhaps he's right. I'm sure that any one of us who does anything develops habits. I'm probably a creature of habit as much as anyone, although now and then I like to think I'm an innovator, and all that bull. But we fall in the old pattern of habit, use what tanks are available, use what help is available, follow the same schedules because help is available now and not then. So I'm sure my wines taste like Heitz wines, and Beaulieu wines taste like Beaulieu wines.

Well, what is the difference? What is the Heitz taste?

People have asked me for years what makes my wines taste—not different—they say "better" than other wines. Tasting better is a matter of personal interpretation, but the only thing I can tell them—as facetiously as I can—is that it's my sweat that went into the bottle instead of hired help's sweat.

You took a Master's Degree at Davis in oenology, is that right? When was that?

This is a little family joke, that I'm a slow learner. I graduated from high school in '38, got my Bachelor's Degree in 1948 and my Master's Degree in

'58 or '59. But a few other things interfered, such as the war, raising a family, and so on. My Bachelor's Degree was in horticulture, although all my work was in viticulture and oenology, and when I finally got my Master's Degree it was in "food science." My first job was with Gallo. I worked in the lab, seemingly by chance, although most of my work with them and other wineries has been in quality control. Maybe it wasn't as much chance as I thought, maybe that's the kind of work I was instinctively looking for. So I worked at Gallo for some months. I was young and not too solid, apparently, and always thinking the grass was greener on the other side of the fence. Then I went to work for Wine Growers' Guild in Lodi, in a quality control program. Next, I worked for Mission Bell down in Madera for a short period of time, also working in the laboratory, not in analysis but in quality control, making the blends. Then I had the opportunity to join Beaulieu in Napa.

When was that?

Early spring of 1951. I came as a chemist and also helped with the blends, quality control, working under Mr. Tchelistcheff, and gradually moved up until I was plant manager. I had a very nice job, I liked it. But frankly it was a job I considered about half time. They had a great winemaker in Tchelistcheff and I was mostly his understudy, their insurance policy if you will. I would have had to wait until he either died or retired, and Tchelistcheff, as you know, is a sturdy individual and only retired a year or two ago. I liked the area, I liked the job, I liked everything but I wasn't using my abilities much. So when the opportunity to set up the oenology program at Fresno State College came long, I decided to take it. I helped evolve the program, design the building, select the equipment, work out the curriculum and, of course, taught viticulture and oenology for three and a half years. But, unfortunately, neither I nor my family could adjust to Fresno. Not that one place is better than the other, but we happen to believe, *know,* we fit better here than we did in Fresno. So we scrounged, looked for work, looked for jobs, looked for a winery to buy, looked for anything, anything, to get back. Finally, we found the little Brendel property who once had the "Only One" Grignolino down the highway.

That's where your tasting room is today?

Right. He only wanted $5,000 down so we borrowed it and moved back to the valley. That's how we started, 1961.

And when did you come up here to Taplin Road?

Oh, that little place down there was very tiny, like a two car garage, really. By 1964 we'd outgrown it, and found this lovely old place empty and available.

Was there a vineyard here before you came?

By the earliest evidence we can find they produced 10,000 gallons of wine here in the 1880s. Their "new" winery was built in 1898, a lovely old stone building. It's a great delight to me.

Where are we geographically? On the far eastern edge of Napa Valley . . .

I would eliminate the word "far." We're on the eastern edge of the valley in a little offshoot valley known as Spring Valley. It's parallel to Napa Valley, and over a ridge, as the crow flies, half a mile away, so we call it Napa Valley. We don't distinguish Spring Valley.

What size staff do you have here?

Well, my wife and I certainly help. Our three children have always helped. The oldest son, David, has now graduated from Fresno State in oenology and has been working for us a year. In addition to the family, we have two other full time men in the cellar. They are both oenology graduates. We may be a little overpowered technically.

About how many cases a year are you producing at present?

We're up to about 20,000.

Do you have plans to go beyond that?

Sure do. I want to make a living eventually. My goal has always been to level off at 40,000 cases. This new building was built with that in mind.

About what percentage of the vineyards where you get grapes do you own?

I grow my own Grignolino, and I do that only because we have a particular strain of Grignolino that's different from anybody else's and I cannot buy it. I like to consider myself a winemaker. Some people may be multitalented, with endless energy. I'm not. I like to make wine. I buy grapes from people who know how to grow grapes and who love to grow grapes.

Where do you buy grapes? All over Napa Valley?

The vineyards are from St. Helena on the north to Yountville on the south, mostly on the valley floor.

Where is "Martha's Vineyard"?

It's south of Oakville against the western foothills. Tom and Martha May purchased this vineyard shortly after they were married. They have roots on the east coast, so as a romantic gesture, he named the new property "Martha's Vineyard." Very romantic, as everything in the wine business is.

Do you attribute significantly different characteristics to these various vineyards from which you get grapes?

Once in a while. I think all my growers produce good Napa Valley grapes, or I wouldn't buy them. I don't put the vineyard designation on the bottle just as a sales gimmick, which is easy to do. Some people are already copying the Martha's Vineyard sort of thing. Being imitated, someone once told me, is the most sincere form of flattery. But remember, the people who do it are always imitators, and they have to sleep with themselves and I can sleep with myself. I don't put the source of the vineyard on the label unless I firmly believe those grapes are distinctly different from, and distinctly better than, run-of-the-mill Napa Valley grapes. Run-of-the-mill Napa Valley ain't bad. But if there is a particular vineyard that stands out, I try to give the grower credit by putting it on the label. I've done that in the past a couple times with Pinot Blanc—McCrea's Pinot Blanc, for example. But it's an easy thing to overdo and therefore destroy.

How many acres is Martha's Vineyard?

About 15 acres, in that range.

About how many tons to the acre does it produce?

Grapes are an agricultural product, so it's extremely variable. I cannot be precise, so I'd better be quiet. If I were a vineyardist, and vineyards were my chief joy and delight, I would know. But I'm more interested in wine.

You don't have any growers in the Carneros region do you?

No. I've got enough grapes from the heart of the Napa Valley where we grow good grapes, better grapes.

Do you imply that the Carneros grapes are not as good as the best?

The growers are very proud of them, and they do make very good wines. I don't have any grapes that come from there, so why should I brag about them?

Is it difficult to control certain viticultural practices which affect quality? I'm thinking about irrigation, pruning, the way grapes are picked. Do you have any concerns over controlling those factors?

I'm concerned about every goddamned thing I do. I think I can get better grapes under my system than if I tried to devote half my energies to running a winery and half my energies to supervising a vineyard. The vineyardists I work with are as proud of their product as I am of mine. Of course, we squabble a bit. You know, a grower would like to have all his grapes in the barn by Labor Day, and I think they should hang on the vines until Christmas, so we're always squabbling. But this is normal, nothing wrong with that.

How much rainfall do you get here?

I've never measured. I think we get the valley average, I don't know. I never worry about things I can't control. If I can change something, then I worry about it. But people ask me, "How hot was it in your vineyard today?" If I don't have a thermometer I don't know, so I get through the day rather comfortably. I've got a hell of a lot to worry about in this business, but I try to worry about things I can control. I don't even keep a rain gauge. When it comes, it comes.

What about overcropping? Is that something you've had any problems with, people trying to produce too much from the acreage, and that having an effect on quality?

Well, grape growers are human, and being human they are greedy, like everybody, like you and me. By and large, I repeat what I said a moment ago, that growers who sell to me are proud of what they produce, they're happy to have me make wine out of it and they do not try to overproduce. They're small growers, they don't have massive tonnages, and since I pay according to quality, they're better off not overcropping.

What about harvesting? Do you get involved in instructing how the grapes are to be picked for you?

You're damn right. If they come in with a lot of leaves and canes and Coca-Cola bottles and milk cartons, I send them back to the vineyard. I've only had to do that a few times. It gets back again to the integrity of the grower. None of my grapes are mechanically harvested. But that doesn't imply I oppose mechanical harvesting. I've seen mechanically harvested grapes that were worse than hand picked grapes, and I've seen hand picked grapes that were worse than mechanically harvested grapes. I'm not against progress.

But couldn't there be a problem with mechanically harvested grapes, since the machine can't distinguish between mature grapes and immature ones?

Do you think a picker out there who is picking by the pound is going to discriminate? He's going to pick every goddamned thing he can get his knife on, unless he's properly supervised. He'll throw rocks and everything else in that gondola. Mechanical harvesters put very few rocks in the gondolas, and you get less damage to your crushing equipment with mechanically picked grapes. The mechanically picked grapes are shaken off or beaten off by some method. The green ones cling, and the ripe ones fall off. I don't see any grave problems with mechanical harvesting.

There are some very small winegrowers who engage in selective picking of grapes, going through the vineyard two or three times.

I wish them luck. I hope they're still in business three to four years from now.

In the major European wine countries, and most elaborately in France, vineyard practices are regulated in great detail by the appellation control laws: pruning, spacing, harvesting, irrigation, and so on. I take it from your earlier comments you don't think that sort of detailed regulation would be useful here?

I believe in democracy, I believe in capitalism, and I think those of us who put good practices into effect are going to survive in the marketplace, and those of us who try to screw the public are going to screw themselves eventually. Without a lot more explanation I think that covers it.

When I told you earlier that I had been thinking of calling this book Winecraft, *you turned a play on words and said you didn't make your wines by "witchcraft or philosophy but by science and common sense."*

I'm not much for artsy-craftsy sorts of things.

Well, my next questions go through the winemaking process and try to probe how that view is reflected in each step. I'd like to ask you first about crushing and stemming. What kind of a machine do you use? Is the bare foot the ideal crusher and all machines less than that ideal?

Years ago, this was when Bacchus was having his revelries, they used to have only the virgin maidens crush the grapes with their feet, but something happened. Either we planted too many vineyards or we ran short of virgins. But I would not trade my crusher in for 100 pairs of bare feet. We use the classic method. You can see the old hopper we bought outside the winery. Fortunately, when we were expanding and built this building, Beaulieu was expanding so we bought their used dump hopper and conveyer. And we were fortunate enough to buy a used stainless steel crusher that somebody else had used and outgrown.

Do you ferment all in stainless steel, both reds and whites?

Yes.

And they're all outfitted with temperature control jackets. You ferment the whites at about what temperature?

Fifty degrees, and the reds about 70 degrees.

Now you don't ferment your Chardonnay in oak, and yet some people swear by that, in new oak no less. You've concluded that that is not a quality factor in Chardonnay?

I ferment my Chardonnays in stainless steel tanks. I like them. I got out of school a long time ago; I'm 56 or 57 years old, and I'm not going to start experimenting now. You may say this is a dumb approach. I like my wines, the customers like them and buy them, in blind tastings they turn out pretty well, so why should I fart around and make life miserable by bringing hundreds of 60 gallon barrels that have to be washed, and are impossible to sterilize, when I can do it neatly and cleanly and efficiently in a method that has been evolved through a period of many generations and which I happen to believe is good? Sanitation and temperature control particularly, I think, are the two prime things in fermentation. And with 50 or 60 gallon barrels, it's awfully costly to cool a whole room, all that bloody air space just to keep your wines cool. Now think a minute. Wine is a business, the same as everything else; the object is to sell your wine at more money than it cost to produce it. And refrigeration is costly. It's better to control your refrigeration cost to *a* tank rather than cooling a whole bloody room just to keep a few barrels cool in that room.

Do you make any wines wholly from the free run juice?

No.

What kind of a press do you use?

Willmes. The pneumatic tube goes down inside and presses like a doughnut, so the pomace is a doughnut on the outside.

Do you always try to get a light, gentle pressing, or are there some wines which you press at different pressure from others?

No, I press them all about the same, red or white. Two or three gentle pressings, but I'll end up at about 60 pounds per square inch.

Do you always start fermentation by sulphuring the must and then inoculating with a yeast culture?

"Always" is a terrible word, but I always *try* to do what you say, yes.

About how much sulphite do you have to use before adding the yeast?

I aim for 100 parts per million, and by the next day when you add the yeast it's dissipated to about 60 or 70 parts per million.

There are many studies done in France on different yeast cultures in various regions and how that affects the final wine. I take it you're with almost everybody I've talked to who think it makes no difference here.

I basically believe Mother Nature is a mean old lady, and mankind has to help make wine.

Well now, there you go, there's an expression of a real philosophy.

But you do it with science, not with crafts.

Do you have to adjust acid often?

Frequently. With tartaric acid.

What kind of fining and filtration do your wines receive?

I'm a great believer in bentonite. We'll rack the wines two or three times, get as much natural clarification as we can, then give a bentonite clarification to remove the excess protein from the wine, get it bright and clear. And sometimes, not always, we'll give it a coarse filtration before we put it away to age.

You don't centrifuge?

No, we fine and filter.

Some people do all three.

Yeah, well they've got a lot of capital coming from some place, because the three are reasonably interchangeable. Usually, just before the wine's ready for bottling, we'll see it if needs fining and then we'll give it a light fining—in the case of whites it's usually bentonite, and in the case of reds it's usually gelatin to remove the excess tannin and soften it. If some problem develops in the wine, then we use one of the commercial fining agents that have a specific purpose. But with normal wines and normal development, bentonite and a little gelatin take care of everything. Then, of course, we give it a nice filtration just before bottling—tighter filtration than the one given when it was just a young wine.

What kind of aging do your wines receive?

The Rosé we like to bottle as soon as we can, which usually means February or March, and it's available on the market in May, June or July. Summertime. The Riesling types—Johannisberg Riesling and Gewürztraminer—we like to keep in upright "1,000 gallon" tanks, bottle in June or July, and we'll sell them September or October or Christmas. Chardonnay—which is now the only white Burgundy type we have, because we no longer make Pinot Blanc—we'll keep that in the upright "1,000 gallon" tanks up until about January or February, and it's been clarified and filtered by then. That's when we bottle the previous year's Chardonnay, so the barrels become available, and we pop it into 60 gallon barrels, and it stays in the 60 gallon barrels a full year.

What kind of oak is it?

The uprights are American white oak, the barrels are Limousin. The more modest red wines—the Grignolino, the Zinfandel, Burgundy—are usually a year and a half to two years in upright tanks, "1,000 to 2,000 gallons," then they're finished off maybe a year in the barrels. I consider Cabernet my finest red wine, so I'll keep that perhaps a year and a half in upright tanks, and then approximately two years in the small barrels; then of course each barrel will vary every so slightly, so we bring it back, put it into a tank which blends the tiny differences that have evolved in the barrels, fine it, filter it and bottle it. So the Cabernet is put in the bottles in July and August, when it's about three and a half years old.

Will you give it any bottle aging?

Oh, sure, we'll not release that until—the very first time—February or March of the next year. And our policy in the past has been to sell only half our inventory at that time, the following year 20 percent, the next year 15 percent, and then ten percent and five percent. We have, every February or March, five vintages of Cabernet available. You simply can't make a fine old aged wine if you sell it all when it's young and fruity.

You produce a range of varietal wines and even some generics and dessert wines. There is a group of wine writers and vintners who have criticized people for trying to produce so many wines. Is there anything to that? How are you able to devote your energies to such a range . . .

I don't waste my time in the vineyard, I told you that half an hour ago. I'm a winemaker; I devote my time to the winery. And also, let's straighten out production. I don't produce all these generics. We produce some of our wines, and we say honestly on the label that we "produced" the wines. Some we "select," we like them the way they are, and we bottle them. Others that we don't think are as good as they could be we "perfect," in our modest terminology. With the lesser wines—the Burgundies, Chablis, and Zinfandels—we'll buy the base wine and then we'll work on them, blending some wines of our own, using our own cellar treatments and our own aging periods. And then we use the term "perfected by." So we do not "produce" these amounts. So many people scream, "We must have more information on the label!" People don't read the information that's there now.

Yes, but it's there in a secret language.

It's not! This says "produced and bottled" doesn't it? What does that one say?

It says "selected and bottled." Sure.

How far did you go in school? Did you go through the third grade? Doesn't "selected and bottled" sound very simple and straightforward? It means I selected the wine, I bottled it. Now what's secret about that?

What percentage of your customers do you think really know these differences?

This is what I'm telling you. Why put a back label on, full of fine print, when they don't even read or care about what's there?

Well, what if it were more straightforward and said, for example, "Heitz Cellars Dry Sherry, produced by . . ." whatever winery actually made the wine. In other words, that's the straightforward way to actually inform people, isn't it?

No. This says it was selected by me. People trust the Heitz Cellars label. This is what reputation is all about. This is what brands are for. One becomes reputable or disreputable. Let's pause a minute and take "produced and bottled." That's straightforward. Now many people, unfortunately, think that means I grew the grapes. That's not true. This is a wine label, not a grape label. It means I produced the wines. You'd be amazed how many people, if you pointed out to them—most don't even care, if they like the wine they buy the wine—say "Oh, 'produced?' Oh, you grew the grapes." "Perfected and bottled": I think "perfected" is a very straightforward word. It would imply I did not produce it.

Well, with all respect, it didn't imply that to me before I had studied the regulations.

What did you think it meant?

I thought that it was a more poetic way of saying "produced." I'm wondering whether consumers who buy the wines have given it any thought.

That's the point. I find most consumers don't read the small print. They don't care.

Is it that they don't care, or is it that they have a tacit assumption that you have made all the wines, I mean, produced all the wines.

Sir, I have explained this in letter after letter. I do my selling by a mailing list, and I have explained this in my letters. I think people who are going to put out over 79 cents for a bottle of wine understand the English language, or if they don't it's not my problem.

Along that same theme, I'd like to ask you about the generic wines, like "Burgundy" for example. There has been criticism of generic labels for decades, within and without the winemaking industry, because the terms have no meaning from one winery to the next, or even within some wineries which bottle both Burgundy and Claret from the same tank. Do you produce consistently the same character in your Burgundy each year, relying on people to know Heitz Cellars Burgundy, and that's why you have no hesitation about putting out generic labels?

Well, you asked about seven things in one sentence. I can understand now why you are a law professor. Why don't you ask me a simple, straightforward question about California Burgundy, and then other more specific questions about Heitz Cellars Burgundy?

Do you think it's confusing to have different wineries put out generic labels, when the Burgundies of one winery are so different from those of another?

Certainly not, because the Cabernet or the Grignolino or the Chardonnay are different from different wineries. The four-door sedans from different manufacturers of automobiles are different. Size ten shoes from different manufacturers are different.

Is Heitz Burgundy always of the same character, do you shoot for the same character of Burgundy?

Within reason, just as I always shoot for the same character with my Cabernet. But they vary. When you're making fine wines, you're not making homogenized milk that comes out of an unending hose the same, day after day, all blended to a uniform mediocrity. My Cabernets or my Chardonnays, which sell for two or three times as much as my Burgundy, vary more than my Burgundy. We try to be fairly consistent, but when we do have a difference, we explain it to our customers through our mailing list.

One more point on the generics. In those European regions from which we've taken these generic names, the winegrowers have never appreciated the fact that we have used those names.

You said the vintners from the regions where "we have taken the names. . . ." Now think a moment. The American Indians didn't start bottling Burgundy. It was Frenchmen, it was Spaniards, it was Germans who came to this country. They brought their grape cuttings with them from home, and they said, "Ah, we're in California now, this is California Burgundy, or this is Rhine Wine." It was a natural transition; we didn't suddenly become a civilized nation and decide to go into the wine business by stealing European names. The Europeans brought those names with them when they came to America and they evolved naturally.

I know the sins are universal and even Frenchmen have tried to take the names of their neighboring districts.

Don't hang it on us now. This is something that we, the present generation of winegrowers, inherited. I would like nothing better than to have a totally different name, but a little peanut like me is not going to go out and fight the world market and say I now make Heitz Cellars or California "Red Table Wine," because that has a bad connotation. "Burgundy" is accepted throughout the world. And it doesn't just say "Burgundy," it says "California Burgundy," or "Australian Burgundy," and so forth. Almost every time I'm in a lunch room I have coffee and "Danish pastry." You go downtown and you buy "English cutlery." So it's a natural evolution, and I get mad when people say "you vintners are stealing these French, Spanish, and German names."

What would your reaction be if Spaniards or Italians or French vintners started selling in third country markets, like Japan for example, wines labeled "French Napa Valley Red," or "Italian Sonoma County White," wines like that?

I think you have a great prejudice, and I think you should wake up and see the light. If Joe Heitz went to this third country, we wouldn't take Napa with us because that's not firmly established yet. We would take maybe Grignolino and things such as that. But *I* did not steal the name Burgundy. The name Burgundy was here 100 years before I was born. I wish things had been different; we would be better off. They are better off that we used this, believe me, because whenever you imitate someone you elevate him.

On the subject of varietals, now, what percentage of the varietal grape is in your varietals?

Normally speaking, 100 percent. I blend the Barbera, because to me Barbera is just too much, too rough and tough all by itself. So I blend it with about 35 percent other, softer grapes. Once in a while, we come out with a nonvintage wine. Perhaps the customer doesn't know this, unless he's an intimate customer and reads about it, but he should be able to tell by the price if he has any sense; when we put nonvintage on something, it really means that it's going to be blended with something else and will sell at a cheaper price. But our vintage dated varietals are normally 100 percent varietals.

Do the best wines in California come from the small vintners? Or is size not a critical factor?

I've felt through the years I've had an unfair advantage by being small. I think my wines have been good, but unfortunately I think some people bought them originally just because I was a small winery. I know a lot of small wineries whose production is crap, and they're still selling it because people say, "This is done by little so-and-so and he does it all by himself." Big money coming into the industry can afford fine equipment, good barrels, perhaps the best of help, and large wineries can theoretically produce some very good wines too. Now, other things being equal, if both the large and small winery have the same know-how, the same fine grapes, the same intense desire, they could both do a good job. Unfortunately, the larger corporation doesn't usually have the same intense desire. Intense desire by itself, though, can be total frustration.

So other things being equal, the small winery may be able to do a better job. But a bunch of amateurs has come into the business lately, because it's a romantic, popular thing to do. And they may have been great attorneys, or great doctors, or great stockbrokers, or shoe salesmen, or scientists . . . and on the outside looking in there's nothing to winemaking: you crush some grapes, put the juice in a barrel, and in a couple of years you bottle it, sell it, and retire. So small wineries per se do not guarantee good wines, but dedicated small wineries with knowledgeable operators, and that intense desire, should have a little better chance to reach the peak than the huge operation with the same basic desires. I don't want to knock the small wineries down, because I am one, but that's not the only answer to making great wines.

Finally, my last question: in your opinion are the best California wines equal to the best European wines?

Is the best blonde as much fun as the best brunette?

People do make such comparisons about wine, though.

Well, I'm a California winemaker, so certainly California wines are the best in the world, Napa Valley wines are even better, and Heitz wines are the best of all! If I were a Frenchman I would scoff at California wines! I'd say French wines are the only ones to drink! I have fun drinking almost all the wines of the world. You get a bummer here and a bummer there, but boy you get real thrills out of any wines from any part of the world. And I have a representative collection in my cellar. Most wines of the world are good if properly presented, and served with the right kind of food. I've even enjoyed a bottle of Algerian wine a couple of times. No, I can't answer your question any more than that, except "Napa Valley wines are best."

Richard Forman
STERLING VINEYARDS

Some very good wines can be made in quantity. But wines of style, of breed and character, can only be made by hand in small batches.

When Sterling opened its glistening white hilltop winery in 1972, replete with a chair lift to carry tourists from parking lot up to winery, the eyebrows of traditionalists raised. There is no question that this winery was designed as a tourist showcase, with ramps leading visitors through the winery to peer down upon fermenting equipment, crusher, and row upon row of oak barrels. But there is also no question that it was artfully done: stained glass windows, white bell towers, and polished surfaces make the visitor feel he is in a monastery devoted to wine. Nor is there any doubt that fine wines are made here.

Sterling produces a variety of wines, all respected, and some acknowledged as among California's finest. Its Chardonnays and Cabernets certainly contend for these honors, along with interesting "secondary" varietals such as Merlot and Sauvignon Blanc. The talent behind the wine is Rick Forman, a young, confident winemaker, highly trained at Davis and then given heavy exposure to European techniques through regular trips to the Continent. We talked in his laboratory office, deep inside the hushed winery. Every half-hour I was startled by the pealing of the carillon, eight bells originally cast in the eighteenth century, formerly ringing in an English church and now stirring excitement about wine in the Napa Valley.

Recommended wine to drink while reading this chapter:

STERLING VINEYARDS
PINOT CHARDONNAY

This winery is perhaps the most visually spectacular winery in Napa Valley. Whose idea was it to build it here on a hill, looking like a Greek monastery?

Mr. Newton and Mr. Stone, owners of the Sterling International Paper Company, also own the winery. Newton's taste is quite refined. He's an enthusiastic collector of European antiques. His home in San Francisco contains a collection which is on the order of magnitude of a museum. Newton and Stone had summer homes up here and Newton, being a fairly shrewd man, realized that the price of land in 1964 was relatively inexpensive compared to what it would become. That year he began buying land and planting varietal grapes. By 1968 they began to think a winery would be in line with their plans. The paper company was doing well and a new venture was exciting. But the winery design was a long time coming.

We used a warehouse at the bottom of the hill as the winery from '69 to '71. We developed plans for the hill winery while operating for the first two years at the bottom of the hill. It seemed very expensive to put in all the equipment down there when we knew we would tear it out in three years when this building was completed, but I think it paid off because we learned so much about how to set up a winery.

I was young and new and had a lot of ideas, some of which didn't work out, and I gained a lot of experience. The plans were developed almost entirely by Martin Waterfield and myself. Dick Graff, who now runs Chalone Vineyard, helped us a great deal, too. At that time Dick operated our winery equipment company and the two of us traveled to Europe looking for equipment to stock that company. Waterfield had a great flair for architecture—at one time he intended to become an architect—and he actually came up with the design of the building, working around the functional plans Dick and I developed. Then we had Richard Keith and Associates, the structural engineering firm which built Chappellet winery, put the plans together for construction and the building was ready by the harvest of '72.

Whose idea was the chair lift?

That was our idea. We wanted to build a winery that catered both to tourists and winemaking. And knowing our winery would be attractive to tourists, we had the problem of how to get them up the hill. We finally settled on the funicular, built by a Swiss ski lift company. I think a lot of people misinterpret it. It's simply a way of getting up the hill which supplies a delightful view and involves a minimum of hassle.

I've heard that when Newton and Stone wanted to start the winery they asked Professor Amerine who his best student was, and he named you.

That's possible; I know they talked to a lot of people. I was in my last year at Davis and I went for an interview. It was a very lengthy process. There must have been 30 interviews and meetings back and forth. I had worked at a couple of other wineries during the harvest. In '67 I worked for Fred McCrea at Stony Hill, for whom I have a great deal of admiration. That really set a theme for me on how I wanted to make wine. In 1968 I worked for Robert Mondavi during the crush—a totally different picture, but I also learned a great deal there, many of the practical parts of winemaking which are virtually unavailable at Davis. Davis is a typical university, all theoretical and not practical. But that's good, I think it's important to learn the theory first. Eventually, it was firmed up that I would work for Sterling upon graduation. That first year we had no winery, and I spent my time gathering information and going to the office in San Francisco designing a winery. I might add I spent six weeks traveling around wineries in Europe gathering ideas also.

That was quite an opportunity for somebody just out of school.

Yes, I was really lucky. I earned the jealousy of many of my peers in school. Actually, in those days there were a lot of opportunities, a lot of new wineries opening up and, as I recall, only five Davis graduates. It was the golden age for Davis graduates.

What made you want to attend Davis and become a winemaker in the first place? Were you raised in a winemaking family?

No, I was not raised in a wine oriented family. My beginnings started with a keen interest in chemistry. As a youngster I maintained a fairly elaborate laboratory in my home and among the many experiments I found the process of fermentation fascinated me most. I would generally distill the wines I produced from all sorts of fruit. One from blackberries grown at our mountain summer home turned out particularly well.

My schooling began as a chemistry major at San Jose State. Soon, through one of my chemistry professors, however, I heard of the Department of Food Science and Technology at Davis. The program sounded fascinating enough to me to transfer schools. I graduated from Davis with a B.S. and Master's Degree in Food Science in '68.

This winery is near Calistoga in the north end of the valley—a bit warmer than the rest of the valley, isn't it?

So people think. We take fairly accurate degree-day temperature readings, and I put this area in a high Region II, low Region III, depending on the year. St. Helena turns out to be very near the same.

How extensive are your vineyards?

We own a lot of acreage, but only 325 acres are planted right now, all within a two-mile radius of the winery. That acreage supplies 90 percent of our requirements. The remaining ten percent comes from a vineyard close to the winery which we have a hand in controlling. It's a nice position as winemaker, since I can really control every aspect.

And how many cases a year does that give you?

We're in the 40,000 case bracket. We'll probably peak out at 75,000 cases of our own production. We are considering buying bulk Sherry, Port and Muscatel from Australia, and we may buy other bulk wine and sell it under the Sterling Cellars label.

How big is your staff?

I have four men working for me in the cellar, and the vineyard crew ranges from 11 to 30. The marketing staff is considerable, I suppose up to 25 people.

Are all your 325 acres on the valley floor?

No, we have a new 80 acre vineyard on a hillside on the Petrified Forest Road on top of the Mayacamas range, some of it so steep it required terracing. It's one of our most promising vineyards, planted mostly to Cabernet, with small sections of Merlot and Pinot Noir. It is well drained, has dark red soil, and very good exposure. The ten percent purchased grapes comes from a piece of land on the Silverado Trail a mile south of here called Three Palms vineyard; it's practically all gravel. In certain sections it looks exactly like Châteauneuf-du-Pape, you see no earth, only rock. The yield is one and a half tons an acre. The quality is most intense, with the Cabernet and the Pinot Noir particularly. Our Bear Flats and Bothé vineyard, which slopes toward the Napa River, is also quite gravelly; the lower section is more alluvial. The upper section, in Cabernet, Merlot and Chardonnay, produces far more interesting wines than the lower section. We have the vineyards around the winery also on alluvial, richer soils. As you drive in the winery, you see five acres of Zinfandel planted on four foot by four foot spacing, the French spacing, which I am finding very fascinating. It's my theory that closer spacing produces better quality, because you have a higher ratio of leaves to clusters. The French certainly believe in this. On an eight by twelve acre you have 450 vines, but on a four by four you have 2,700, so vine costs alone are staggering, and the cultivation costs are incredible. But the French wouldn't dream of doing it any other way, and they might be right—so I'm trying it on a small piece of acreage.

We have a couple of other vineyards nearby, also on flat alluvial soils, and finally we have our vineyard in the Palisades area, directly across from the Eisele vineyard (from which Ridge made a unique wine in '71). Our vineyard has an identical makeup and is budded with a special Cabernet clone obtained from the old Martin Ray Cabernet.

Why don't you keep the wines from these vineyards separate and give vineyard designations on the labels?

We do keep them separate, but I blend them before bottling. They all have different characteristics that blend quite nicely into something a little nicer than any one alone. The Cabernets are the one case where we have a big variance between the vineyards, but rather than separate them by vineyards we've decided to separate them by wine types. With the lighter ones we'll make a Cabernet Rosé, with the medium grade Cabernets we'll produce our regular vintage Cabernet, and with our very best Cabernet grapes we'll make our Private Reserve Cabernet wines.

How do you achieve your undercropping to cut the yield down?

I don't believe in pruning severely because I'd rather let the vine produce the maximum amount of leaves it can, although pruning is one way to cut the crop. I don't think it's the best way: it's the cheapest. We thin the clusters in spring. On some sections, we thin severely, taking as much as half the crop.

Who does the thinning, and who harvests the grapes?

In the last few years we've found we're capable of using our own crew. It's a good psychological feeling to have worked the entire year nurturing and cultivating these vines and then be able to harvest the fruit. It's a mistake to allow a contractor to come in and take their glory away.

Is it all done by hand?

Yes, with knives. We don't have mechanical harvesters. They pick into 40 pound lugs, which are dumped into three ton gondolas and brought to the winery. From the time the gondola is filled, through crushing, usually is no more than 20 minutes.

Do you pick the vineyards all at once, or do you go through two or more times as the grapes become more mature?

We normally pick all at once. I set the time for picking each vineyard. We have picked vineyards selectively by blocks, but never selectively by individual vine.

Here you are in a new, multimillion dollar winery, very artistically done, and with the finest equipment that can be purchased. How do you make wine in such a winery? Do you make it as a modern, technologically oriented winemaker, or as a traditional artisan winemaker?

When I was very young and a bit naive, I was thrust into the European winemaking scene by Newton. Once a year I still go somewhere out of the United States to see what other countries are doing. That's been important in molding my winemaking style. Before I had ever made wine here, I spent a long time in France and I was enthralled with it. Also, my experience at Fred McCrea's Stony Hill winery instilled in me the methods of a very small, traditional place. So I came into my first harvest knowing that I wanted to make wine in the European way. I wanted nice equipment, but I didn't want any equipment of the do-it-quick type. My ultimate excitement is this Private Reserve Cabernet program. I'm terribly excited about some of the selections I've been able to make from the Cabernet in certain sections of our vineyards since 1973. We have a good deal of Cabernet so it's the easiest to concentrate on. I've dedicated myself to the perfection of this selection. I use an absolutely strict, to-the-letter Bordeaux treatment, from crushing and fermentation through the ancient hand method using only barrels. The wines are fined in the barrel, racked every quarter—by gravity, not with pumps. I even managed to get French equipment. I visited France last spring and studied very carefully at a number of châteaux exactly how they treated the wines, and purchased the equipment to do it. We'll produce about 5,000 cases of it each year. If I had my way, I'd probably make only the Chardonnay, which I love to ferment in barrels, and my Private Reserve Cabernet—it's my real love.

Are you saying, then, that the very best wines must be made this way, in small quantities?

You have to define "best wines," because some very good wines can be made in quantity. But wines of style, of breed and character, can only be made by hand in small batches.

How far does that go? Does it mean, for example, that you should crush by foot? I'm being facetious.

Of course you are, but you know that is a very good process. Probably the abandonment of crushing Port grapes by foot in Portugal might be the end of a certain quality factor. It's not to be pooh-poohed, really. We have a Healdsburg stemmer-crusher. It's a very good machine; they've been perfecting it for years. It's designed for a minimum shredding of the grapes, has the slowest action possible to do the job. You never see broken seeds.

Do you ever ferment any wines with a portion of their stems?

Yes, in certain years I find it advantageous to ferment Pinot Noir with a portion of the stems.

And from the look of all the stainless steel, you must ferment your wines in those tanks.

All but the Chardonnay, which is always fermented in 60 gallon, Limousin barrels. It's quite a chore but definitely worth it. I was indoctrinated with that idea on many visits to France, and I wanted to see for myself whether it makes a difference. In '69, '70 and '71, I fermented half the Chardonnay in stainless steel and half in barrels, and every year I found the barrel fermented wines were different. They had more of the bouquet I prefer, were rounder.

Was it merely increased oakiness that made the difference in bouquet?

No, it wasn't necessarily the oak because I used barrels from one to three years old. Also, the wines fermented in stainless steel then went into oak barrels for the same length of time. So the week of fermentation in oak wasn't making a difference in oakiness. The temperature curve the wine goes through during barrel fermentation, the fact that the lees and extra yeast are naturally gotten rid of by spilling out of the barrel, and probably other reasons I'm ignorant of, make the subtle differences. The Chardonnay juice is quite cool when we put it into the barrels, because it's settled overnight in jacketed stainless steel tanks. Then it does as it pleases, controlled only by the 58 degree room in which it ferments. It starts slowly, rises to a peak of about 70 degrees, and gradually falls back to room temperature.

What temperature do you use in fermenting your other wines?

The whites 60 to 65, the reds 75 to 80 degrees. That's warmer than some winemakers ferment their white wines, but I've experimented and prefer warmer temperatures. Riesling might be a different story; perhaps coolness benefits that wine. In the varieties we ferment we're after varietal character, and that develops better from warmer fermentation. There is more fermentation bouquet produced from cooler temperatures, but that tends to disappear with bottle aging; sometimes it lasts for only six months.

How long do you leave the reds on the skins, particularly the Private Reserve Cabernet?

Depending on the balance of the fruit, from 10 to 18 days. I have gone as long as 22 days with good results.

Do you start fermentation by adding yeast?

Yes, we inoculate with Montrachet yeast for everything. I've allowed a few lots of red to ferment spontaneously without a yeast starter, but I couldn't detect any differences. I don't really believe that different characteristics are formed by different wine yeasts. I had an interesting talk with Pascal Ribéreau-Gayon, a very famous professor at the University of Bordeaux. He's done research on it and also believes there is no noticeable difference in character among different wine yeasts, unless yeasts produce off characteristics.

Do you ever add acid to bring up the acid levels?

Oh, every year we have to adjust with tartaric acid on something, but not everything, and we never adjust to extremes.

Do you centrifuge the wines at any point?

We just got a small centrifuge last year. I intended to put the Sauvignon Blanc, Chenin Blanc and possibly Traminer through—never the Chardonnay—and I found it was too small, and settling the wines overnight worked perfectly well. But I did put the lees through and extract wine from them. It amounts to our press wine: we put all the sediment and pulp through it, and it makes a fabulous white wine which will be the basis for our White Table Wine. That's the sole use of the centrifuge. I think it's a little unnatural.

Do you also use the press wine from your regular press?

We have a bladder type press, and I don't press very hard.

What do you do in the way of fining and filtration?

The whites are fined with bentonite, and the reds fined with egg whites, never gelatin. Egg white is a very gentle fining, it clarifies without stripping character or color. After bentonite fining, if the whites are clean, we give a simple racking and further aging. If they're cloudy, as they may be 50 percent of the time, we rough filter them, and then before bottling they receive a fairly tight filtration. The reds are usually lightly filtered once just before bottling, but the Private Reserve Cabernet is never filtered. The regular reds are racked out of the barrels with pumps and it's difficult to do without picking up a bit of the lees. The Private Reserve is racked without pumps, out of the head of the barrel as they do in Bordeaux, and the wine is absolutely brilliantly clear. That's done every quarter for two years.

Why don't you do that with all the reds?

It's terribly time consuming. You just can't possibly do it on all of them.

How long are the reds aged and in what kind of cooperage?

They are all aged about two years. The Pinot Noir and the Private Reserve Cabernet are in small cooperage all that time starting January or February after the harvest. The regular Cabernet spends its first nine months in 3,000 gallon Nevers tanks, then goes into the small barrels. The Pinot Noir and Chardonnay are in Limousin. The other barrels are all Nevers. We have no American oak. The Sémillon goes half into barrels and half into tanks, and the Chenin Blanc and Gewürztraminer are aged only in the upright tanks. We're talking about a matter of months for the whites, whereas the reds spend years.

Your Chardonnay ferments in Limousin oak and stays there until it's bottled. How long would that be?

Eight to 11 months.

Are your varietals 100 percent, or do you blend some?

One hundred percent, except for the Cabernet which has about 20 percent Merlot in it, and the Sauvignon Blanc which soon will have some Sémillon. We're about to produce two generics, house wines we call Sterling Red and Sterling White. This is another way to separate some of our Cabernet. We have the regular Cabernet, Private Reserve, Cabernet Rosé, and we may extract some lots of Cabernet which won't fit into those niches and put them into Sterling Red, plus whatever else we might have around. We may also buy some Zinfandel for that. It will be under the Sterling Cellars label, our secondary label which is also used for a few wines we don't produce ourselves, like the Ports and Sherries. Sterling Vineyards is our primary label.

You've avoided using the usual French terms of Burgundy and Chablis for those red and white generics.

Yes, we don't think that's fair. They're not Burgundies or Chablis, they're red and white table wines, attractively packaged and very sound value wines, but not Burgundies or Chablis.

Would you say your wines have their own particular style, different from other Napa Valley wines?

I think you can usually tell whether they've come from the same stall. Winemakers are different, they develop different styles, and whether it's a reflection of their personalities or practices or what, I don't know. I think certainly our area gives us a style. If someone wants to know what Calistoga Cabernet is like, or Calistoga Chardonnay, they can rely on us because our grapes come only from this area in close proximity. Just as when you go through the Medoc and you know what Margaux tastes like, St. Julien, Pauillac, and St. Estèphe, so we have the Napa Valley areas, all the way from Carneros to Calistoga. Ours is a regional wine.

Do you believe the best California wines are as good as the best European wines?

You wouldn't think so if you looked at my cellar. I suppose I have five percent California wine and 95 percent European. But I think it depends on the variety. With Chardonnay, California is producing wine that is *very* close to the best French Burgundies.

How long would you say Californians have been producing Chardonnays of that greatness?

I'd say the past five years. Stony Hill was the originator of fine Chardonnay, but the new Chardonnays are different in style. With the advent of barrels, small cooperage aging, they've gone beyond Stony Hill and are very Burgundian. If you make a Burgundian style Chardonnay, it's not going to be a light bodied wine; you must pick the grapes very ripe, and the wine must be big, heady, pungent wine. With Pinot Noir, we have miles to go and I think we'll never get there. I think our own Sterling Pinot Noir is one of the unique Pinot Noirs in California, but it's not French Burgundy. Cabernet is another wine California winemakers are continually improving and in many cases show better than their French counterparts. This trend, I believe, will continue—and in time there will indeed be California Cabernets which on occasion will rank well with even the first growth Bordeaux.

Robert Mondavi

ROBERT MONDAVI WINERY

You have to live it, a wine is a reflection of yourself.

If Robert Mondavi were drawn in a cartoon he would have little lines whisking by him to show perpetual motion. The man is a dynamo. When not rushing around his winery, he is rushing around Napa Valley rallying his fellow vintners or jetting to Europe promoting exchanges of wine knowledge with the great châteaux. For all this, he has been called a visionary, and a leader. The phrase "Bob Mondavi says," can be heard wherever California winemakers gather.

Yet it is his fate to be surrounded by controversy. A bitter family feud erupted when he left the Mondavi family's Charles Krug winery in 1966 to start his own. Although he treated the subject delicately in our interview, the continuing feud was recently dramatized in a courtroom where Robert pressed a lawsuit against his mother and brother to dissolve the Charles Krug partnership. At the same time, Robert Mondavi is sensitive about the image his winery presents. For example, he prefers not to disclose the size of the operation. His wines, however, are rarely controversial. They are generally respected as setting a very high standard, and a few, particularly Cabernet Sauvignon, are among Napa Valley's finest. I talked with Mondavi in his executive suite at the Spanish-mission style winery on the Napa Valley floor at Oakville. Characteristically, the interview was briefly interrupted twice while Robert rushed outside to be interviewed by television news teams.

Recommended wine to drink while reading this chapter:

ROBERT MONDAVI
CABERNET SAUVIGNON

As a member of the Mondavi family you have been a winemaker most of your life, haven't you?

Yes, upon graduating from college I was at the Sunny St. Helena Winery producing bulk wine and then in 1943 I talked my father into forming a family partnership and buying the Charles Krug Winery. I've continued over the years to have my interest there, but in 1966 I came here with my son Michael to establish the Robert Mondavi Winery.

Why did you want to start another winery?

Michael was interested in going into the wine business and I felt this would be an opportunity to do many things that could not be done at the older winery. I also felt the time was right, that the public would pay extra money for a California wine if it had an extra dimension of quality. Before that time, if the public wanted a better wine they would normally buy a Bordeaux, a Burgundy, a Rhine or a Moselle. I, and my son Michael who is very interested in fine wine, wanted to challenge that. We felt we had the soil, the climate, the grape varieties. By developing the winemaking techniques and presenting the wine to the public with the proper image, we could compete with the so-called truly fine wines of the world and eventually get the prices they are getting now. So we started our own winery; it is owned by our family plus our partners, The Rainier Companies, Inc., of Seattle, but its operation is the sole responsibility of the Mondavi family.

The winery is fairly big, isn't it? What size is the staff?

Frankly, I don't know the number. I would say 60 or 70.

Small winemakers commonly tell me the finest wines can only be made on a small scale. Yours is a fairly big winery, isn't it?

Compared to Spring Mountain or Stony Hill, for instance, yes, but not compared to many others. I'd say 95 percent of the time the finest wines *are* made by the smaller wineries. But there are exceptions to rules. I've concluded you can produce wines in reasonable quantities that are equal to those of the smallest producer. If you have climate, soil, grape varieties grown in a proper location, and you add dedication, desire, the will to train your people, and the proper facilities, you can duplicate what the smallest producers can do. In fact, I believe that once I get a group of people with me as I'm doing, I can do not only as good a job, but possibly a better job. Once I get people with the same feeling, the same understanding, the same will to do it well, there's no reason we can't do it. And if you go through a blind tasting, and talk to other people, even the smallest producers, I think you'll find there is a great regard for what we're doing.

Let me say just one thing to you. We do everything the smaller wineries do except it takes us five or six years to train people who have this feeling. I sit and taste wines every day with our key people. During fermentation season I check every tank every day, sample them all the time. We're totally involved. If you want to produce fine wines you have to follow them from grapes, through fermentation, to the selling. You have to taste the wines of the world, understand the subtleties. You have to live it; a wine is a reflection of yourself.

One school of winemaking says you should interfere with nature as little as possible, and the other school emphasizes the need to control nature with technology to a great extent. Where do you fall in relation to those schools of thought?

I say this, what the Dickens, let's be practical. You can be destroyed by Mother Nature. What they're trying to say is, do what Mother Nature will do under the best conditions. I certainly do not believe in excess pumping, I want minimum movement, minimum clarification, minimum filtration. You should see that the grape matures fully so the skin, the tannins, are soft and fully mature, then make wine naturally to get the maximum from the grape. Some say that when the sugar no longer continues to rise and the acid drops, pick the grapes then. Well, I say, in addition, chew that skin first to see if the tannins are astringent, or soft as they should be.

Do you own most of your own vineyards?

We have about 300 acres bearing. There will be close to 650 acres in another two years. In addition, we farm 200 to 300 acres under long term agreements. Together, these will amount to approximately 70 percent of our total crush.

Where are those vineyards?

They're all located in Napa Valley. We have 300 acres near the winery, plus the Oak Knoll ranch on the Silverado Trail about six miles northeast of Oakville.

Are those all valley floor vineyards?

The majority are valley floor, but we have a few mountain vineyards.

Are the vineyards from which you purchase grapes also all in Napa Valley?

Basically, they are all Napa Valley vineyards. We did experimental work on other north coast county grapes, even Monterey and Amador county, to see if we could produce a special type of wine. We concluded that since we have enough Napa Valley vineyards we're better off concentrating here on grapes that produce the distinctive Napa Valley character. All our varietals are from Napa Valley.

Some vintners prefer hillside vineyards to valley floor vineyards. Do you think there is any quality difference?

We crush certain hill vineyards ourselves. Most of our own vineyards don't happen to be in the hills. The great Bordeaux are not on hilly areas at all, the great Burgundies are on flat or gentle slopes, and then again you get the beautiful Rhines from hills and steep slopes. Hill vineyards are not usually overcropped. On the valley floor some growers might tend to overproduce. But quality will be subject to climate first of all, then soil, proper drainage, and the right selection of grape variety with the proper yield.

What is the climate here around Oakville?

It's an upper Region I or lower II. We find this is better for Cabernet. We find definitely that Oakville is the outstanding location for Cabernet Sauvignon. It's been that way for the last 100 years, and I think for the next 100 years we'll even find it more so. Carneros is Region I, too cold, I believe, for Cabernet but excellent for Pinot Noir and Chardonnay.

Have you made any attempt to separate out the grapes from single vineyards and make a distinctive wine, as some wineries are doing now?

Oh, definitely. For the last two years we've had one man working full time and four men working half time in research, separating grapes crushed from various vineyards, comparing production techniques. We even made wines in five gallon containers and compared them with our normal operation, and we've gotten a lot of valuable information. So yes, we are separating out vineyards, and those we prefer we set aside and they will come out in our "unfined" or our "reserve" lots of wine.

You don't name single vineyards on the label, though, do you?

We haven't yet. We may do it when we have what we want, and the vineyard is what we want.

Are you satisfied that you're able to control the viticultural practices on the vineyards from which you buy grapes, so you're not getting overcropped grapes and they're of the quality you want?

Now that there is a surplus of grapes, I can assure you the grower will cooperate to give the highest quality grapes possible. You find better pruning and viticultural practices than in the past, because wineries aren't interested in buying grapes which don't have the maximum quality. In order to get our growers to deliver maximum quality grapes, eliminate overcropping, etc., we've introduced a bonus system where the grower will get a 55 percent bonus for excellent grapes.

How do you prune your own vineyards? Severely, lightly?

It depends on the vine; each requires different treatment. But we prune to get the best quality possible, and we're even experimenting with thinning our grapes to see what effect it has on quality. On our vineyards we get from one and a half to four and a half tons an acre. We hear a lot higher figures.

Which vines give you as little as one and a half tons?

Some of the Pinot Noir and Chardonnay back here used to get one and a half to two tons, but now we've pulled those and replaced them with better selected wood with the idea of getting two and a half to four and a half tons. We have a tough time averaging the so-called four and a half tons that people expect on Cabernet around here.

Do you harvest by hand or mechanically?

We have a mechanical harvester but we're experimenting with it. We don't use it nearly as much as we could. We're trying to find whether it's better for us or not. On some of the whites it worked out well, but then on some of the reds it didn't. We have mixed results at the moment. If it doesn't damage the vines, I think there is a good chance of making it work, and work well.

Do you harvest selectively, sending the pickers through the vineyards more than once?

No, we haven't done that—nor is it done anywhere now.

Who does the harvesting, and what do they pick with?

Mainly seasonal workers who come through. They use knives or scissors. They pick into buckets or containers of 10 to 30 pounds and transfer into four or five ton gondolas.

What is the Robert Mondavi style of wine? How would you describe it?

Well, we've gone into quite a few new techniques people are now picking up. We were the first to really introduce using new barrels. We brought in Nevers oak, Limousin, Yugoslavian and American oak and compared them all, aging Cabernet, Pinot Noir, Chardonnay, Sauvignon Blanc. We more often liked the Nevers, but we also like a certain amount of

American oak in the Cabernet blended with the Nevers oak. I've always thought American oak was little more authoritative, had a more pronounced and heavier character, while the Nevers is softer, more subtle. I prefer 75 to 80 percent Nevers with the balance American oak.

Would you characterize your wines as big, intense, subtle, or just what other words would you use?

We're not trying to make big, heavy wines. Even if they are big, I want them to be full, palatable and pleasing. We're trying to make a wine with what I call a middle body—full, round, completely dry to the taste. I'm referring, naturally, to our Cabernet, Pinot Noir, Chardonnay, Fumé Blanc, and Gamay. I want a fullness in the mouth which leaves a dry, clean taste and invites you to drink. We make wines to be consumed with meals; we don't want them too heavy, too coarse, or so pungent it will take 40 years to soften out. Yet they can be big, full, round and pleasing.

A good example of this is my first experience at the Pyramid restaurant in Vienne, France, the finest restaurant in the world at the time. I had been wined and dined the entire week and had eaten a huge breakfast. My wife and I were passing through Vienne at noon but we could not miss the opportunity of eating at the Pyramid. We expected only to taste each dish. The first course was a sole from the Saône River, floating in butter. The sole was light, delicate and full of flavor—we finished it all. The same was true of the Chicken Alexandria and the desserts. After eating everything, we felt better than when we arrived. I then realized you could have food which had fullness, flavor, yet was not overpowering and heavy. This was dining to the finest degree. I realized the same could be true of wine.

Do you ferment everything in stainless steel, and at what temperature?

Yes, all temperature controlled stainless steel. The whites mainly around 55 degrees, under 60 degrees. The reds we used to ferment between 75 and 80 degrees, but now we're beginning to ferment at a warmer temperature—85 to 87 degrees.

Do you start fermentation with a yeast starter?

Yes.

Do the reds always go through malo-lactic fermentation?

Yes, we won't bottle unless we complete the malo-lactic fermentation.

Do you make wines from free run juice?

I used to because we didn't understand how to handle press wines. There is a lot of character to press wine and if handled properly it will give additional body and fullness, yet with the necessary softness required in a truly fine wine. For this reason, we began to use some of the press wine.

During fermentation of the reds, do you pump over the cap?

We do two things. We pump over and also we have roto-fermenting tanks which we rotate three times a day for ten minutes—five minutes one way, five minutes back at three revolutions per minute. The tank is on an axis, and a motor turns the whole thing around like a cement mixer. And we find we get a better extraction that way.

Do you often adjust acid on your grapes?

Sometimes we do, depending on the year. We use tartaric, malic and very little citric acid.

And what about adjustment of sugar levels with concentrate?

I don't believe in concentrate. If you use concentrate you have an entirely different character. Any wine we have which has a small amount of residual sugar, such as our Johannisberg Riesling, is made by adding a natural sweet reserve. It makes your wine lighter, more delicate, with more of the natural flavor.

Do you fine and filter your wines?

We were the first to come out with unfiltered and unfined wines. Certain wines, because of their condition, may have to be filtered, but we try to eliminate filtration when possible, especially our Cabernet, Chardonnay and Fumé Blanc. We try to eliminate filtration and fining, because wines without this process are slightly fuller and a little more natural. At times our Cabernet or Pinot Noir may have an excessive amount of astringency which will not soften even in aging. If this is the case, we will fine with egg white. On white wines we may use isinglass or casein.

You don't use bentonite?

We may use a little bentonite during fermenting season to clarify it for heat stability.

Haven't you received a little criticism for those labels that say "unfined" and "unfiltered" because of the fact that you centrifuge the wines? Isn't centrifuging doing pretty much the same thing?

Let me put it this way: it depends on how you use it. You can take a lot out, or you can take nothing out. We've compared wine we've put in barrels without centrifuging that have just been racked, wines that have been lightly filtered, wines that have been centrifuged. The best wine we've made to date is the wine with a very light centrifuging right after fermentation. So we use the centrifuge to take out a small portion of the pulp, fibers and yeast cells. It's similar to what you'd have if you put the wines directly into small barrels and then racked them, because they clarify more quickly that way. But we prefer centrifuging to the method where wine is naturally settled in 4,000 or 6,000 gallon tanks and put into the barrel.

How long are the wines aged in wood?

The Cabernets typically spend from 22 months up to 30 months in barrels, the Pinot Noir from 18 to 24 months, the Chardonnay from 9 to 12 months, the Fumé Blanc seven to nine, Gamay about six to eight, and

Chenin Blanc we give just a kiss of oak. Our Rieslings we'll age in 300 to 600 gallon oak casks for two to three months.

Do you blend the varietals or are they 100 percent of the varietal grape?

Well, Cabernets are about 93 percent Cabernet Sauvignon and seven percent Cabernet Franc. Pinot Noir is 100 percent, as are the Riesling, Gamay, Zinfandel, Chardonnay. Our Fumé Blanc is usually 90 percent Sauvignon Blanc and approximately ten percent Sémillon. Sometimes I find Sauvignon Blanc a little heavy in character and blending with Sémillon gives more complexity and vitality.

Would you like to see the legal requirement of 51 percent for varietal wines raised?

I think that'd be fine as far as I'm concerned, because we're doing it; but each to his own.

What would you think of the idea of leaving the legal requirement at 51 percent to allow maximum blending flexibility, but also requiring the other varieties used to be listed on the label for the consumer?

That might be a good idea. I think the public would like to know, and I think it would be of interest.

You've just recently added generic wines to your line, a Robert Mondavi Red Table Wine and a Robert Mondavi White Table Wine.

Yes, I refrained from doing that until we had our name established, because any time you do that people feel you're going the way of all flesh. I feel there's a need for a dry, rounded table wine that sells at a reasonable price, aimed at the knowledgeable wine drinker who likes dry wines instead of the usual inexpensive "mellow" table wines. We didn't want to call it Burgundy or Chablis; I wanted to get away from French nomenclature and call it exactly what I thought it was, very simply Red Table Wine or White Table Wine.

Would you like to see the European geographical names for generic wines phased out generally in the industry, as you have done?

I would, yes. I don't see why we have to bank on the European tradition. Let's use our own. That's why we came out with Red and White Table Wine, we wanted to stand on our own two feet, we wanted to be honest and forthright in what we're doing.

In your judgment, are California wines today equal to the best European wines?

From time to time they are. I think we have not consistently gotten as much out of the grape. But in the next few years a few of the fine wines of California will be ranked among the truly great wines of the world.

How many wineries in California today are in that truly top category?

Everyone thinks his winery is producing the finest wine. There are many good wines produced in California, but ony a few vintners have the complete devotion, total involvement and knowledge to produce truly fine wine—just as is true in other wine growing regions of the world.

Louis P. Martini

LOUIS M. MARTINI WINERY

I don't put much stock in these wines you buy and wait 20 years to drink. I don't buy them to wait 20 years, I buy them to drink now.

I drove into the Martini property just south of St. Helena on Highway 29, the spine of the Napa Valley, and entered a suite of business offices in the large, concrete winery. Louis P. Martini greeted me, then sank his six foot four inch frame into a chair and spoke in a businesslike and deliberate manner—not at all the salty, argumentative Italian his famous father was reported to have been. Near the beginning of the post-Prohibition era, his father, Louis M., turned Martini virtually overnight into one of the top selling premium wine names in the country. Louis P. is now firmly at the helm, and his children are involved in the operation, continuing the family tradition. In the trade, Martini is renowned as the winery that "discovered" the Carneros region for Pinot Noir, and as the producer of the unique dessert wine Moscato Amabile. Among consumers, the Martini label is known as eminently reliable for sound wines at moderate prices. Some of the special selection Cabernets are particularly good values, and uncommon Martini varietals such as Folle Blanche, Barbera and Merlot are worth seeking out.

Recommended wine to drink while reading this chapter:
LOUIS M. MARTINI
FOLLE BLANCHE

When did your father, the founder of this winery, start making wine?

Back about the time of the San Francisco earthquake he and his father had a winery of their own. He went back to Italy to study oenology for a year and came back again. He started working for wineries in the central valley and in 1922, after Prohibition was already in effect, he and two investors purchased a winery in Kingsburg below Fresno.

Why would they do that in the middle of Prohibition?

He decided it was a good time to get into the wine business instead of going out of it. You could easily produce sacramental wines, and, being Italian, he believed the experiment of Prohibition was only an experiment and it would be strictly a matter of time before it was over. In '32, when it looked as if Prohibition would be repealed, he decided that to go into the table wine business he had to get up into the north coast counties. He looked for a couple of years and bought this piece of property and built a winery on it which was completed in '34.

You pretty much grew up in a winery, then, didn't you?

Yes. Actually, as a youngster I worked more in the vineyards than I did in the winery. I did put in some time in the winery during summers when I was in college, but before that I preferred the outdoor work.

Did you then go to Davis and study oenology?

No, I studied food technology at Berkeley. The Davis program was under way and I did spend a year there and took all the oenology courses they offered, but I wasn't sure I wanted to go into the wine business and I didn't want to lock myself into an oenology program. I wanted more outlets. I graduated from college, came back to work at the winery for six months and then Pearl Harbor came along. I spent four years in the service and then returned to the winery and started taking over production.

Your dad passed away just in 1974 didn't he?

Yes, he was 87.

Are there other members of the family involved in the winery?

Well, we're slowly getting there. My oldest daughter was working in the East, but she has come back to join us and is now our assistant manager. We have a son who will graduate from Davis in oenology next year.

How would you place yourself between the two schools of winemaking, the school that says you shouldn't interfere with nature, you should do as little as possible, and the other school that says modern technology should be applied to the extent possible?

If you don't interfere with nature you don't end up with wine, you end up with vinegar. That was facetious, but I believe very definitely that on a commercial basis—you can do what you want in your back yard if you're making only 100 gallons—you need modern, scientific technology to successfully run a winery. I wouldn't think of trying to run one without it.

With or without that technology, can wineries your size and larger produce some of the very best wines made?

I think the difficulty in producing the very best wines comes about when your principal winemaker can no longer know everything that's going on. You can still make technically sound wines, but I'm talking about the best wines possible.

How many cases a year does the winery produce now?

About 300,000 cases a year. We plan to expand about four or five percent a year until we get to 350,000 cases, and then if we're going to expand much beyond that we'll have to make some major capital changes in the winery. Whether we want to do that, or whether we want to eliminate some items and stay under 350,000 . . . we'll cross that bridge when we come to it.

I take it you are not at that stage where the winemaker can no longer know everything that's going on, even at 300,000 cases?

No.

How can you control the great number of different wines you produce? Some say wineries must specialize in only two or three wines to make the very best, that they can't keep their attention fixed on a dozen or more, as you do.

I don't think it takes 100 percent of your time just to make two or three wines. After all, you make a year's supply at one time, and if you only make three wines what are you going to do the rest of the time? I really think the biggest factor is the availability of good grapes, and after that it's the care and the time you take to do the proper things at the proper time. And then make the final blend to the taste of your philosophy.

Yes, you are known for having some fine vineyards. About what percentage of your wines come from your own vineyards, and where are they?

About 70 percent. Our vineyards are all over the map. We have practically no grapes at all around the winery. We have about 350 acres in the Carneros district, mostly planted to Pinot Noir.

Is it true you were the first to plant vineyards down there in Carneros?

I think we were. There had been some old vineyards there, from many years back. But as far as I'm aware, none of the right varieties were planted. We did start the Pinot Noir down there. My dad had crushed grapes from the old Stanley ranch, and he liked their character, and it looked to him as if it would be a good area for early maturing varieties. So he bought part of the Stanley ranch in 1942. And over the next 10 to 12 years he built it up until it was all planted. Since then we've added another 40 acres to the original ranch, and we've added 140 acres about four miles from it.

Didn't you disregard the conventional wisdom which, at that time, held that the area was too cool to grow grapes?

Well, it *is* too cool to grow grapes generally. The Carneros area is limited to certain varieties, so we are specializing in Pinot Noir down there. We have a little Chardonnay there but we've also found a better spot for Chardonnay.

Where is that?

West Side Road in Healdsburg, Sonoma County, which is also very cool. The land is benchland and it's better drained. It's right on the west side of the Russian River about five miles south of Healdsburg.

Why do you think it does better there, since both areas are cool?

We have better soil drainage there than in Carneros. We have deeper soil, to begin with; we get a little better crop of Chardonnay, and it seems to be more aromatic and have a better texture. The Pinot Noir does well there too, but we have so much Pinot Noir planted in Carneros we don't need to plant much more up there. So we have there some Pinot Noir, Chardonnay, Gewürztraminer, Merlot, a little Malbec, some Napa Gamay, about ten acres of Cabernet and a little French Colombard.

Where is your Barbera grown?

Mostly at Monte Rosso. We buy some. The Monte Rosso vineyard, the first one we bought, is up on top of the hills.

That's in the Mayacamas range on the Sonoma side isn't it?

Correct. We're approximately two miles beyond the Mayacamas winery's vineyards, but we're on the other side of the ridge, facing the south slope. Our white varieties are up there now, with the exception of the Chardonnay. Our best Cabernet and our best Zinfandel also come off that vineyard.

I thought you had a vineyard very close to the winery here which produced your best Cabernet.

We do have, but in volume it doesn't amount to much. It definitely produces some very good Cabernet, but there are only 20 acres and nine are really outstanding because they are up on the hills. We were going to sell it. The Sonoma vineyard turns out five or six times the volume of grapes that one does. In the Napa Valley itself we really don't have anything, unless you consider Carneros, and of course the Chiles Valley ranch is about five miles due east of here, within Napa County. We're going to plant that, probably, mostly to Zinfandel and Petite Sirah although a trial block of Cabernet Sauvignon looks very good. Again, it's cool. We didn't realize at the time we were putting these vineyards together that they are all as cool as they are. Carneros and Healdsburg are all low Region I, and Monte Rosso and Chiles Valley are low Region II. In Chiles Valley we have only about 80 acres planted so far, but we have a potential of a couple hundred.

You don't have any vineyards on the valley floor, then?

No, and we deliberately avoided it because when we were buying vineyard land in the 50s and 60s we couldn't see how this valley floor was going to keep from becoming another Santa Clara Valley—full of suburban houses—and we didn't want our vineyards destroyed, so we searched around for places of comparable quality.

Do you think the temperature of those areas is just about the whole game, or do the soils and topography influence grape quality equally?

I don't know about "equally." Of course, slope determines vine temperature to some extent, depending on how the sun hits the vine. Probably temperature is the most important thing, but soils are also important; how well drained, how heavy, and how rich they are. Of all our vineyards, we have only about 40 acres on the Healdsburg ranch which is really lush, river bottom loam and silt; it produces good tonnage but poorer quality than the grapes from the other sections.

Would you like to see different viticultural areas, like those in which your vineyards are located, have officially defined boundaries and carry appellations of origin?

Yes, I would. We wouldn't use them, because we believe in blending and we like to have wines from different places with different characters to blend. But I do think it's a good idea to be able to have specifically defined viticultural areas with corresponding appellations of origin. We make a point every year to keep all our Cabernet from our own vineyards and from our growers separate. We taste each in the spring, and they're different, way different. Two or three will be almost of comparable quality, and others will complement each other. One will have a big nose but lack body, another big body and no nose. And by making a blend you can make an exceptionally good wine.

I see the advantage of that blending philosophy. Have you also considered taking advantage of the distinctiveness of the grapes from a specific vineyard, by making that one vineyard's production into wine and naming the vineyard on the label?

Yes, but we don't think we're ready for it yet. For a couple of reasons. If you're just a little operation and you sell half your wine directly to consumers and the other goes out to a few local stores, that's one thing. But if you have nationwide distribution, as we do, you can't take a shotgun approach and throw out 15 Cabernet Sauvignons at 15 different prices from 15 different vineyards. You'd have the most confused bunch of consumers ever seen. You can do this only if you're selling to all your close friends in the wine and food society. People in the Midwest and in parts of the East could care less whether it's this location or that location. We simply haven't developed that far; eventually we'll have the same situation as the different French chateaus, but it's doing to take several generations to do it.

Where are the vineyards from which you buy the other 30 percent of your grapes?

All in the Napa Valley, with the exception of a couple in Sonoma. Between our own vineyards and our growers, we're growing about 50 percent in Sonoma County and 50 percent in Napa County. So we don't put "Napa Valley" or "Sonoma" on our label, we say "California" because we want to take advantage of blending from the two areas. There would obviously be some economic advantage in using the "Napa" appellation, because Napa has developed the better reputation. For many years Sonoma did not have enough interest in premium wines to develop a reputation, even though in many areas they have comparable grapes. Now we see more good wines coming out of Sonoma, but up to about five or six years ago there were not many with a national reputation.

Do you prune your vineyards to limit the yield of fruit?

Oh, yes, we follow normal practices. Our vineyards average, overall, about three tons to the acre. We listen to other people who get four, five and six tons, and I don't see how they can do it. Now the Carneros vineyards get less simply because the varieties down there are smaller producers—Pinot Noir will get two to two and a half tons to the acre. In Healdsburg, we get about two and a half tons on Pinot Noir, maybe three tons on Chardonnay, only about three tons on Cabernet and Merlot. We're making up for the low Pinot Noir tonnage by getting eight tons on French Colombard, and about five tons on Gamay.

Do you normally harvest by hand?

Yes, but we do have two machines. We have some spots in Healdsburg and Napa where we can use them for Pinot Noir, Merlot and Cabernet. We've run experiments for four years in a row where machine harvested grapes and hand harvested grapes were picked side by side, and the wines made side by side, and we can't tell the difference.

Who does the hand picking?

We just hire people. We set up a little boarding house at each of the ranches and we hire about 20 pickers in Napa and 20 in Sonoma.

What size containers do they use?

They pick into a pan and dump the grapes into a two ton tub which we set on a truck and take to the winery.

Do you ever send pickers through a vineyard more than once to get the fruit as it matures?

Not unless it appears there is so much second crop that it's worthwhile to go in again. We have done that a number of times. We do some bunch thinning and removal of second crop on our Cabernet at Healdsburg. The good soil there makes it too vigorous to control just by pruning.

Which wines are you putting out now? You cover the whole range of wine types, don't you?

We've cut out a few whites now. But we still make several varietals: Cabernet, Pinot Noir, Zinfandel, Barbera, Merlot and Gamay Beaujolais. In addition we make Claret, Chianti, Burgundy and Mountain Red. In whites, we make Johannisberg Riesling, Gewürztraminer, Folle Blanche, a dry Chenin Blanc, a Chablis and a Mountain White.

You have two types of generics, those named after geographical regions in Europe and those simply called "Mountain Red" and "Mountain White." Now, the latter just means red or white wine; does it also mean the grapes were actually mountain grown?

I'm not sure what "mountain grown" means, but we generally consider the north coast counties area as being mountainous area. Sometimes we grow in the valleys of these mountains. Chiles Valley, for instance, is at 900 feet elevation but the vineyards are on the valley floor—is that mountain grown? I don't know.

Why do you make a distinction between "Mountain Red," and your Burgundy or Claret or Chianti?

We make a different wine. Mountain Red is a fairly light, soft, year and a half to two year old wine, and the base of it is mostly Zinfandel, probably

60 to 65 percent Zinfandel, and the balance is whatever we've got left over of other varieties. The Burgundy generally is a blend of Petite Sirah, Gamay and Pinot Noir, often about 55 to 60 percent Petite Sirah.

Why not call that Petite Sirah, since you have more than the legally required 51 percent?

The distributors wouldn't let us do that, we're selling too much of it as Burgundy. They'd scream.

Do you foresee the discontinuance of the European geographical names?

Yes, but it'll be a long time. They're a wine type now—it's just coincidental they're European names.

But how can they be described as a "wine type" when the only thing they have in common is their color?

Well, the Burgundy, in contrast to the Claret, is supposed to be a heavy bodied red wine.

But that's not consistent from winery to winery. I've heard of wineries filling their Burgundies and Clarets from the same tank.

I don't think they should do that. We try to make ours quite distinct, primarily by keeping the Petite Sirah out of the Claret and keeping the Zinfandel out of the Burgundy.

Do you put close to 100 percent of the varietal grape in your varietal wines?

I don't pay much attention to what percent is in there. I try to make the best wine we can. Naturally it has to be a reasonably high percentage or it's not going to have the characteristic of the variety. Our philosophy is to make the wine taste like the grape from which it's made, if possible. Whether it's 70, 80, 90 or 100 percent is not important.

Are your Cabernet and Barbera blended?

Yes. Barbera is blended with Petite Sirah, Cabernet with Merlot, Malbec, sometimes Zinfandel.

Should the legal requirement of only 51 percent be raised at all?

I would like to see it raised to about 65 percent. If people buy a varietal wine they should at least be entitled to get two-thirds of the main variety. You can't cut much below 65 percent and get the predominant character of a single grape, although sometimes you may make a better wine.

Would you have any objection to a legal requirement that the names of the other varieties used also be listed on the label?

Yes, I would, because it's of no value at all to the consumer. It makes a bigger difference where that variety is grown. The same variety grown in two different places is very different. Also, blending could be considered a trade secret.

Might that be an argument for also indicating on the label the region where the grapes are grown?

That would make more sense. But the most important thing on the label is the brand name, the name of the winery that's putting it out. Everything else is of minimal importance. Vintage doesn't mean that much, variety doesn't mean that much because it depends on where it's grown, appellation of origin doesn't mean that much because you can make a lousy wine even out of Napa grapes if you don't know what you're doing, "estate bottled" and all that junk doesn't mean anything at all. It depends on the winery, on the name on the label.

Yes, but with all the heavy advertising done now by ordinary wineries passing themselves off as fine wineries, not to mention the prestigious names that have been involved in wine fraud here and in Europe, consumers may shy away from reliance on the brand name as a guide to quality. I think that's why they're asking for more information on the label.

I don't agree. Advertising will influence a consumer to buy a brand only once. If he doesn't like it he won't buy it again and no winery can exist very long without repeat sales.

How would you describe the Martini style?

Our style, if you want to call it that, is to try to produce varietal wines as distinctly varietal as we can make them. And we try to make the grape flavor the predominant flavor. If we have wood, we want it so subtle you can hardly pick it up. We like wines aged enough to be smooth, but we like them to retain their freshness and fruitiness. And this is why we don't use a lot of small cooperage aging. We have a couple thousand barrels, but we always blend barrel wine with the wine we keep in larger tanks, because if it were completely barrel aged it would destroy too much of the fruitiness.

How do you ferment the wines?

We still have our old concrete fermenters in addition to the new stainless steel ones, and the reds are fermented in both. All the whites are fermented in stainless steel at 50 degrees, and the reds at anywhere from 70 to 85 degrees.

You initiate fermentation with a yeast starter. Have you had any thought of experimenting with spontaneous fermentation with the wild wine yeast on the grapes?

No, can't chance it. You don't know what's going to come out, and I don't think it'd make much difference anyhow because we spread the pomace back out in the vineyard and I'm sure the natural micro-flora is close to what we inoculate with.

What kind of yeast do you use?

We use the Champagne strain.

What kind of press do you have?

We have two Willmes presses: one—the bladder type—we use for the whites, and the other—the plate type—we use for reds. The reds don't need quite such delicate treatment, and also the plate press is twice as big.

Do you have a centrifuge?

Yes. We are using it to clean up white musts, and later for racking off the lees.

Do you fine and filter all the wines?

Most of them. We fine the whites with bentonite and the reds with gelatin. We don't fine some of our Special Selection wines that we make separately, but we filter all the wines.

Why would you not fine the Special Selection wines when you do it to the others; are you looking for different character?

Well, they're aged longer than the others so if they have a few corners on them it doesn't matter as much because those corners will naturally get knocked off if we keep them in bottles five or six years. The other wines go right on the market, and I feel when you put a wine on the market it should be ready to drink. I don't put much stock in these wines that you buy and wait 20 years to drink. I don't buy them to wait 20 years, I buy them to drink now.

Do you have to adjust the acid levels on your grapes?

Sometimes, depends on the year. We'll use tartaric acid.

Do you ever adjust the sugar level with concentrate?

Once in a while, we have done this. I'm not too crazy about that procedure. If we have a bad year and the grapes come in late with low sugar, I prefer to make the wine and adjust later with brandy. Instead of adding concentrate to produce more alcohol, we can bring up the alcohol with high proof brandy later on.

What kind of barrel aging do the different wines receive?

We try to bottle Cabernet after three or four years, Zinfandel and Pinot Noir after two and a half years, and the Barbera after about three years.

And where has that Cabernet been for three or four years?

It's been in all kinds of wood. Part in 50 gallon American oak barrels, part in 500 and 1,300 gallon casks, and part in redwood; then it's all blended together. The only white wine that receives barrel aging is Chardonnay, and we put that in French Nevers oak for about a year. It doesn't all go into oak—we hold some of it and blend it back in.

Do you believe the best California wines are equal to the best European wines?

You stuck that word "best" in there. No, they're not. The reason is we haven't really found the places to grow the grapes. I don't think Europeans know anything we don't know, except that for 500 or 1,000 years they've been growing grapes, and they know which grape does best on which slope. We have areas in California we're not growing grapes on yet which will make a substantial difference when we discover them. After my trip to France this year, I certainly think we can match all but their very best vintages and generally we offer a far better dollar value. I don't put much stock in competitive wine tastings. I wonder how many of the results could stand up to statistical evaluation. Also I think there is a large difference between taste preference and drink preference.

Brother Timothy

THE CHRISTIAN BROTHERS

"Take a little wine for thy stomach's sake and thy frequent infirmities." (*1 Timothy 5:23*)

Yes, there really is a Brother Timothy. The tall, cassock-clad Brother pictured in countless Christian Brothers advertisements strolling through vineyards or checking wine casks, has in fact been making wine for The Christian Brothers for over 40 years. A serious and disciplined man, I admired his sense of detail (*sine qua non* of winemaking) revealed when he spotted a misspelled name in my interview notes and quickly grabbed a pencil to correct it. Although the winery is staffed mainly by lay workers and the Brothers are rarely seen in clerical garb, the atmosphere of a religious institution somehow prevails on Mont La Salle. Other religious orders sell wine in the United States, but The Christian Brothers is one of the few still carrying on the medieval monastic tradition of producing the wine itself. There has always been ambiguity about the wines: the winery is so large (the largest in this book) it seems to fall into the class of mass-production wineries. But the general wine quality is consistently above average, and some special bottlings compete surprisingly well in blind tastings.

Recommended wine to drink while reading this chapter:

CHRISTIAN BROTHERS
NAPA FUMÉ

Is Christian Brothers the largest winery in Napa Valley?

Yes, the largest by far. We make close to a million cases per year of table and sparkling wines produced and bottled within Napa County.

Many smaller producers state that the finest wines can be made only on a small scale. Does your huge size put you at any disadvantage?

We were a tiny winery when I started here in 1935, and certainly I'm proud that our winery has grown to its present size, and quite likely will continue to grow. To regret that we've grown to this size is, to me, just insane. Look at the people who are small today: aren't they working to generate more sales, working toward growth? And if not, they're not likely to be viable in the long pull of time. It's one thing to make a very fine wine, but if you don't sell it you won't last long. So if you're a dreamer who wants the finest thing in the world regardless of price, and then finds out the product won't sell, your business life is very short. Also, there may be some tiny wineries who are meticulous in their approach but may not be able to produce the finest thing possible, simply because they don't have money enough to afford the necessary equipment or personnel.

How many wineries do you operate, and where are they?

This one at Mont La Salle, just northwest of Napa, is our parent location. The Brothers acquired this property in 1930. In 1945, we acquired property at Reedley, southeast of Fresno. In 1950 we acquired the old stone cellar on the north side of St. Helena, commonly called Greystone Cellar. We acquired a lot of vineyard property in 1954 on the Napa Valley floor, and on one of those properties, at the south end of St. Helena, we built a winery in the '60s and on into the '70s. And also in the early '60s we bought the old Biscelgia winery in Fresno itself. So we're running five wineries.

Do the Brothers themselves constitute a large portion of the staff operating the winery?

No, we've always had a small number of Brothers operating the winery. We have just five Brothers attached to the wine and brandy operations right now.

How long have the Christian Brothers been making wine in California?

The Brothers started shortly after 1879 when they bought property at Martinez and found there were 12 acres of vineyard planted. One Brother decided the grapes should not be wasted, so he got a long wooden trough and crushed the grapes in it with a wooden club. We think the club was a tree branch that must have looked like a mule leg because "mule's leg" was the nickname they gave it. The Brothers used the wine at the dining table, but neighbors or local clergy came around asking about wine and in the 1880s the Brothers started to make some sales. And our wine business continued to grow very slowly right through Prohibition.

We were permitted to continue during Prohibition, producing sacramental and so-called medicinal wines sold on doctors' prescriptions. I entered the Order in 1928 during Prohibition, a little prior to the stock market crash of '29. That was before the Brothers had acquired this property, so I knew that old Martinez property firsthand, and I knew two or more old Brothers who had known the Brother Cecilian who made the first wine there.

The Christian Brothers is a teaching order. How extensive is it in the United States?

We have around 3,000 Brothers in the United States and about 15,000 throughout the world. We're in about 80 countries. The principal work of the order is the educational work in our schools, mostly boys' schools, though we are very slowly going coeducational now.

And is the winery the principal source of support for those teaching endeavors?

Our winery operation, although it seems large, doesn't support the Order or all the Brothers in the United States. Our activities in the United States and throughout the world are so large. Also, each province is autonomous from the others. So our activity at the winery mainly supports our San

Francisco province, which covers the west coast, from the Rockies out to the coast.

When you entered the Order in 1928, I take it you were not a winemaker. How did the Brothers develop your interest?

In 1928 Prohibition was in effect, and I was only 17 years old, so certainly I knew nothing about wine at that time. I joined the Order to become a school teacher, to teach science principally. Biology was one of the things I was interested in, but at the time I was ready to teach, most of our high schools dropped biology as a "nonessential" subject. That left such things as chemistry and physics. So I began to teach high school chemistry, and also taught high school English literature. I taught for four years before being invited to the winery to be the wine chemist in 1935.

Do you think of Christian Brothers wines as possessing a style distinct from other Napa Valley wines?

Yes, I do think of them that way, and I guess there are some definite reasons for believing that is true. We do no vintage dating, so we're not leaning heavily on each year and saying, "Well, that's the way this year turned out." We've never had a vintage date on our bottles for all the 90 years of the existence of our company. We've always believed in blending, with all the inventory at our command in our extensive cellar, to achieve what we thought was best. We like freedom, the expression of our own artistry in blending. It depends on the man doing the blending, his palate, his judgment, his memory—everything about him and his experience comes into play. One of those little nebulous ingredients we try to blend into our wine is complexity, an intriguing and mysterious complexity. We can achieve that with blending more than with wines all of one vintage. Also, by blending different years, an older wine gives mellowness to a certain blend, and a younger wine gives freshness and fruitiness. And we think it's good for the continuity of our wines. You can buy the same wine and find it will be the same from year to year, so you have reliability and continuity.

Do your vineyards supply most of your grape needs?

No, in Napa County we grow about half of what we need for table and sparkling wines, and buy the rest. In the San Joaquin Valley, where we produce our brandy, dessert wines and vermouths, we grow only about five to ten percent ourselves.

Where are your Napa County vineyards situated?

We have vineyards in each of the three recognized climatic zones. First, on this property we have between 200 and 250 acres of hillside vineyards, all in beautiful soils, with a northeastern exposure for the morning sun. We have vineyards just north of Napa, east of Oakville, south and north of St. Helena, and another sizeable vineyard halfway between St. Helena and

Calistoga. With the exception of the Mont La Salle vineyard, they're all on the valley floor.

Are any of those unique vineyards?

Well, I like the quality from this vineyard on the slopes best of all. But in the valley floor vineyards we have a variety of soil conditions and climates; from here to our northernmost vineyard it's 30 miles. They're all different. This vineyard is cool, a high Region I, or low Region II in some years.

What varieties are planted here?

Pinot St. George is the main grape. We also have Sylvaner, Johannisberg Riesling, Chardonnay, and smaller amounts of other varieties.

Do you ever keep the grapes from this vineyard separate, make them into special lots of wine?

I'd like to just be able to say yes, but the answer is really no, with one exception. All the Pinot St. George on the market now is exclusively from the Mont La Salle vineyard.

Over several decades here in the Napa Valley, have you come to any conclusion whether hillside grapes are normally better than grapes grown on the valley floor?

I agree with the general thinking, that slope grown grapes are better than grapes grown on the valley floor. I think there are demonstrable reasons for this. Grapes grown on hillsides usually have good drainage, their root systems penetrate deep in search of water. As a result, hillside grapes never have excess water, which might be true on the valley floor. There, vines might be planted over a water table, with no difficulty getting water, and the berries may be larger. If this is true, each gallon of wine made from hillside grapes may require twice as many berries as each gallon made from valley grapes. A lot of the flavor and color components of the grapes are associated with skin tissue and cellular structure immediately under the skin, so it stands to reason that if you crush a lot of properly ripened small berries from hillside vineyards you get a heavier and more flavorfull wine than if you crush fewer of the larger berries from valley floor vineyards.

Can you gain the same effect from grapes on the valley floor by deliberately undercropping—pruning or bunch thinning for a smaller crop?

I think the answer is no. If you thin you improve the quality of the grapes left on the vine, but those berries will be big and fat, because the vine is vigorous and healthy, richly supplied with nutrients and moisture.

Do you limit the yield on your vineyards by pruning or thinning?

Yes, everybody does; pruning is designed for that purpose. For instance, we had large crops back to back in 1973 and 1974 and our vineyard people calculated it was time to give some thought to closer pruning. So we did a reasonably close pruning in 1975, to raise the quality a little. Although the quality in 1974 was beautiful, it was beautiful because we had an Indian summer. We can't count on that ideal Indian summer situation every year, so we pruned closer.

On the scale you operate, I imagine your vineyards are mechanically harvested.

No, we have no mechanically harvested grapes and no plans to mechanically harvest. We like the hand picked grapes better, that's very definite in our, let's say, opinion structure here. However, there's another reason too. All our vineyard operations are in the hands of the United Farm Workers Union. And César Chávez and his UFW people have not authorized the use of mechanical harvesters.

What do your workers put the grapes into?

They pick into little pans and dump those into a one ton trailer pulled by a little tractor.

Do you ever have them pick a vineyard more than once, to get the fruit at a better point of maturity?

Yes, we do a little of that, to get a better quality grape, but we don't do it with many varieties, and we don't do it every year. We might do it with Pinot Noir, and we've also handled some Johannisberg Riesling that way. I don't think we'll expand that technique, because we aren't convinced it's absolutely crucial for quality.

You produce almost the full range of varietal wines.

Almost, yes; there are a few we don't make.

You also produce generics and I read a quotation attributed to you that the California use of generic names such as Burgundy and Chablis, geographical areas of France, amounted to "the sins of the fathers being visited upon the sons."

I'm sure I said something more or less like that, that it's too bad it ever got started. But you and I are sitting here speaking English, a language imported from overseas. Well, the wine names and grape names were also imported from the old world. When our grandparents and great-grandparents came to this country, they brought those names with them. When they made wine here, they may have called it "Napa Valley Sauternes." They used "Sauternes" in pride of their motherland and in pride of their accomplishments of producing wine something like the wine they knew back home.

Certain words have acquired a generic meaning. Champagne, for instance, to most people means a naturally sparkling wine. You must admit the word has a general, generic meaning. In French, "champagne," if I understand anything about French, means something like a grassy field, or pasture, when you get to the roots of the thing. And now the French legislation says Champagne means a natural sparkling wine produced in a certain way only from certain districts. But that ignores its generic meaning. Here in California we produce "Rhine" wine; now that may be a goofy one. But on wine labels we always state "California" preceding the generic name, indicating its actual origin, so I don't consider there is any misrepresentation to the consumer at all.

Would you object if a French company produced wine, labeled it "French Napa Valley Red Wine," and sold it in third countries?

I wouldn't agree to that. This may be a one-way thing. The European people who brought those names from over there came here. It's not necessarily a two-way street.

Are your wines usually 100 percent of the varietal grape on the label?

Just a few years ago, they were almost all 100 percent. The Grey Riesling has been an exception right along. We think we can improve the Grey Riesling considerably by adding a little Sylvaner and a little White Riesling. Then in '72 we had a very poor crop and our inventory was getting low, but our sales remained good, so we began blending the other varietals too. We did it for other reasons as well, for balance in the wines and so forth.

Will that situation reverse itself with the current glut of varietal grapes on the market?

Yes, I think and hope so. Our varietal content is high now, but I'd like to see it a little higher.

Since none of your wines carry vintage dates, they are only legally required to have 75 percent Napa Valley grapes if the label says Napa Valley. Do you blend grapes from other areas in your wines, and where are those areas?

Yes, we use minor amounts of grapes from Sonoma and Santa Barbara counties in a few of our Napa Valley varietal wines.

How do you ferment the wines?

All in temperature controlled stainless steel. For the whites, we maintain the temperature at or below 50 degrees. For fermentation of red wines, we think the ideal temperature is 72 degrees.

Do you start the fermentation with a yeast starter and have you ever tried letting it start spontaneously with the wild wine yeast on the grapes?

We use a starter. We object to spontaneous fermentation, because you're in a no-man's land of science; you don't know what you have or what the heck you're doing. We did that a long time ago, 30 odd years ago. I lived through that period, and you need only one bad fermentation to change your mind.

You have a unique way of circulating the must during fermentation. Would you describe that?

We circulate the red fermentations with pumps of infinitely variable speed, the fermenting wine being distributed over the cap by a rotating device of our own design. The pumping speed and the number of hours of circulation are carefully controlled to give each wine the optimum color, grape aroma and flavor.

Do you fine and filter all of the wines?

Yes, we fine almost all the white and the reds with bentonite, and, later, we fine the reds with gelatin and if necessary with something like egg whites. But we stopped using egg whites a couple of years ago. We had been using fresh egg whites, and our boys separated the whites and yolks, took the yolks to the school kitchen, and the cook would bake cakes with them.

How many filtrations do the wines go through?

Several. In the cellar they get a rough filtration and in the bottling department they receive a final filtration through pads and through the millipore. All except the dessert wines go through a millipore filter before they get into a bottle.

Do you use a centrifuge at any stage?

No, we've tried centrifuges and we've never found one we thought fully satisfactory. However, in the initial fermentations we have a couple of big vacuum filters. We do a good deal of vacuum filtration and we think this obviates the necessity for centrifuging. We probably have more money tied up in vacuum filters than anybody has in centrifuges. The vacuum filter is a big rotating drum; the filter powder—diatomaceous earth—builds up around the outside of the drum and there is a very sharp knife along the side of the drum that shaves off the solids the filter has just taken out of the liquid.

Do you ever adjust the acid, or adjust the sugar level with concentrate?

We use almost no concentrate, but we do use special blending wines for sweetness sometimes. For acid adjustments we sometimes do use some citric acid. We may use a little tartaric acid, but more likely it would be citric.

But tartaric is preferred generally, isn't it, because it's naturally present in grapes much more than citric is?

No, tartaric is used less, citric is used more. Tartaric acid is not really very soluble, so you can have crystals form in the bottom of the bottle or adhere to the cork. It's less likely you'd have that with citric acid. Tartaric acid is naturally present in the grape but much of it precipitates out during fermentation.

Since you blend your wines from different vintages, you must have an extensive aging program so you'll have older reds to blend with.

Yes, our reds average close to four years in the cellar. This is in oak and redwood—very seldom we might have a red wine in stainless steel.

Take the Cabernet Sauvignon as an example: how long would it be in the cellar and in what kind of cooperage?

It would average four years. Now as to the cooperage, we have some 50 gallon barrels, but most of our oak cooperage is 2,000 gallon casks; we have more of those oak casks, probably, than anybody else in the industry. But since others don't have casks (which are expensive and now more difficult to obtain than they ever were), many wineries find it expedient to use 50 gallon oak barrels.

What kind of oak are the casks?

Well, we don't know. They're pretty old and most of them were installed by a San Francisco cooper many years ago, a company which hasn't existed since before Prohibition. His name was David Werner, and I haven't traced the history of his company but we think they got most of their oak from Europe.

We hear a lot these days about California wines rivaling European wines. In your view, are our wines as good as the European?

I'd say yes, absolutely, without a question. And if there is any argument about it, I think you should try to settle the argument on the basis of the general technology available and the understanding of the technology. In other words, are California winemakers fully acquainted with wine technology as it is in this modern day and age, or are they wedded to the past? I think our California wine technologists stack up favorably against technologists of any other country in the world. If you find that hard to prove take the general level of California wines compared with the general level of wines in any other country, and I'm sure you will find our general quality is better.

And if you move above the average level, go to the top of the premium scale? Can our technology make wines equal to the very best of Europe?

What I've already said indicates the broadly based foundation for that pinnacle of success you're talking about. I think California does reach higher up that pinnacle than any other wine producing country today. Remember, although in one way the California wine industry is only 40 years old because it's been only 40 years since Prohibition, we did have a very fine and honorable history before then. Prohibition damaged and destroyed things that have not been replaced at all, but after Repeal the whole California wine industry was ready to accept new ideas and techniques; we were not hidebound by tradition, not wedded to the past or governed by senile thinking. We've been extremely progressive, wedded to science, extremely eager to listen to new ideas from the University of California. So California is at the point where we can challenge any winemaking country of the world with even its top-ranking products.

Well, thank you; do you have any further comments?

I'll give you my favorite quotation, from Paul to my namesake Timothy: "Take a little wine for thy stomach's sake and thy frequent infirmities." Paul was telling Timothy that wine was good for his health, and I think it is as good today, or better, for your health as it ever was in the past.

Sonoma County:

THE HEART OF HISTORY

Sonoma County produced wines earlier, and once had more vineyards and wineries, than Napa Valley. But Napa eventually gained the ascendency and today Sonoma's glories are largely those of the past. The past starts in the town of Sonoma, a quaint village centered around a grassy plaza where the Bear Flag was first hoisted in 1846 declaring California an independent republic. By then, wine grapes had already been growing for nearly 30 years at the Spanish mission across the street. And the Mexican General Vallejo had a winery nearby before and after California separated from Mexico.

Hungarian Colonel Ágoston Haraszthy really put Sonoma on the wine map. A swashbuckling, heroic figure (or something of a con man, depending on who tells the story), Haraszthy brought fame to Sonoma. He crusaded to make winegrowing California's leading industry. Among other bold moves, he singlehandedly collected over 100,000 European grape cuttings and gave them away in California. (Some believe those vines may have included the original Zinfandel cutting, a grape of uncertain origin now found only in California.)

By the turn of the century there were scores of wineries and many miles of vineyard in the county. But after the trauma of Prohibition, Sonoma never managed to live up to its past. It struggled into the 1960s with few wineries, and even fewer of note. Hanzell winery and a revived Buena Vista were virtually the only ones attempting great winemaking before the 1960s wine boom.

But today, promise is in the air. Many small new wineries devoted to fine wine have opened; some of the older ones—such as Simi and Sebastiani—have taken a new interest in fine wines. The main wine activity lies in two subregions of the county. One is the Sonoma Valley stretching north along the Mayacamas Mountains from the town of Sonoma. The other is the Russian River area, particularly the stretch of the river which flows west to the Pacific, and Alexander and Dry Creek Valleys which lie next to the river in the county's northern end. Each has its distinct micro-climate, and the wineries are competitively exploring vineyards as if in a treasure hunt.

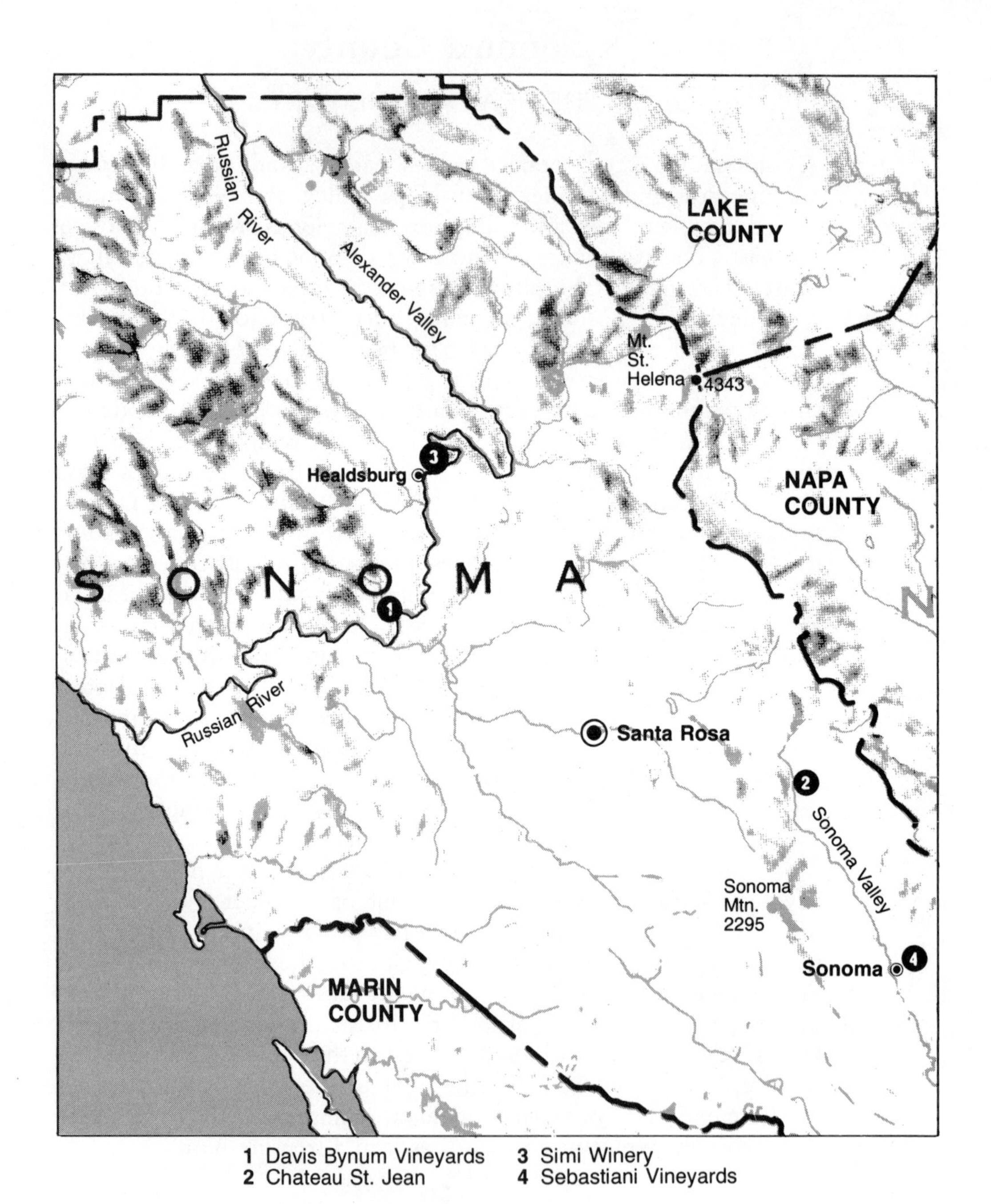

North of San Francisco Bay
SONOMA COUNTY: The Heart of History

Davis Bynum and Hampton Bynum.

Davis Bynum

DAVIS BYNUM WINERY

That's what winemaking is, physical labor. Any idiot can make wine, but he has to be a tireless idiot.

Just where the Russian River changes its southerly course and bends westward to run for the coast, stands an old hop kiln remodeled to house the Bynum Winery. In earlier days, kilns were scattered all over Sonoma County, but the hop business was eventually lost to areas whose hops were milder and more acceptable for beer brewing. Paradoxically, Davis Bynum speculates those strong Sonoma flavors show up today as a beautiful *goût de terroir* in some of the area's wines. The coolness of this Russian River stretch has stimulated vineyardists to anticipate great futures for Pinot Noir, Chardonnay and other fine varieties rarely planted there until recently. The Bynums are among the first to explore this area for fine wine and possess the experimental attitude it will take to find the region's greatness. As I spoke with Davis, a man whose wit is as dry as his wines, his son and co-winemaker, Hampton, joined us in conversation in their home near the winery.

Recommended wine to drink while reading this chapter:

DAVIS BYNUM
PINOT NOIR

You were a home winemaker before you became a professional, weren't you?

DAVIS BYNUM:

Yes, and there are times I wish I still were. We started making wine at home in 1951. I didn't start the winery until 1965, so we had 14 years of it, buying grapes from people like Louis Martini and August Sebastiani, until they didn't want to sell grapes any more. I was in the newspaper business, with the *San Francisco Chronicle,* on the staff of *This World* magazine; I was garden editor and did several things. Then I went to Southern California to run weekly newspapers for Scott Newhall, the editor of the *Chronicle.* I was born and raised in Southern California, but after a year I decided it had changed so much I really wanted to come back to the Bay country. So I quit and started the winery on San Pablo Avenue in Albany, adjacent to Berkeley. San Pablo Avenue is noted for its auto shops, not for wineries. But we had the building we needed, and also, being close to the University of California, we drew heavily on the faculty, graduate students and others. Almost 50 percent of our original business came from the

University. We didn't have the wherewithall to buy a vineyard and build a winery. We started out buying bulk wine from other wineries, and we would age and blend, and I think occasionally come up with a better wine than we started with. But there was a big surge of interest in wine, and wineries no longer wanted to sell bulk wine. There we were, with a market for our wines and our normal supplies were cut off, so we were forced to buy a vineyard in the Napa Valley in 1971.

Wasn't your father a wine buff before you?

DAVIS:

My father was a wine buff for as long as I can remember. Professionally, he was a California historian. His office was at UCLA but his principal concern was the Bancroft Library at Berkeley. He wrote a book on wine, was a wine judge at the State Fair and Los Angeles County Fair for years, and when he retired he moved to Napa Valley and bought a vineyard.

Do you still make wine in Albany?

DAVIS:

We still make mead there, honey wine. Not my favorite glass of wine, but we have a wine chemist who worked with us for a long time who developed this formula and wanted to make it, so we did because he was so high on it. All of a sudden there is a market for mead. All our other operations are here now.

How many acres do you have near here?

DAVIS:

We own 74 acres here, but it's not planted. About two years ago we took in shareholders to acquire this property and remodel the building which used to be a hop kiln. Our shareholders have vineyards around here which supply us with all our grapes. We're not going to use the Napa vineyard any longer, it's such a long haul, and we prefer the Sonoma grapes. Our principal grapes in the future will be Johannisberg Riesling, Sauvignon Blanc, Chardonnay and French Colombard for the white wines. For the reds it'll be Pinot Noir, Cabernet, Petite Sirah, and Zinfandel from Dry Creek. All but Zinfandel come from this area, and they all come from the five growers who are shareholders.

How is the climate in this area?

DAVIS:

It's a fairly cool Region I. One problem for grapes like Cabernet is getting sufficient sugar. One of our growers, Joe Rochioli, who is one of the most conscientious growers in the whole north coast region, has pruned his Cabernet very heavily this year to help get the sugar up. Last year we averaged 23.5 Balling on the Cabernet, which is good, and it's just a lovely, fragrant wine. It will take some time to age out, but it has a certain vineyard characteristic which is also true of our French Colombard and Sauvignon Blanc. The Sauvignon Blanc is a very fragrant wine, which I think is a combination of the soil here—benchland, well-drained . . .

HAMPTON BYNUM:

It's very deep soil also. There's a top layer of loam, but underneath there is gravel from the Russian River which goes down, I've heard, almost 30 feet.

DAVIS:

This is called the Russian River Valley. That's not a very adequate description of the area for a label appellation because it could technically include anything within the Russian River drainage basin which starts north of Ukiah in Mendocino County. We're eight miles south and west of Healdsburg.

Do you think the soil here is more important in determining the wine's character than weather?

HAMPTON:

They're both important. It's purely speculation which is dominant; it'd take long range studies to really find out.

DAVIS:

I recently read an article on soils in Bordeaux. Some viticulture professor said he didn't think soils made much difference. I think he's wrong, but he pointed out that ten of the leading châteaux are grown on highly different soils.

Did he talk about soil drainage, was that similar on the ten?

DAVIS:

That's the key—drainage and cool nights that extend the ripening period. As you know, one problem with warm regions is that you lose acid and this happens both in the central valley and coastal areas. Calistoga in Napa Valley, for example, is an area where grapes ripen too quickly. Our harvest is usually later than most areas. In '74, for instance, we crushed Chardonnay September 12th, and people elsewhere were crushing Chardonnay about the first of September. This area has never had a chance to show what it can do with premium varietals. Most vineyards here are very recent plantings. And all the old vineyards were farmed by Italian families for high yield, so they planted Carignane, Zinfandel and Colombard. Only about four years ago did anybody begin planting grapes like Pinot Noir, Chardonnay and Riesling. Last year we made Petite Sirah, about half from our Napa Valley vineyard, and half from Fenton Acres vineyard down the road. And that was an outstanding wine, I think it reached 25 Balling, a big black wine that will take forever to age, similar to some wines Ridge has put out . . .

HAMPTON:

Which aren't really our style.

What is your style, how would you characterize it?

HAMPTON:

We emphasize varietal character more than wood. Rather than trying to make a full bodied, high alcohol wine that must be appreciated by itself because it would dominate a meal, we make wine to accompany a meal.

DAVIS:

This year we didn't put our Sauvignon Blanc or Johannisberg Riesling in wood at all. Some people might argue Sauvignon Blanc should have wood, and I won't dispute it, but I still say the varietal character is tremendous and I hate to deaden it any by a conflict of wood on the palate.

Do you and your son make the wine alone?

DAVIS:

Hamp is the only one at the winery full time. I'm here two or three days a week, and we have a couple of fellows who work part time. When I was first getting into the wine industry I talked to Joe Heitz, whom I had known for some time, and he said a winemaker should never get into growing grapes, just make the wine. I disagreed with him at the time, but now I must agree that it makes more sense to let somebody else grow the grapes.

HAMPTON:

You have to work closely with the grower, though, and he has to want to work with you too.

DAVIS:

We're sort of involved here in a winery co-op, because the growers are also minor shareholders and so it's in their interest to supply the best grapes. So they don't overcrop, they prune for a low crop and also do some bunch thinning.

What tonnage to the acre do your growers' vineyards produce?

DAVIS:

Well, French Colombard is a very productive grape, I'd say somewhere around seven tons.

That's certainly high.

DAVIS:

Yes, but not compared to what it produces in areas like Dry Creek where they get perhaps 12 tons. That grape has another name: West's White Prolific. I don't know who West was, I've never inquired. Now the Cabernet will yield at most three tons, and the Pinot Noir gave us four last year.

How is the harvesting done?

HAMPTON:

All by hand. They put the grapes into four by four bins, which hold half a ton of grapes, and bring the bins right up to our winery. They don't go into gondolas. The come to us right after they're picked. They don't sit in gondolas, and the distances are short between vineyards and winery. It's the next best thing to field crushing.

Do the growers ever pick selectively, sending the harvesters through more than once to get the fruit as it ripens?

DAVIS:
No.

How many cases did you produce last year?

DAVIS:
Around 15,000 cases. I'd like to reach 25,000 to 30,000 and call it quits.

Do you ferment in stainless steel?

DAVIS:
Yes. We have fermented whites in oak tanks, but our reds are all fermented in *open* stainless steel, very small fermenters.

Why did you emphasize the "open"?

DAVIS:
I don't know, maybe we like to work harder. That's what winemaking is, physical labor. Any idiot can make wine, but he has to be a tireless idiot. Seriously, most wineries ferment in closed tanks, but we like open ones so we can pump over the cap more, we feel we get better color and certain complexities you might not pick up otherwise.

HAMPTON:
In a closed fermenter you almost have to control your temperature because there's less heat loss. Whereas with an open tank you lose heat, get oxygen working with yeast and creating a different type of fermentation. And we ferment in small enough quantities so it can't get too hot.

DAVIS:
With the reds we have ten 700 gallon fermenters and four others that hold 1,200 gallons each. Only once or twice has the temperature gone too high; it never exceeds 82 or 83 degrees. Now the white wines ferment cool, we pump them through a heat exchanger. The Riesling ferments between 50 and 60 degrees, while other white varieties get to around 70 degrees and then we chill them to 55 degrees. Some wineries ferment their whites awfully cold. I think that's silly.

Their theory, of course, is that it retains more of the fruitiness.

HAMPTON:
And less complexity.

Do you inoculate with yeast to start fermentation?

HAMPTON:
Yes, Champagne yeast.

DAVIS:
I know a commercial winemaker who always uses just wild yeast to start

fermentation. There are things to be said for doing it that way. If it goes right, you may end up with a more complex and stable wine than if you sulphite and inoculate. Who knows?

What kind of a press do you have?

DAVIS:

Two Vaslin presses, they are beautiful machines. I've never used another automatic press, but I couldn't ask for more. On the larger, the two heads move together pressing the wine, and we can set it at six different pressures. We use free run and light press, and keep the heavy press separate. I hear about wines made from free run juice, but I'm not sure anybody really does this. I like to blend in *some* of the press wine.

Do you have to increase the acid level by adding tartaric, or do you always have sufficient acid naturally?

DAVIS:

We don't add acid, our grapes have it, though it's fairly common practice over in Napa and even in Sonoma County.

What about adjusting sweetness with concentrate?

DAVIS:

Never, I wouldn't do that. I'd rather not crush the grapes if they don't have the sugar naturally.

Do you fine and filter the wines?

DAVIS:

Only one filtration, just before bottling. We always fine. I haven't yet made a completely stable white wine that didn't need bentonite fining. On the reds, we normally fine with a little gelatin. The Riesling has about .7 residual sugar, and we chill the Riesling and take it off the yeast before it's completely fermented dry in order to retain that bit of sugar. We give it a sterile filtration so we don't have viable yeast in the bottle which could re-ferment. If I had a centrifuge, I could just stop fermentation by centrifuging. That'd be easier than racking it off the lees as we do now. But I'm for doing as little as possible to stabilize a wine. The biggest problem with unfined wines is their instability. If you sell it from the winery you can explain it, but it's exasperating to a retail dealer when customers return wines because of sediment in the bottle.

How long do you age your red wines?

DAVIS:

The Cabernet will be in French and American oak for two years. The French oak is 135 gallon cooperage, and the American 800 gallon ovals. Our '73 Pinot Noir was exclusively in French oak, 135 gallon, for a year and a half.

Your cooperage is about twice as big as the usual small barrels used for such wines.

DAVIS:

We have many 60 gallon barrels but they are not new. Certain complexities come from long aging in relatively small containers, but if the oak is new it can be too overpowering.

Do you get those complexities with your 135 gallon cooperage?

DAVIS:

Oh, yes, not quite as much as with a 60 gallon barrel, but we definitely get the effects.

Are your varietals 100 percent of the varietal grape?

DAVIS:

Some are, some aren't. The white varietals all are. The Pinot Noir is 100 percent, the current Cabernet is 85 percent Cabernet Sauvignon and 15 percent Sonoma County Ruby Cabernet. And I did that because the acid was a little low on the Cabernet Sauvignon and high on the Ruby Cabernet, and also the Ruby Cabernet had some nice characteristics. The Zinfandel we're bottling this week is 100 percent, but I have put a little Petite Sirah and Carignane in other Zinfandels. We bottled a Merlot also which was about one-third Cabernet Sauvignon and the rest Merlot—a very good wine.

Do you have an opinion on the requirement that a varietal need contain only 51 percent of the grape on the label?

DAVIS:

I think it should be raised to 75 percent. I'm all for that.

Would you object to listing on the label the other varieties blended with that 75 percent?

DAVIS:

No, I wouldn't object, but it might be difficult. In making a blend like Burgundy, for instance, you may have pumped portions of Zinfandel, Carignane, heavy press wine from Cabernet. It'd be very difficult to determine what percentage of each grape was present if you wanted to blend some with your varietal Cabernet.

What if you didn't have to list the exact percentages, just had to give the names of the blended grapes?

DAVIS:

That's fine, that's fine. If you had a requirement that it had to be 75 percent of a varietal grape to carry its name, then the consumer would know those other varieties were 25 percent or less. I think the main thing is not to mislead consumers.

In addition to your varietals, you also put out generic wines under the "Barefoot Bynum" label with a big purple foot on it. How was that witty idea born?

DAVIS:

When my father retired from the University and bought the place in Napa

Valley his friends kidded him about what he would do, and one of them joked that he would be making "Barefoot Bynum Burgundy." So when I started the winery we came out with that label, and unfortunately it's grown so popular I wish I'd never done it. Out-of-state sales for Barefoot exceed our Davis Bynum label sales in gallonage. I remember when I first discussed with our New York broker which wines he would sell, I asked "How about the Barefoot?" And he said, "None of that country boy stuff for New York, we're too sophisticated." He first went to The Wine Merchant in New Jersey and they wanted the Barefoot. Then he went to a big New York liquor store where he was trying to sell his imported wines. They said "Tell you what, we'll take your wines if you'll give us an exclusive on Barefoot Bynum." Last month we shipped 509 cases to New York, and over 400 were Barefoot.

Is it popular only because of the label, or also because it's good?

DAVIS:

It's a good wine, all north coast, but it's young. The Burgundy is Petite Sirah, Carignane and a little Zinfandel. And the Chablis is primarily French Colombard and Sauvignon Vert, all Sonoma County.

Do you have any misgivings about using the European place names Burgundy and Chablis on your labels?

I can't get very excited one way or the other. I'd just as soon call it Red Table Wine or Sonoma White. But we've tried to use such names and in every case the Burgundies and Chablis continue to outsell the others, even if the customer pays more for Burgundy or Chablis. But if it's going to be called Burgundy or Chablis there should be government regulations setting the grape types that may be used. That would secure some consistency in the California Burgundies or Chablis.

In your judgment do the best California wines come from small wineries, or are the larger ones just as capable of producing the best?

Oh, there are some very nice wines produced by big wineries. For example, the Wente Sauvignon Blanc is very fine wine, year in and year out. But the potential for making great wine is better in a small winery because they can concentrate on given lots of wine. They can also get good grapes on given lots of wine, without blending them out with poor grapes as the big wineries sometimes must do.

Do you think our California wines are as great as the great wines of Europe?

I'm prejudiced. Yes, I think our potential for a good Cabernet is as good as the potential for a good Bordeaux. We haven't yet rung a bell on Pinot Noir but I think this area does have the potential to do something with Pinot Noir. And we have a good potential Chardonnay; we'll find out because we're just beginning to get a crop of Chardonnay.

Richard Arrowood

CHÂTEAU ST. JEAN

Let me tell you the reason most people don't have centrifuges: they are terribly expensive. But the improved quality of the finished product justifies the expense for us.

The "château" of Château St. Jean is a country home built in the 1920s and remodeled into business offices and a tasting center for the winery. Polished wood paneling and a vaulted portico give it the air of a small museum. Dick Arrowood's office, cloistered on the second floor, continues the theme with white walls and shelves displaying empty bottles of some of this century's greatest French Burgundies. Arrowood talks at machine gun speed, is full of ideas, reactions, comments, plans for this new winery. The winery is owned by three grape growers from the San Joaquin Valley and it must be their favorite hideaway, for nothing could be further from the massive winemaking operations of the San Joaquin Valley. Château St. Jean is a small, elegant operation, emphasizing limited production wines from individual vineyards in Sonoma and Mendocino Counties. Given Arrowood's training and predilections, the Rieslings, Chardonnays and Sauvignon Blancs are the wines to watch. The first releases were stunning.

Recommended wine to drink while reading this chapter:

CHATEAU ST. JEAN
WILDWOOD VINEYARD
CHARDONNAY

I understand you are about to break a record by producing seven different Chardonnays all from the '75 vintage. Why are you doing that?

It's done in Burgundy. You can go out and buy a bottle of Vosne-Romanée, but you can also buy the wines of the vineyards of that village; you can buy Richebourg, La Tâche, Echézeaux, Grands Echézeaux, whatever it happens to be. We're trying to do that here, because there *is* a difference. You taste those seven Chardonnays and every single one of them is different. I have 100 cases of some Chardonnays, I have 1,000 cases of others. When they come on the market, many will be sold exclusively here at the winery, a few will be in California retail shops and they'll disappear off the shelves as fast as they go on. We've already seen this happen.

Is it fair to ask which of the seven Chardonnays you produced is your favorite?

My favorite would probably be the Sonoma Valley Chardonnay from the Wildwood Vineyard. It's just down the road, and they have some very old vines of Chardonnay, Zinfandel and Cabernet. They're giving us unreasonably good wines. But they're all so darn good, it's hard to say; even our least expensive Chardonnay, a blend of four different growers from Sonoma and Mendocino Counties, is very fine.

Do you think a blend of wines could sometimes be better than one from a single vineyard?

The Château Montelena Chardonnay that placed first in the Paris tasting was blended from Alexander Valley and Napa Valley vineyards.

Yes, one was Belle Terre vineyard in Alexander Valley where we've gotten grapes also, and if you don't think it cost me more this year! I generally prefer not to blend vineyards. Belle Terre is owned by the Henry and Ron Dick family; they're cautious, conservative vineyardists. Their vines are 10 to 11 years old, and they probably get three tons to the acre. It's on a little bench on the west side of the Alexander Valley, right above the Russian River. It's a little cool for Cabernet and a shade warmer for Chardonnay than I think it should be, yet the fruit is gorgeous. We calculated it's a high Region I, low Region II. In '75 he got about 24.5 sugar, with about .95 acid. We are publishing this data in a brochure that talks about each of our wines. It shows sugar and acid at harvest, alcohol, residual sugar if any, number of cases produced, harvest date, and other data. We do not put information like, "Serve it with lamb chops and candied curry," and useless information like that.

Compare your Wildwood with the Belle Terre vineyard: why are they different?

Wildwood is on a very steep hillside, at about 1,500 feet, while Belle Terre is about 500 feet on a little bench. The Wildwood is volcanic soil, well drained, iron-oxide in color, easily leachable, and I think it's lost many of its nutrients. The vines struggle to produce two to two and a half tons on a hillside. Belle Terre is on gravelly, river bottom soil from the Russian River. Belle Terre has a tremendous amount of fruit, and the Wildwood has a nutmeg-clove character which come probably from both the soil and the Nevers and Limousin oak it ages in. The berries from Wildwood came in last year with 24.8 Balling and .97 acid. It's unreal, you couldn't ask for a better balance! Made 240 cases of a big, rich, full Chardonnay. It isn't going to go very far, but that's all right. The point is, it's unusual. People say Sonoma Valley doesn't produce rich, lush Chardonnays as the Napa Valley does. Well, my '75s haven't hit the market yet, so let's wait and see what happens. I'm very excited about them.

Are your growers' vineyards all in Sonoma County?

Eventually 80 percent of the grapes will come from the Sonoma Valley area within the county. We also are going to Alexander Valley within the county, and three specific vineyards in Mendocino County—Redwood Valley vineyards for our Pinot Blanc and Mendocino Chardonnay, another grower in Potter Valley with Riesling, and a third grower in Mendocino County with Sauvignon Blanc. We have an unusual contract with our growers. We don't pay bonuses for sugar points, we pay a set fee for a sugar point range. We ask for a certain minimum sugar and acid. If any grapes fall below our set standards, we have total refusal rights. Now we pay dearly for this, but it's worth it. We're one of the few wineries doing this.

What kind of grapes are planted in your own vineyards around the winery?

Chardonnay, Johannisberg Riesling, Gewürztraminer, Pinot Blanc, Sauvignon Blanc, Muscadelle de Bordelais. Fifty acres on the hillside, 50 acres down below on flat land. We did two years of thermograph studies and decided we were in a high Region I, low Region II area. That is why we chose those varieties, plus we feel whites are going to be the "in" thing. There are a few other varieties I don't want to mention because we don't know how they'll work out. Although all our white wine varietals are usually 100 percent varietal, we plan to use these experimental varieties in our special bottling of Sauvignon Blanc Demi-Sec. We're trying to do a Sauvignon Blanc in the Sauternes style. When our grapes come into fruition in the '78 and '79 vintages we hope to have that style, with botrytised grapes.

Do you get the botrytis here?

We have, and we get good fog, and afternoon sun, so we have a good chance for development of it. I did my graduate work on botrytis culturing, and I've done it in the vineyard with a little sprayer; you can actually inoculate a vineyard to get it going. We haven't done that yet on anything we've produced, though we have produced some very interesting botrytis wines. We have five '75 Rieslings from five different vineyards, which range from a *kabinett* style to a *trockenbeerenauslese* which is very heavily infected with botrytis. We haven't had to induce it yet, it occurs naturally here more than people ever thought.

Where did you study oenology and how did you get interested in winemaking?

I was studying for my degree in chemistry and found summer employment at Korbel Champagne Cellars in 1965, and from there I came back and bugged them enough to finally get into their laboratory. I worked under Alan Hemphill and Adolf Heck, two of the most knowledgeable Champagne and sparkling wine men in the industry.

Did you study chemistry at Davis?

No, I took my bachelor's at Cal State Sacramento and then I went to Fresno and did some work in oenology. But my interest in oenology first came after I started at Korbel in 1965, and about '66 I decided the science of winemaking interested me. I had done everything from shoveling out fermenters to cleaning the rest rooms. I begged them to give me a job in the laboratory, even though they didn't really need anyone, but I talked them into letting me work in the lab on weekends. They found out I was competent and interested, and so I ran their night crews during one summer working 12 to 14 hours a day. I graduated from Cal State

Sacramento in '68, did my graduate work at Fresno, spent a very short time at the Davis summer session.

I was married in 1968 and moved to Fresno where I taught chemistry as a teacher's assistant while I took oenology courses at Fresno State College. I also traveled to Korbel on weekends. I then decided to leave Korbel and I went to work for Joe Vercelli at Swiss Colony at Asti. I spent abut a year there as chief production chemist, in charge of Champagne quality control. In January 1970 I joined Sonoma Vineyards under the able direction of Rod Strong as oenologist and winemaker. In 1973 I was promoted to vice president of production. In May of 1974 I left Sonoma Vineyards to join Château St. Jean as vice president and winemaker. The company was formed in 1973 by Robert and Edward Merzoian and Ken Sheffield, all agriculturists living in Visalia and Porterville. In November 1973 the trio purchased the Goff estate in Kenwood and embarked on the capital intensive wine business.

How many people do you have on the staff?

We have a cellarmaster and a cellarman who work full time, and we hire three or four others during crushing. We have a quality control manager, Milla Handley, who is a graduate oenologist; a very talented vineyard manager, Bernard Fernandez; sales manager, Robert Merzoian, Jr.; a maintenance man; plus other office people—probably a total of 15 full time persons.

How many wine types do you produce?

Three reds: Cabernet Sauvignon, Merlot and Zinfandel. In the whites: Chardonnay, Gewürztraminer, Riesling, Sauvignon Blanc, and a white Pinot Noir which is a by-product of our Champagne *cuvée.* All our wines are 100 percent varietals, with the exception of our Cabernet which we may blend with some Merlot and Cabernet Franc. And if a vineyard designation is on the label, it's 100 percent from that vineyard. We top with the same wine, we don't use the five percent from another year you're allowed. We have all the records to prove it. Our alcoholic contents stated on the label are exact, though you're legally allowed plus or minus one and a half percent. If we say it's 12.2, it's 12.2.

Is it difficult to keep track of and print labels for all your wines?

Not for a small winery.

How small are you?

When we finish in about two years, we'll reach about 30,000 cases per year.

What kind of yeast do you inoculate with to begin the fermentation?

For all whites but Riesling we use a Champagne strain, and for the Riesling I have a strain from Geisenheim. For the reds I have a yeast from the Pasteur Institute. At the crush we inject CO_2 through a little tube which ends down in the crusher, so once the grapes are crushed they're immediately blanketed in CO_2. From that point on through the processing, they are handled under an inert gas atmosphere. One thing carbon dioxide allows you to do is add less sulphur dioxide at the crush. We add just 60 to 70 parts per million, enough to inhibit the polyphenyloxidase browning, and that's it.

Do you ferment all in stainless steel?

Mostly. And we have many different sized fermenters to take care of the separate lots that come in varying amounts. We have 500 gallon fermenters, 1,000 gallon, 2,000 gallon, and 3,000 gallon. But Chardonnay and Pinot Blanc are also fermented in new French oak barrels.

What temperatures do you use in fermenting?

Chardonnay ferments at 47 to 50 degrees for the initial 10 to 12 degrees Brix, then finishes in new barrels without any temperature control, although it rarely exceeds 60 degrees in the barrels. The other whites ferment at 45 to 55 degrees, depending on the variety, and the reds at 75 to 80 degrees.

Do you let the Chardonnay sit on the skins for any length of time before fermenting?

Yes, depending on the condition of the fruit at the time of the crush, it would vary from several hours to several days.

Do you crush or ferment any of the wines with a portion of their stems?

Yes, some reds, and an occasional Chardonnay for style differences.

The Burgundians ferment Chardonnay entirely in new oak barrels. Do you think there is a difference in the wine if barrels are used rather than stainless steel?

Definitely. There seems to be better flavor extraction from new oak during fermentation in the barrels. But it must be done with care to avoid high, damaging temperatures.

How heavily do you press the wines, and how much of the press juice do you add back into the free run?

The bladder press is perhaps the most gentle of all presses; you get less juice yield but higher quality. The maximum pressure we use is 45 psi, approximately. Although we do separate free run and press juice, on occasion, I back blend some press wine with free run after fermentation and aging. The press wine often carries more character than the free run.

Do you have to adjust the acid on the grapes sometimes?

We try not to, and we don't normally. If we did we'd add tartaric; but I frown on that, I'd rather blend juice with juice to get the proper acid level.

I see you have a centrifuge.

Yes, that's $68,000 sitting right there, and I feel it's very important. We use it to clarify the juice before fermentation on almost every white wine. We also use it on some whites after fermentation, and I've experimented with centrifuging reds after fermentation rather than racking, and this has allowed us to market some "unfined and unfiltered" red wines.

Will you put "unfined and unfiltered" on the label?

Yes, but we'll also explain it was centrifuged. In some cases when we choose not to centrifuge, the label will say only "unfined and unfiltered."

Isn't that misleading, because centrifuging essentially does the same thing that fining and filtration do?

Absolutely not. Centrifuging removes insoluble solids. Filtration removes insoluble solids, but also absorbs some soluble compounds. Filtration takes out much of the beneficial odiferous substances, while I feel centrifugation, when properly used, does not. Taste and smell are chemical reactions. The things you taste and smell are soluble. If they are insoluble, you can't taste them or smell them—and we remove only the insolubles. The argument of some winemakers that the centrifuge removes too much just has no bearing on the matter, as long as the centrifuge is used properly. I'm glad you brought the question up. Let me tell you the reason most people don't have centrifuges: they are terribly expensive. It is hard to justify the expense, but the improved quality of the finished product justifies it for us. If you use the centrifuge improperly the wine becomes almost water white and tastes like not much of anything. You must know what you're doing. With Chardonnay, we start with probably 14 percent insoluble solids and bring it down to three to five percent insoluble solids. Riesling we take down to about three percent insoluble solids. All this does is hasten a settling technique. People who ferment without settling are only fooling themselves if they expect to produce a quality product. If you are making fine white wines you can either settle them before fermenting or you can centrifuge. Settling takes three days to three weeks, centrifuging does it right away and does it scientifically and precisely. Being somewhat of a scientist I like to use what I know best. The main reason I want the centrifuge is to start with clean juice. I like to sleep nights, and this is one of my insurance policies. Another insurance policy is a totally sterile bottling line, $150,000 worth of the finest equipment money will buy. It's made by Seitz in Germany, and at this time there is probably no other like it in this country.

Do you also filter the whites?

Yes, and the reason is we make some sweet wines. We stop fermentation by chilling before all the sugar is gone; if you leave any yeast in, it can start fermenting the sugar again.

Can't you remove all the yeast by centrifuging?

Bob Mondavi says you can, and has been very successful, but I haven't been able to accomplish it yet. I'm not sure you can with a sweet wine. When we have a sweet wine, we centrifuge, filter through cellulose and diatomaceous earth, then polish filter through a millipore filter which will remove particles of yeast and bacteria down to .65 microns.

Do you find a detectable difference between sweet wines done your way and those produced by adding a muté of sweet grape juice or concentrate?

Yes, there is a difference. The Germans are doing it, though, more now. I am quite a fan of German wines and probably have 50 or 60 cases of the '71 vintage alone in my cellar. Riesling is my favorite wine. I was at one of the best known wineries in '74 and they were saving their reserve of sweet juice and then adding it after fermentation, for a *spätlese.* It made me a little unhappy. There's definitely a difference in taste; to me, it tastes artificial, even though it's only juice.

What kind of cooperage do you have, and how long do you age the various wines?

We have new French oak we started with this year for Chardonnay, 60 gallon hogsheads, mostly Nevers and Limousin, some Allier and Tronçais. The Chardonnays are in all of these kinds of French oak for three months to a year depending on the age of the barrels. The Fumé Blanc is in American oak for three to six months, the Pinot Blanc in Limousin and Nevers for three months to a year, and the Riesling, Gewürztraminer, and sweet Sauvignon Blanc are not aged in wood at all. In the reds, I put the Cabernet Sauvignon and Merlot in Limousin and Nevers for one to two years, depending on the age of the wood, and the Zinfandel in American oak for the same length of time.

Do you think our best California wines are equal to the best wines of Europe?

Certain wines made in California are equal to if not better in some cases than their European counterparts. Chardonnay and Cabernet Sauvignon are examples. Pinot Noir still has a long way to go. Riesling is just breaking through as a top varietal. My vineyard manager, Bernard Fernandez, took our *trockenbeerenauslese* to Germany a month ago and was going to give it to somebody at the Seitz factory as a present. They were tasting the '75 *beerenausleses* and *trockenbeerenausleses* from the Rheingau area at the Geisenheim Institute and wanted to taste ours.

He was embarrassed, he said he hadn't brought it for a comparative tasting. But they said, "Let us taste it blind with the others." They put it in the blind tasting, and we got first place! They wouldn't believe it was really California wine, they just wouldn't believe it. Our quality for the present as well as the future rests primarily with the vineyards and winemaking techniques. It should be an exciting next ten years.

Mary Ann Graf

SIMI WINERY

Wines are like children: when they're born, they're dirty, smelly, hard to manage, and as they grow up they go through an adolescence . . . some of them have better breeding than others.

The lovely stone walls of Simi Winery grace the outskirts of the dreary little town of Healdsburg in northern Sonoma County. The Simi building, a contemporary of the railroad age, sits just yards from the tracks where its wines used to be loaded directly from cellar to boxcar. I stepped gingerly across the tracks and entered the winery, dim and cold inside, but warmed visually by endless rows of beautiful oak cooperage. Mary Ann Graf interrupted her work in the laboratory to sit and talk with me in the adjacent office, a room with high stone walls and thick window ledges giving a feeling of permanence you don't encounter in modern structures. Indeed, Simi wines have been appreciated in Sonoma for as long as anyone can remember. Nationally, the reputation of these wines has had its ups and downs over the decades, but in the 1970s—despite several rapid turnovers in ownership—Simi is once again a rising star. The reason lies in the consistently better winemaking techniques of Mary Ann Graf and the consulting aid of Andre Tchelistcheff.

Recommended wine to drink while reading this chapter:

SIMI
ROSÉ of CABERNET SAUVIGNON

You are one of the few women winemakers in California. Do people comment about that to you?

Sure, I get a lot of comment about it. I have never personally felt it was unusual for me to be in the business. Even through college I didn't think it was unusual to be the only woman in the class. I never gave it much thought. I was having a hard enough time staying in college to think about it. Oenology classes were the ones I did the best in, though. I think as long as I'm not reminded how unusual it is, it won't bother me. People ask me whether it was hard to find a job, whether I was discriminated against. I graduated from college at a very opportune time—there was a crying need for oenologists. I was able to work at a winery right away where I could get my hands dirty. I learned a hose from a hammer. A lot of *men* don't even get that opportunity now. And I've had a lot of jobs since then and I can't really say I've been discriminated against, but then discrimination is often such a subtle thing.

You are the fulltime winemaker, and you also have Andre Tchelistcheff here as a consultant don't you?

Yes, he and I started here at the same time, three years ago. Hopefully they'll keep me on! I am relatively new to this. Some of the things I'm saying may be shown to be wrong in the future but I'm learning, and I couldn't ask for a better teacher. I've gotten where I am more because of physical type of labor, rather than esoteric things. I'm more of a practical person, rather than a theorist. There are good male winemakers and mediocre male winemakers. You'll have to ask Andre whether he thinks I have the potential to be great someday, but I'm going to be judged as anybody else is judged.

How did you become interested in a winemaking career?

I don't come from a winemaking or even a wine drinking background. I do come from a California agricultural background. We didn't live on a farm but my father taught vocational agriculture in high school. In college my academic strengths were more in sciences than in letters, so I majored in food science. Late in my second year I took Introduction to Wine Appreciation, which I think every undergraduate at Davis takes, and I really got excited about it. Winemaking encompassed all the things I was interested in—microbiology, plant pathology, engineering, the whole range. I graduated from Davis in 1965 with a major in oenology. I've been at Simi for four crushes now. Before coming here I worked at Sonoma Vineyards for a few months, did some consulting for Scott Laboratories, and worked for United Vintners in product development at Asti. Right out of college, I worked for the Gibson Wine Company.

You know winemakers are jacks-of-all-trades and masters of none. When I was in college, my future seemed to be in quality control for some food canner (which didn't interest me) or in doing research, and I frankly don't have the drive, or what at the time I felt was the genius, to go into research. It was the production aspect of wine I liked the most, working with your hands, though connected with your head. That's inspired from the way I grew up.

Is it essentially true that Simi was a bulk winery until Russell Green took it over in 1970?

Immediately before he took over I think it was. But in the past it produced premium wines. Its heyday was before and after Prohibition. When Mr. Green bought it from the Simi family, there were some 1935 and 1941 wines in the bottle here, and we were selling some 1935 Zinfandel, Pinot Noir and Cabernet. Also some old Carignane.

Were they good?

Yes, especially in an academic sense. When wines get to be that old there's great variation from bottle to bottle. They were all recorked in '71 or '72.

When was the winery built?

The winery was started in 1876. These buildings were built around 1904. Pietro and Giuseppe Simi had a winery in San Francisco and came north looking for sites. They called it Montepulciano for many years, after their home in Italy. They died shortly after it was completed, and Isabelle Simi and another relative carried it on. She was then about 14 years old and she is still here. She keeps track of receipts, works in the tasting room, and greets a lot of the customers who have been coming here for years and years. It's fascinating to talk to her. Mr. Green bought it from her in '70 and sold it to Scottish & Newcastle Company in '74 who produce Scotch and beer in Europe. Then it was just sold once again, to the Schieffelin Company in '76.

Is this a large winery?

We bottle 75,000 cases a year, about two-thirds of it red wine and one-third white. So it's medium sized, as north coast wineries go.

Does the winery own its vineyards or buy its grapes?

We own only three acres of Johannisberg Riesling, and we contract with Russell Green to buy his grapes. Green owns about 250 acres, of all varieties. We buy a few grapes from others in Alexander Valley, for example, some very old Zinfandel.

Are they all nearby?

Yes, they are in the Alexander Valley which stretches between Geyserville to just southeast of Healdsburg in Sonoma County, adjacent to Dry Creek Valley. I think other winemakers would agree that the Alexander Valley does have certain characteristics that appear in the wines, just as Dry Creek or Sonoma Valley do. We talk about the earthiness of Alexander Valley wines. Whether that is complimentary or not remains to be seen. We're only dealing with ten years, which is a very short time to learn about an area. But I think it's interesting that we're developing the Alexander Valley as an appellation area.

What is its temperature region classification?

It's a high Region II, but there are micro-climatic differences within it. That regional classification system has limited use; there's much more to it than temperature. The exposure is important, whether it's hillside or river bottom soil is important, the viticultural practices are crucial.

Are Green's vineyards hillside or river bottom areas?

About half and half.

How is harvesting done?

Some grapes are hand picked, into buckets which go into little bins, about two tons each. We do some mechanical harvesting on our Cabernet; Mr. Green was one of the first in the area to harvest mechanically. The final results aren't in yet on mechanical harvesting of certain white varieties. You can provoke a lot of arguments on quality of the must, though I think it can be done if you crush in the field along with the harvesting. It will be quite a few years before we have the answers. Cabernet, however, can be successfully harvested mechanically. You get good separation of the grapes from the vines and little juicing.

Do you get any immature grapes picked along with the mature ones?

No, those stay on the vine. That's one advantage of mechanical harvesting. The second crop which is usually less mature remains behind.

With the hand picked grapes, do you ever have the pickers harvest selectively, in sections of the vineyard that are more mature than others?

We obviously can't say, "Pick this row, don't pick that row." We have to be flexible. But just before the grapes mature, I'll go out twice a week and check for maturity, and I'll tell them we'd like the Riesling, for example, to be brought in tomorrow if at all possible, or let's wait until next week. Communication between the winery and the vineyard manager is of utmost importance. Some parts of the vineyard mature at different times than others. Then, yes, we may only pick one section before the others. Pickers aren't always available, but what we try to do is get the grapes at the right time. Most of the acreage, by the way, is in Cabernet and those grapes do mature at different times.

How many wines do you produce?

About nine. The reds are Cabernet, Pinot Noir, Zinfandel, Gamay Beaujolais. We make a Rosé of Cabernet Sauvignon which is 100 percent Cabernet. The whites are Chardonnay, Johannisberg Riesling, Gewürztraminer and Chenin Blanc.

Are the varietals all 100 percent of the varietal grape?

Pretty much. The Cabernet has anywhere from 10 to 30 percent Merlot, that's a discretionary thing. Pinot Noir is 100 percent, Zinfandel 100 percent, Gamay Beaujolais is 100 percent.

What is the Simi wine style? Can you describe it, is it different from other Sonoma County wines?

Yes, in the past, and even now, Simi wines seem to have a certain inherent style probably due to the cooperage in the winery. There seems to be some continuity in taste, a certain mellowness. This is my third year here, and I'm not sure yet what it's derived from. It could be a combination of the winery and where the grapes have come from.

Our winemaking philosophy *has* changed in the last two years. When Andre and I started here we changed the production practices. Press wine is now immediately added back into all the red wines. We induce malo-lactic fermentation right after the primary fermentation. They were getting a malo-lactic fermentation before, but not as controlled. I think it makes a difference whether it occurs right after the primary fermentation or a year and a half later when it's aging. Sometimes you have to control the natural events.

Are you a naturalist, then, or are you of the scientific school?

Neither really. In the naturalist school there are hit and miss things, and I think as winemakers we should use the available tools of winemaking. I don't want to rule out the University of California as being a total waste of time! Research is certainly a very valuable part of winemaking. On the other hand, I'm not saying wine is built strictly from science either; there is tremendous art and luck to it, and feel for it. You have to be open to learning new things. Take Andre, he's still learning. There's no room for complacency. Winemaking isn't the same day after day—you have winemaking and production problems that come up and are exciting. Science hasn't explained all these problems, that's what's fascinating. Even when we can explain them, we may not be able to control them.

How do you ferment the red wines?

In open redwood fermenters. There are pros and cons regarding redwood or stainless steel. I'm not going to promote either open redwood fermenters, or stainless steel, but I like the redwood because they are built so you get an efficient cap-to-juice ratio in pumping over. The heat transfer is more efficient, though occasionally pockets of heat do build up. The stainless steel fermenters cannot be built as wide, they're taller and narrower. If they are not designed for efficient pumping over, then they're not as useful. One real advantage stainless has, though, is cooling jackets and versatility as storage tanks. We have some stainless steel which we use for reds when we have an overage when the redwood ones are full. So each winery has equipment that is suited for its specific needs—those needs are usually not obvious to the layman who is anxious to give all kinds of advice.

How do you control temperature in the redwood?

We pump the wine through a heat exchanger.

Are the whites fermented in stainless steel?

Yes. They're crushed and go through a dejuicer. We pump the juice directly into a chilled stainless tank and it settles. The skins are pressed lightly and we take that juice too. We also have a centrifuge. We're learning about that. We don't usually centrifuge the juice, we settle it and then start fermentation in a cooled tank, about 55 to 65 degrees. I'm learning about that too. It isn't arbitrarily better the cooler you do it. Each year you learn that maybe you're going to make some changes the next year. Hindsight is always 20/20.

Do you start fermentation with a yeast starter?

Yes, we get two yeast cultures from the Pasteur Institute in Paris. I believe they are both polycultures, that is, a mixture of various strains. Each culture results in different characteristics in the final wine as dictated also by the grapes, the climate, and an infinite number of variables.

Prior to adding the yeast, you add sulphur at the crush to stun the wild yeast. How much do you add?

For a white wine, between 50 and 60 parts per million, which I'm sure sounds low to you. We feel it isn't necessary to go any higher. With a very low fermentation temperature and a high SO_2, it's possible to get off flavors. We don't get excessive browning or wild yeast taking over, we get a good, clean fermentation. Of course the grapes must be in excellent condition.

Why not rely on the natural wine yeast on the grape skins to ferment the wine?

That's academically interesting, and excellent wines have been made that way, but it's been adequately shown there is more danger of picking up off flavors and odors that way. It isn't practical; we have to also think of the commercial aspect.

When do you use your centrifuge?

Immediately after the wines are fermented dry. We're talking about the white wines and rosés, as we rarely use it on the reds. Its function is to remove the wine from the gross lees. It is really beneficial to separate the wine from its lees as soon as possible after fermentation. Economically, it frees fermentation tanks for subsequent musts. People object to the word "hastens" when you tell them a centrifuge hastens the process, because they think you're artificially accelerating aging, and traditionally wines are supposed to "sleep" for years. But all it does is allow you to get the wine off the lees faster. Nobody likes to sit around in their own —— and wines are the same way. Andre and I talk about how wines are like children: when they're born, they're dirty, smelly, hard to manage, and as they grow up they go through an adolescence . . . some of them have better breeding than others.

Do you also fine the whites?

Yes, we do judicious fining, just as we do judicious centrifuging. The naturalist school says no fining is the best fining. But fining is what the word implies. Each wine requires different fining but generally the whites require some bentonite. The reds get some gelatin fining. They're cold stabilized at about 40 degrees, given this gelatin, and then bulk filtered—coarse filtered, to get out the rocks—and then they are ready to go into barrels.

What kind of barrels are they?

Our small cooperage is divided between American oak in which we age Cabernet, and Limousin and Allier barrels for aging Pinot Noir and Chardonnay. We partially ferment the Chardonnay in those barrels, incidentally. We ferment them down to about eight degrees sugar in stainless steel and then finish off the fermentation in the barrels.

Why do you divide the fermentation of the Chardonnay that way?

Partially for temperature control. In the barrel the heat during fermentation can build up rather rapidly. The other reason is that room has a wooden floor and barrel fermentation is very messy in the initial stages. The wine spills out of the barrels onto the floor, and we can't hose down the wooden floor very easily.

What does that method give to the Chardonnay that fermentation entirely in stainless steel would not give it?

What I think it gives it, and this is a limited observation, is that it gets a jump on the development of the Chardonnay character.

Are you talking about oakiness?

Fermentation and aging in small oak enables the wine to clear itself more efficiently; it requires less handling. I'm talking about the character, the class that Chardonnay develops, which can only be developed in wood—depending on the style; there are several styles. I don't think we'll ever have a Montrachet in California, at least in the numbers I'd like to see. I don't think this area is particularly capable of it, but that's not to say the Chardonnay isn't good, it's just a different style.

You fine, filter and centrifuge. Is it really necessary to employ all three, do you risk taking character from the wine?

That's why I say we do it judiciously. We may do all, we may do one, depending on the wine. That's why I have a job. You can't really cookbook them. I can't tell my cellarmaster go down there and do all these things to each wine. That's why you have to live with them, to know what they each need.

How many years do you hold the wines in the barrels?

Because of the age of our cooperage, particularly the French barrels, the wine stays from a year to 18 months. The American barrels are relatively new, and I could try to impress you by saying we keep them in there a minimum of two years, but that doesn't apply, because your wine would reek of oak. The oaky character is certainly something you want, but the other benefits that are derived are much more important.

Do you rack the wines?

In the case of reds, we rack the wines after the light gelatin fining we give them, and after the malo-lactic fermentation, which is a very odorous process, there is a great deal of racking and aeration that goes on then as a sort of cleaning process.

Do you bottle age the wines before selling them?

Definitely. On Chardonnay, I demand and usually get at least a year. Same with Cabernet, usually a year in the bottle. The Chardonnay is usually in oak about six months, though that varies with the age of the barrels too.

What is the effect on winemaking when a winery is bought by a big corporation like this one has been twice now in two years?

When wineries are bought by corporations, there's usually a great advantage gained because of the corporation's marketing abilities. And also, you are able to make improvements that probably couldn't have been made otherwise. For instance, we bought a centrifuge, and installed the dejuicing system, and those things are expensive.

Is the winemaker ever reined in by the board of directors?

No, I don't feel that way, though I've seen it with some of my friends elsewhere. Certainly there are compromises to be made but in our case they are not compromises of quality, but rather matters such as how much of which wine will be bottled, whether we will produce this wine or another wine, that sort of thing. You have to remember I'm working for a commercial winery. I don't feel inhibited in my creativity, but if I were independently wealthy and had my own winery I could treat it as my toy. That's not the case here.

Earlier, you were comparing our Chardonnays with French Montrachets. How do you rate the best California wines compared with the best European wines?

Good question. There really is no answer. I recently spent three weeks in France with a group of vintners and viticulturists guided by Andre. We saw great châteaux, cooperatives and some very small, little known wineries. We tasted over 300 wines and talked and listened and questioned for three solid weeks! It was an intensive learning experience but one that, for me, raised more questions than it answered. Basic winemaking is the same the world over, the methods are all "cousins." The wines are different but the same in many ways. Quality is often measured differently by the oenologist than by the connoisseur or by the consumer. The French wine drinker does not mull over the chemical aspects of his wines. For example, how long the juice remained on the skins is not information he uses to make a quality judgment. He enjoys each wine only for what it is.

So, to rate the best French against the best American is an exercise. Does it matter? The consumer has to make the choice and in many instances in America, he is not prepared adequately to do that. I don't think that giving him all the specifics on the back of the label is the answer. We'd be promoting a quality judgment based on the consumer's knowledge of winemaking practices.

August Sebastiani

SEBASTIANI VINEYARDS

Look, my dad taught me this stuff and some of it I don't tell anybody but my kids.

He likes to pose as a "dumb farmer" (his phrase), and you might mistake him for one if you were to see him striding through his winery in bib overalls and straw hat, letting loose earthy expletives and joking with the tourists who stand three deep in the tasting room. But August Sebastiani has been out-maneuvering city slickers for a long time. His overalls happen to be custom tailored, and his earthy speech disguises marketing skills that have dazzled Madison Avenue and have built Sebastiani Vineyards into one of the largest premium wineries in California. When I interviewed him in late 1975, he indicated the previous year's sales were 500,000 cases, but when the '75 figures came in sales had more than doubled to over a million cases, an increase due largely to August's innovation of putting varietal wines in half-gallon jugs. His son Sam signs a newsletter to customers every month filled with reports on dad's birds and wild ducks (his hobby), mama's spaghetti sauce recipe, or sister's new baby. But between the lines of homespun gossip, the newsletter is professionally written and provides viticultural and winemaking information of such caliber that the issues could be bound into a wine encyclopedia. That seems to be the Sebastiani plan: project a homey image, but make no little plans for the wines.

How good are the wines? The Sebastiani forte has been sound, reasonably priced wines with noticeable, if not intense, varietal character. Some of the well aged Cabernet Sauvignons, the Barberas, and a new "Swan's Eye" colored Pinot Noir Blanc, have inspired wine critics to utter superlatives. We may hear more such superlatives now that the Sebastianis' financial success is enabling them to replace some of the ancient winery equipment and to concentrate occasionally on small batches of wine.

I talked to August Sebastiani in his office, a cramped, converted house across from the winery—no pretentious executive suite for him! He sat there in his striped overalls, and seemed right at home.

Recommended wine to drink while reading this chapter:

SEBASTIANI VINEYARDS
BARBERA

How long have the Sebastianis been making wine in Sonoma?

My father founded this winery back in 1904. He immigrated from Italy as a youngster, went to work in a San Francisco vegetable garden, saved a few bucks, enough to get him up here to Sonoma, worked in the hills as a woodcutter and driving a team of horses, and when he had enough money together he bought himself a 500 gallon wine tank and started from there. We still have the same tank.

The Sonoma region was already famous at that time for its wines, wasn't it?

That's right. In the late 1800s the Sonoma Valley was covered with vineyards. At one time there were 50 or 60 wineries: nearly every ranch of any size had its own winery. The whole valley was a blanket of vines. They'd make wine, then sell it to the bigger firms with facilities for filtering and bottling. Then, close to the turn of the century, phylloxera moved in here and wiped out most of the vineyards. My father came after the phylloxera plague, when all was being reestablished. But it never recovered to what it had been in the 1890s.

You must have grown up and spent your entire life around a winery.

I was born 14 feet from a wine tank. And by 1928 I started to help my dad's old bookkeeper doing government records and so on, because I was one of only two people who could understand my dad's hieroglyphics, his Italian writing. He never did go to school. He couldn't read English, and learned to read and write Italian the hard way. My dad passed away in 1944, and I've been running the winery since 1937 when I got out of college.

Since you grew up at the winery, I guess you had no need for any training at Davis.

No, my dad had his ideas, and we still have our own ideas. We have people from Davis, but we superimpose our wills on them when it comes to certain facets of winemaking methods and taste.

What is the size of your annual production?

Right now, between 400,000 and 500,000 cases a year. We're getting close to the point where we're going to level off. We don't want to become so large that we lose control of our quality, where it is a grind instead of a pleasurable business.

Is it tougher to make fine wines for a large winery like yours than for a small winery?

You can't be a big winery and make good wines unless you have the proper facilities. You can't make special little lots of wine if you have only large tanks. This is why our new fermenting room has batteries of 800 gallon tanks. They're a pain in the neck for most wineries, but we have them. Actually, we have better control than a small winery: better equipment for temperatures, for storage, more know-how, more supervision. Being a boutique sized winery is no insurance of quality, any more than—if you go a step further—home winemaking is an insurance of quality. Some of the worst slop I ever drank is the stuff I've been exposed to by home winemakers. Size is not all of it, you have to have equipment, know-how, and, more important than anything, dedication for damn hard work.

Do you own a large percentage of the vineyards where you get grapes?

No, we only own around 300 acres of vineyards. I maintain those as a nucleus for certain kinds of wine. I contract the rest of our grapes, and I've got farmers I buy from without contracts we've been buying from since the days they came in here with teams of horses. If I could have my way, I wouldn't have a grapevine because a farmer can do a better job, easier, than I can while I'm also trying to run a winery. It would be like trying to run a glass plant and owning a cork grove—you can't do everything.

Which varieties are planted on your 300 acres?

I have Barbera, Green Hungarian, Traminer, Pinot Chardonnay—some of your top varieties used for special purposes.

Are your growers all located in Sonoma County?

The majority are Sonoma County growers. However, I do get a few grapes out of Napa, Mendocino and Solano Counties, special grapes for special purposes.

Do you have special vineyards which give you grapes you like to keep separate, to make wines from them alone?

We have done that in the past, though we haven't identified them as such. We are in the process of keeping them separate and some will be so labeled in the future. I take great pride in the Cabernet that comes from what we call our old cherry block. It's right here next to my home, up on some real rocky, red soil; it makes one hellish good wine. We've kept that wine separate in the past, but it wasn't identified separately. Starting this fall, those things will be earmarked.

About what tonnage to the acre does that vineyard produce?

It varies, naturally, it'll go from three to four and a half tons to the acre. It's not a big yield, but they're darn good grapes.

Do you believe hillside vineyards generally produce better grapes than floor vineyards?

Oh yes, I think your hills do. I think grapes forced to suffer and fight a little always taste better. I don't know if you've ever hiked in the hills and come across an old pear or apple tree growing wild, fighting for existence, and eaten fruit off the tree that's never been pruned, sprayed, cultivated or irrigated. Remember the taste of that apple compared with an apple grown on the flat, fertilized and watered to hell. If you've done that, you know the answer yourself. It's like going out and picking a wild blackberry and comparing its taste with something you get from the truck farmer.

Would you like to see the appellations of origin in Sonoma County and other north coast areas more fully developed?

No. And I'm very outspoken when I say no. Not until there is a quality control standard set up. There are Sonoma County grapes not worth a hoop, Napa County grapes that are just as bad, and grapes in Mendocino that are even worse. Why should we hold an umbrella over that quality, at the expense of true quality, without some sort of a panel to approve quality? To give a blanket endorsement to a region is no good.

So you envision a tasting panel of experienced people who would pass on the quality of the wines?

Yes, and say this wine is fit to bear this seal. Otherwise it'd be a phony.

Would you favor a change in the requirement that only 75 percent of a nonvintage wine come from the appellation area stated on the label? Should it be higher?

There again, there should be some tie-in with quality. If 75 percent of the grapes come from Sonoma County, and 50 percent of those come from an area I consider no good, what the hell does the 75 percent mean? It's just 75 percent junk. If they're going to do it, they should go a step further, and control cultural practices.

You mean pruning, vine spacing, irrigation and so forth?

Exactly, and when to pick them, the whole works. If you preclude certain areas from being entitled to an appellation of origin, and you give this privilege to a select few in choice locations, they may become greedy and start overcropping, leaving 20 eyes on cane instead of five, force watering.

So what you'd really like to see is something like the French appellation control system that does regulate those practices.

Actually, I wouldn't like to see anything that involves work, red tape and more Amos and Andy stuff. Being a family controlled winery I'm against anything that involves more red tape, more routine, more slow up. In my particular case, I have my own appellation control with the name Sebastiani. I put nothing in the bottle that isn't worthy of the name. I figure that's better than any appellation.

What is the Sebastiani style of wine?

You might say it's a Sonoma style wine. About the only one with a similar wine is Louis Martini. Of course, they have a large vineyard here in Sonoma that poor old Louis was very fond of.

How would you describe that style?

I can't describe taste to you any more than you can describe it to me. How would you describe the taste of a banana if you didn't have something to compare it with? I'd say our wines are less earthy than Napa wines, have more body than Solano wines, are bigger than Mendocino wines. We have less oak in our wines than many north coast wineries, for several reasons. Some wineries, for economic reasons, try to speed up their aging by putting wines in 50 gallon oak barrels. Others do it because they want the character of oak, whether it be American or Limousin oak. I can't say it's an unpleasant taste, I just don't feel heavy oak taste is desirable to a majority of the American public. We give our heavy bodied reds about three and a half years in redwood of various sizes, and then finish them off in American oak barrels—and we use a few French in combination with them—for an average of about six months.

You market nearly a dozen varietal wines plus some generics. Are your varietals 100 percent of the varietal grape, or does that change?

It depends on the bottling, we don't have any fixed rule. Naturally we have the 51 percent rule, you can't go below that. But some wines we produce at a higher percentage than others. It's all a matter of taste. This is not a computer-run operation, it's a matter of tasting and comparing.

As you approximate 100 percent of the varietal grape in a wine, the more varietal character of that grape will come through. Do you have any wines in which you shoot for virtually 100 percent to get that strong varietal character?

Actually, very few. This is a misconception of the American public. Take Cabernet Sauvignon. They think a French Bordeaux from a chateau is 100 percent Cabernet Sauvignon. This is the furthest thing in the world from the truth. In France, they not only blend, but some of your better chateaus actually interplant their vineyards with Cabernet Franc, and Merlot. And if you ask the chateau owner for the basis of his blends, he promptly, clearly and very firmly says it's none of your business.

There has been talk for many years about raising the 51 percent requirement. What is your view on that?

I don't think it's necessary for this reason: the wine business is competitive. I know the only reason we are as successful as we are is that we're meticulous with our quality. I won't cut my nose off by putting out something inferior and doing something short range. But if I think that 55 or 60 percent tastes better than 90 percent of the grape, I'm going to put it at 55. After all, I have 200 million people out there to judge those wines for me. So just because some author says he thinks it should be 95 percent, and he's never made wine in his life, I could care less what he thinks. See what I mean?

What would you think of the idea of leaving it so a wine could carry the varietal name at 51 percent, but also requiring the other grapes used to be listed on the label for the consumer? The notion is that a wine named after a grape which is only 51 percent of the wine is not wholly forthright to the consumer.

When you buy a package of Betty Crocker cake mix do you ask what kind of grain was used in the mix? I'd be opposed to it. We're very jealous of what we've got, and if you were to ask me a question about certain things, quite frankly, and I hope you wouldn't be insulted, I'd simply tell you I'd rather not answer that question. People come in here and ask me where do you get your grapes, what kind of grapes do you use for this and that—that's like asking me for the combination to my safe.

Look, my dad taught me this stuff and some of it I don't tell anybody but my kids. This is the difference between me and some other guy. What else do you have? Anybody can send to the University and get an oenologist trained by Dr. Amerine and the other professors up there. They all go through the same school, same books, same methods. What have you got? You've got a bunch of canned peas.

Well, nevertheless, let me try some general questions about your winemaking methods. First, what kind of fermenters do you have?

Until this year we've used open top concrete tanks. This year we installed stainless steel tanks, all beautifully temperature controlled to within one degree, and we'll use them primarily for fermentation of the whites. However, we won't complete fermentation in stainless steel, we'll use wood in conjunction for certain problems. People who use stainless steel exclusively have developed some horrible off tastes and odors. Apparently some of the hydrogen sulfide escapes through the wood, or because of the wood, and in stainless steel it is trapped. I've seen some whites produced entirely in stainless steel and you couldn't walk in the same room with them or they'd stink you out.

Do you inoculate with yeast to get fermentation started?

At the beginning of the season, yes.

What kind of yeast do you use?

Well, that's one question I'm going to take a pass on.

Do you fine and filter all the wines?

In the case of the white wines we'll occasionally use gelatin, or on rare occasions isinglass, but mostly plain old bentonite. And we filter and we cold stabilize so the wines don't break down when exposed to the cold.

In the case of the reds we fine and filter them too. Then, with Zinfandel and Gamay Beaujolais, they peak out in a year or two, and we sell them relatively young. In the case of your bigger red wines, your Barberas, your Pinots, your Cabernets and others, they average about three and a half years in redwood, six months in small oak cooperage and then a year in glass. We're firm believers in bottle age. When I bottled our 1968 Cabernet I could have sold every bottle right off the bottling line, because there was a terrific Cabernet shortage. But it needed bottle age, and we kept it in glass for almost two years. Most of our vintage wines sit in glass for darn near a year before we turn them loose. We're fortunate in that we get a malo-lactic fermentation in many of our bottled wines, and this is the difference between a good and a great wine.

You don't mean you get it in the bottle, do you?

In many cases we get it in the bottle. You can't be sure when you will get it, or even if you will get it. The bottle age we give the wines is good, for many reasons, and one of them is I'd be afraid to release them for fear I'd get a delayed malo-lactic. People would call in and say "I've got a fizzy wine." So we keep it beyond the calculated danger period.

Do you ever adjust sweetness with concentrate, or add acid to adjust acid levels?

No, we don't use concentrate here, we're fortunate to get proper sugar in our grapes. Occasionally, we will add a little citric acid when the grapes are deficient and need toning up.

In '75 you came out with jug wines with varietal labels: Cabernet Sauvignon, Pinot Noir and Pinot Chardonnay. That caused quite a stir. How did you decide to do it?

We were sitting here looking at close to three quarters of a million gallons of all ages of Cabernet Sauvignon, and saw a mountain sized wave of the same grapes coming at us this fall and a bigger mountain next fall, and out there we had an American public clamoring for something they could afford. I was sitting here with it, they were out there wanting to buy it. People were telling me don't sell it in half gallon jugs, that's sacreligious, you're destroying your image, you'll ruin yourself. I said B.S. and we did it. It was just a matter of horse sense. We became national heros for just using horse sense. We got write ups in I think 2,000 newspapers because we broke the phoniness barrier by giving a person a good buy.

How were you able to do it—the grapes in those wines a few years ago were very expensive.

Fine, so I should sit here and cry in my soup because I paid $1,000 for grapes that I'm selling on a basis of $400? I know I'm going to replace them for even under $400. You don't have to be a mathematical genius, you just have to figure to even out, get rid of it. A lot of people had the same idea, but they didn't have the back-up stocks I had to play with. We'd been accumulating excessive stocks of these wines. The half gallon thing was a relief valve because I had more than I needed.

Did those wines receive less than the usual aging period?

Much less: the Cabernets and Pinot Noirs averaged two and a half years of age. And they're blended down, blended down with a softer wine than we use for our regular Cabernet and regular Pinot Noir, to round them out and make them more drinkable at an earlier age. But I'll tell you something, for the money they're a terrific buy. Sometimes I wonder if they're not *too* good for the money.

When you compare California and European wines, do you find our best wines are equal to their best?

I think you've got good wines in both. Are bananas better than oranges? I'd rather let the public answer that question.

Mendocino County:

THE NORTHERN FRONTIER

You feel far north in Mendocino County. It lies beyond comfortable commuting distance of San Francisco and you encounter only an occasional small town, the highway, mountains and trees—lots of trees. This is California redwood territory, lumber country more than wine country. But a glance at the map shows it is a natural extension of the coastal ranges and valleys that host so many wineries in Sonoma and Napa. Its northern latitude does not make it cold; growing season temperatures are much like those in the Napa Valley, ranging from Region I to III. But Mendocino has never developed the winemaking prestige of its southern neighbors, apparently because no one attempted to make truly fine wines there until recently. Now, the Fetzers and Parduccis have created a runaway fine wine business based in the Russian River Valley. Additional vineyards have been planted in the cool mountains nearer to the coast and a couple of tiny, new wineries have opened in the same area. Mendocino has become the northern frontier of fine California wine.

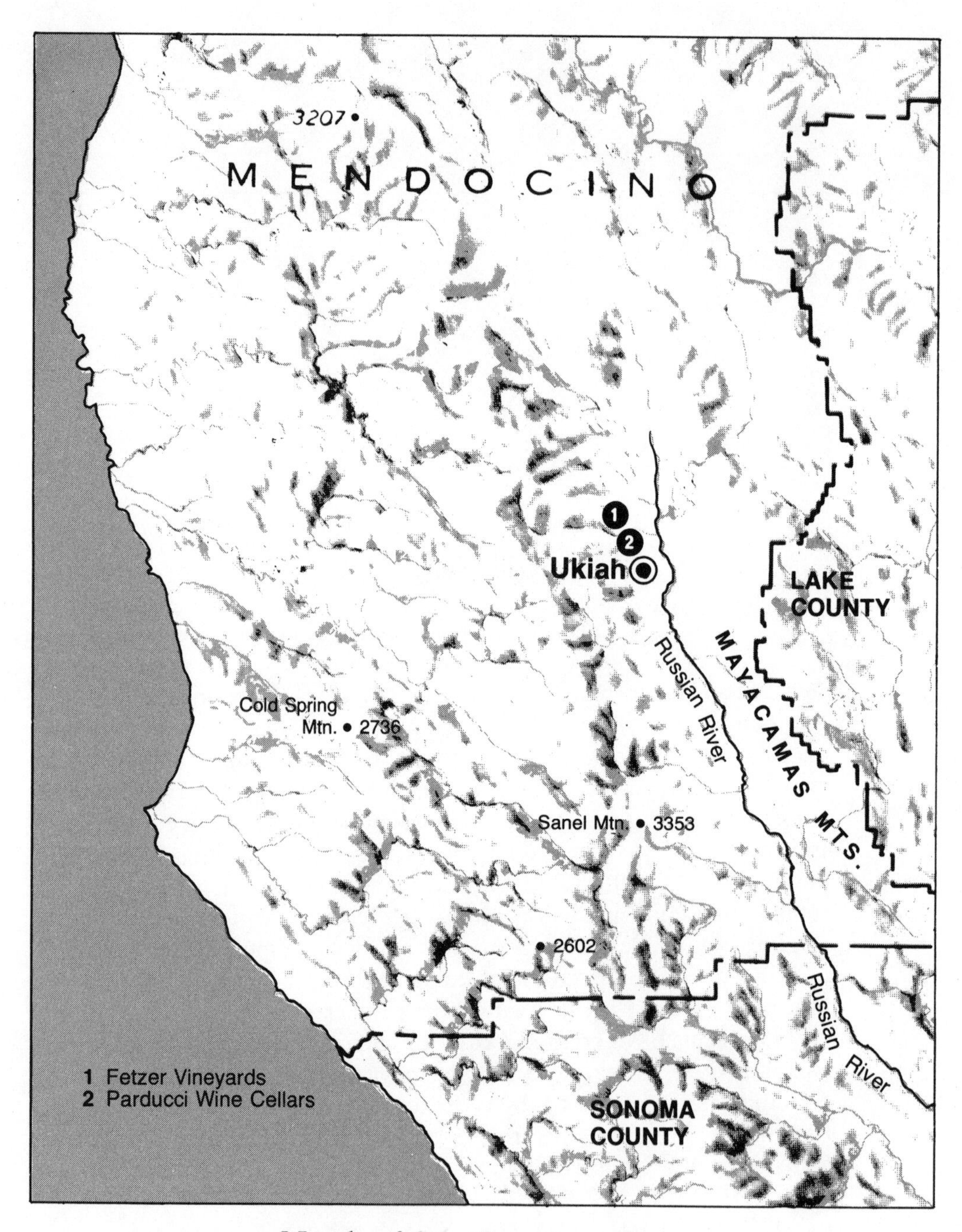

North of San Francisco Bay
MENDOCINO COUNTY: The Northern Frontier

Bernard Fetzer

FETZER VINEYARDS

You don't make fine wine with people who at ten minutes to five look at their watches and say, "Let's start rolling up the hose, boys, it's five o'clock." You have to have dedication.

The Fetzer ranch is tucked against benchland hills at the end of a long country lane, the white house surrounded by grassy shade—the winery standing across the way where you would expect to see a barn. This is one of the northernmost reaches of fine California winemaking, and the Fetzer family seems isolated and self-sufficient. But in no time at all the Fetzers have become major competitors in the fine wine market, their sales multiplying twenty-fold from their tiny beginning in 1968. The Fetzer formula for this success appears to be moderate prices, good varietal character and sometimes a pronounced oakiness. Though it is perhaps too early to tell whether there is a "Mendocino flavor" or a "Fetzer style," it is clear there are fascinating tastes at reasonable cost in Fetzer wines.

We sat and looked out at the woods while we discussed wine in Bernard Fetzer's comfortable, book-lined study on the winery's top floor. As I was leaving, a middle-aged Austrian couple on a tour of the United States arrived. Their surname was also Fetzer, and they had come thousands of miles to meet their American counterparts whose wine label they had somehow spotted in Europe. The Fetzer winery is not so isolated after all.

Recommended wine to drink while reading this chapter:

FETZER
PETITE SYRAH

Your winery is relatively new, isn't it?

The winery was built in 1968; however, we've been here for 20 years, planting vineyards and shipping varietal grapes to home winemakers throughout the United States. I had been in the lumber business, but now I spend my full time in the wine business, as do my three sons and three of my daughters.

Does a small, family winery like yours have an advantage over large wineries in the making of truly fine wines?

In my opinion, big wineries will seldom make great wines with any consistency. In the first place, they can't isolate small, beautiful lots of grapes. They say they can, but you will find that they have mostly 20,000 to 100,000 gallon tanks. We started this winery pretty much as a hobby in the beginning. As a result, we probably have more small fermenters than most wineries in California and we can isolate small lots of special grapes. For instance, you may get ten tons of beautiful Cabernet Sauvignon off a certain slope. To isolate that lot you have to have a 1,500 gallon fermenter, and you have to keep the grapes separate while they are fermenting, and then you must separate the wine in the aging cellar. It requires tremendous effort and recordkeeping. If the winemaker at a big winery wants to ferment a certain red wine for two weeks, he finds it impossible. As he looks out his window he sees 100 grape trucks lining up at the crusher. He has to get the fermentation vats emptied and ready for the next surge of grapes. Fine wine must be made at a leisurely pace—its making doesn't fit into corporate production schedules.

The wine business in California will evolve down to two types of wineries: big, giant corporate owned factories that turn out jug wines, and small, family owned châteaux which turn out the great wines. The corporate winery that attempts to make fine wines producing 50,000 to 100,000 cases per year will not be a feasible financial endeavor. You don't make fine wine with people who at ten minutes to five look at their watches and say, "Let's start rolling up the hose, boys, it's five o'clock." You have to have dedication. The small premium wineries have a place in our market, and I think as our young people become sophisticated about wine, the small wineries will have an expanding market.

How many cases a year do you make?

Roughly, 50,000 cases per year.

Was the great wine boom of the late 1960s instrumental in your decision to open a winery in 1968?

I think it was primarily the desire to have an integrated operation, to see our grapes go down the driveway in the form of a bottle of wine rather than in a gondola full of grapes. Another great incentive was the fact that Mendocino County was an unknown region and we wanted to let the world know about our region and what great wines can be grown here. Also, we sold grapes to amateur winemakers, most of them very scientific people—a lot of nuclear scientists, doctors, dentists, architects, engineers—who would buy our Cabernet Sauvignon, Sauvignon Blanc and other varietals to make their wines, and return each year with samples. They believed these Mendocino wines from this far north area possessed a lot of finesse and quality. I decided if it was their opinion that the wines possessed these qualities, we should build a winery. We started by making just 6,000 gallons the first year, and each year we've expanded.

Do you own all your own vineyards, or do you buy grapes from others in the area?

We have about 120 acres here. We buy about 50 percent of our grapes from other growers.

Which varietals are planted on your own 100 acres?

Mostly Cabernet Sauvignon, Sauvignon Blanc and Sémillon. I felt this soil and climate were similar to the Bordeaux region, so we selected basically Bordeaux varieties.

What is the soil like?

It's all benchland, very gravelly and heavy clay soils. Good drainage, and none of the deep loamy soils you get along the river bottoms.

How many tons per acre do these vineyards yield?

Our Cabernet yields two tons per acre. Another interesting way to put it is that each acre produces roughly 120 cases of wine per year. I think you first start making wine when you go into the vineyard in the fall with your pruning shears. We prune as do many of the châteaux in Europe. Château Lafite-Rothschild has boasted that each vine is pruned to yield one glass of wine. Their production is about two tons to the acre. We keep our vines restricted to that level. Of course, in Europe, they have many more vines per acre. Most of our vines are planted 6 by 12 feet. We find that's best on our benchland soil.

Are the vineyards from which you buy grapes all in Mendocino County?

Yes, we've never made any wine from grapes other than Mendocino grapes. We believe wineries should restrict their crush to a definite region, so they can offer consistency in the product. We will be crushing some Lake County grapes which is a region very similar to Mendocino.

Where is the Redwood Valley geographically?

It lies six miles north of Ukiah, which is the county seat. It's approximately in the center of the county.

It used to be said by vintners in Napa and Sonoma that fine wine grapes couldn't be grown in Mendocino County. Now you and a handful of others have probably turned that thinking around. But why were they saying that in the first place?

People are sometimes motivated by one of the strongest basic instincts of mankind, that known as territorial instinct! Mendocino's viticultural history goes back for many years, but being so far north we were always isolated. In fact, there was no rail transportation to get grapes or wine out of this region in the early days, until 1910 when they completed one of the most difficult rail projects in the world, bringing the line up the Russian River. And there were few commercial wineries here. The Italian families who planted the first vineyards planted predominantly varieties like Alicante Bouschet, Carignane, and the other grapes that made huge volumes of just plain red wine. It wasn't until the last 15 years that the growers became interested in fine varietals. But those few fine varietals that were grown here were certainly recognized as being outstanding grapes. Wineries in Napa, Sonoma and Livermore bid for the production of this county, particularly Grey Riesling, Pinot Noir and Pinot Blanc.

What is the climate of the area?

Originally Winkler classified everything north of Cloverdale as Region III, and this hurt the region severely because people really believed that it was a hot area. Later a weather recording station in the heart of Redwood Valley produced data that reclassified this particular area as a cool Region II. As a result of its mountains, Mendocino is full of micro-climates. Here in our own valley where our vineyards are situated, at the headwaters of the Russian River, our climate normally on hot summer days is four to ten degrees cooler than it is in Ukiah. The county has a series of canyons that run inland from the coast southeasterly and these canyons are like air conditioning ducts. Every afternoon during the summer at about two o'clock these ducts start bringing the Pacific marine winds up into the inland valleys. We're in one of those ducts, about 22 miles from the ocean.

Is temperature the most important factor, then, in the quality of your grapes?

It plays a significant part. I just read an article yesterday in *Scientific American* by Philip Wagner whom I've always regarded as one of the greatest contributors to our winemaking in America, and he claims that climate is the predominant reason for the great variations in wine. I contend that soil plays an equal part, along with cultural methods. Technology can do little to make a good bottle of wine. Wine is primarily a product of soil, and exposure. Someday Mendocino may be regarded as the Pauillac of California. Wine is a product of the soil, and you don't get good wines in the river bottom soils, you have to have benchlands to get wines of real finesse and quality.

Do you think small micro-climate areas should be defined and used on labels as appellations of origin?

Yes, we've been doing that for some time. We label right down to the very vineyard on many of our wines. Our Recetti Vineyard Zinfandel is an example, where we mention on the label the vineyard, the elevation, what sugars the grapes were picked at, and other information.

Do you get sufficient rainfall to dry farm the vineyards here?

Many of our vineyards are dry farmed in Mendocino County. We get from 35 to 50 inches per year, 40 inches on the average. The rain comes from November to March, so there's a long dry spell in between. However there's a myth among wine consumers that irrigation makes an inferior wine. Irrigation with moderation is beneficial to the crop. We irrigate once a year, around June. Certainly irrigation after the month of July can be detrimental to the crop, and we do have many growers who practice this, irrigate right up until time of harvest simply because by flooding their vineyards with water they can get more weight when they sell by the ton. This makes a very inferior wine.

How can you control those kinds of practices on vineyards which you don't own?

We don't buy from those growers. We know just about every vineyard in the county and who follows what practices; it's common knowledge who is irrigating.

Can you also get your growers to prune as severely as you do?

Yes, you see we're very small, and we couldn't afford to take even one load of inferior grapes, because we don't have all those vast inventories of wines to blend mistakes out with. One mistake would be disastrous for a small winery. So over the years, we have learned which sites and which growers produce superior quality, and these are the vineyards we have sought out and entered into long-term contracts with.

Is the harvesting all done by hand?

Yes, all by hand. I wouldn't consider machine picked grapes. I'm sure that the whole industry is fast realizing this; they've been very disenchanted with mechanical harvesting.

Why?

Because you get all kinds of material besides grapes, and you get a lot of immature, second crop grapes. You just don't make wine picking grapes in this manner. Besides our vineyards are too steep and rough to ever be machine picked.

Who does the picking?

Our pickers come like the birds each year. We always worry about whether they'll be there. However, as machine picking becomes more prevalent in the southern counties, it makes labor more plentiful up in this region. And the second source of labor are housewives and school children in this area.

What do they use to pick the grapes with?

A curve-bladed or hooked knife.

Do you ever pick the vineyard more than once, going through once and getting the most mature fruit, and then repeat the process?

Yes, we do. We pick Cabernet Sauvignon usually in the last week of October, sometimes as late as Armistice Day. Then on our Sauvignon Blanc and Sémillon, we go through and pick a second time, after the main operation is shut down. We pick all the botrytis affected clusters. Botrytis comes naturally here some years. We always make three or four barrels of excellent botrytis late picked wine for our family and our friends.

Do you think of your wines as having a style that's different from other California wines?

I think the real discriminating taster is a better judge than I. I've been told many times by people throughout the United States that if there were 100 red wines on the table and seven of them were Fetzer wines, they could pick out the Fetzer wines blind because of the soil and style of winemaking.

What flavors do you get from the soils?

I think we get a very spicy, cinnamon-like flavor in our red wines from this soil, lots of body, big noses, high acids, lots of tannin.

Which varietals do you produce?

Cabernet Sauvignon, Petite Syrah and Zinfandel in red varietals. Another red we call Mendocino Premium Red. It's 100 percent north coast Carignane. We have lots of Carignane in the county. One of our great problems in Mendocino is that we're heavy with these generic type grapes, especially Carignane, but when it's grown in this region it really has complexity. If properly made and aged it turns into excellent everyday wine. It's interesting that some of the most famous connoisseurs on the whole west coast have been sure it had other varieties in it. One of them said he picked out definite Petite Syrah in it, and another was sure it was at least half Zinfandel!

That Premium Red is your generic red wine. Why didn't you call it Burgundy?

It would be unfair to the Burgundians to call it Burgundy. People are becoming turned off by French nomenclature on American wines. One of the greatest impediments to wine drinking in our society is our complicated system of naming wines. That's one of the reasons wine like Green Hungarian is so popular. Everyone can pronounce it!

Which white wines do you produce?

Fumé Blanc and Mendocino Premium White. The latter is a blend of Chenin Blanc, Sémillon and French Colombard. We are also making a Chardonnay.

Are all the varietals 100 percent?

Most are 100 percent varietal unless otherwise specified on the label. Zinfandel has always been 100 percent, Carbernets have all been 100 percent but we're thinking it may be necessary to do some blending on the Cabernet, to make it more complex.

What will you blend with?

Well, we'll consider that more or less a trade secret.

Do you ferment in stainless steel, or in wood?

Entirely in stainless steel, all temperature controlled.

At what temperatures do you ferment whites and reds?

The whites at 55 degrees and the reds at 85 degrees.

Do the reds go through a malo-lactic fermentation?

Very definitely. They all go through it without any problem.

Do you start fermentation by inoculating with yeast?

Yes. We use Champagne yeast for everything.

Do you make any wines wholly from the free run juice?

Not in the past. We have always felt that our press wine is essential to add good flavor and balance to our wine. We have French presses. Our yields are very low, this is the reason we do not separate the press wine.

Are these the bladder type presses?

No, they are opposing plate type presses. Our yields are roughly 150 gallons per ton with those presses.

Do you have to adjust acid frequently?

No. We have exceedingly high acids in our grapes in this region.

Do you have to use concentrate then sometimes to raise the sweetness?

No.

What kind of fining and filtration do you give the whites?

Whites have to be fined. We use a minimum amount of fining material. We find we have a great advantage in Mendocino because our winters are cold. We throw the doors of the winery open. The cold nights do tremendous things for clarifying our wines.

Do you own a centrifuge?

No, and we have no plans to install one.

Why do you say that with such assertiveness?

It's our opinion that fine filtration and centrifuges and pasteurization and all the other processes can whip all the good things out of the wine. You come up with a product which is like American cheese: it offends no one, but doesn't excite anyone either.

How do you treat the reds?

Many of the reds have no fining at all. Each batch of wine is a personality in itself. Many of the reds require no filtration and some of them no fining. This requires a lot more work, more racking and more time in the cellar. We filter some wines just before bottling.

How much time do they spend in wood?

All of our red wines that get barrel aging—one year to 18 months. I'm a firm believer that that's the only way to age red wine.

I think I have tasted a good deal of oak character in even your Carignane.

Yes, you have. Some of those wines have been in the barrels for 18 months.

Are your barrels new?

Yes. We add new barrels each year.

What kind of wood are they, and what size?

All are 50 gallon barrels, some Burgundian, some Nevers and some American oak.

How often do you rack?

We don't put wine into the barrels until January or February; prior to that it's been clarifying in this cold weather I told you about. After that, we probably rack a couple of times per year after the wine is in the barrel.

Do the white wines spend any time in wood?

Most of them spend four to five months. These are Yugoslavian casks, 2,000 to 2,500 gallons.

Do you think the great California wines are as good as the great European wines?

I certainly do. I was recently at a tasting at the Waldorf Astoria, and had the privilege of tasting a number of 20 year old California Cabernets, alongside some older French Bordeauxs. New York has a lot of sophisticated wine drinkers and I picked up a very definite enthusiasm among them for our California Cabernets. I thought the California wines stood up to any of the French wines. Zinfandels, well made and cellared for 10 to 15 years, turn out to be more magnificent than many of the Bordeaux wines. I think our Petite Syrahs will stand up alongside any Côte Rôtie or Rhône wines. However, we'll never make nice Sauternes like Suduiraut or d'Yquem. And we'll never make a Riesling like some of the fine German Rieslings. I do believe we'll make some great Sauvignon Blancs in California. And I believe it's already proven that in a few isolated areas we can grow some beautiful Chardonnay. California premium wines are here to stay and in the next ten years they'll consistently outscore the French and other European wines in all competitive tastings.

John Parducci

PARDUCCI WINE CELLARS

I am a great believer in micro-climate definitions. If an area is found to produce an excellent wine consistently, my opinion is the area should be defined on the label for the benefit of the consumer.

John and George Parducci have never been shy of championing Mendocino County wines or of complaining about too much oak in wine. As a result, they have been tagged "controversial" in some wine circles, "leaders" in others. Nor are they shy about meeting the demands of the market: while sticking to no-oak principles for their wines generally, they recently began producing an additional line with definite oak character especially "for the wine buff." Paradoxically, the no-oak wines have been winning high honors in county fairs and other blind tastings. Italian families have been making wine in Mendocino for many years, but the Parduccis are one of the only families to turn their typical, small vin ordinaire operation into a dynamic competitor in the fine wine field. With financial backing of a new majority partner, the winery has been transformed in the last several years and today old redwood tanks share space with stainless steel, there is a new showcase sterile bottling room, and a tasting room crowded with tourists. I talked with John Parducci in his office, then we examined the winery and ended up late in the day at the tasting room.

Recommended wine to drink while reading this chapter:

PARDUCCI
CABERNET SAUVIGNON

What is the Parducci style of wine? How would you describe it?

Number one, I'm not a believer in oak. You won't find large amounts of oak complexities in any of our wines, except for some of the special bottlings that are made for the wine enthusiasts who want to lay away wines for further aging. I've always highly criticized wines that are overshadowed with oak so that you don't even know what kind of grape they're made from. It probably comes down through the years from the people who are buying French imports and have acquired a taste for such wines. My personal opinion is the majority of those people don't know what they are drinking. I recently had 16 retailers here from San Jose, and I let them taste the Cabernet out of the tank that had not had one day of wood. They said they had never tasted anything like it, and thoroughly enjoyed it.

To prove a point, we divided our 1973 Vintage Cabernet Sauvignon in two lots. We kept one lot in stainless steel containers without any wood contact and bottled it early this year. We aged the second lot in redwood, then oak, and bottled it a few months later. It's going to be interesting to see the consumers' reaction on a large scale. We expect the final results next year when the wines will be released. So in general you'll find our reds are delightful and fruity with no wood in them and our white wines are also full of aroma and flavor.

How many white wines do you produce?

We were the first to bottle a French Colombard and now there are 13 wineries or more doing it, and we make Chardonnay, Chenin Blanc, Sylvaner Riesling, a Chablis, Green Hungarian, Sauvignon Blanc and Flora.

No Johannisberg Riesling?

No, I have never fallen in love with Johannisberg Riesling, never tasted one from Mendocino County that I thoroughly enjoyed and I just don't think we can produce a good one yet.

What is the Flora like, the hybrid grape developed by the University of California?

We have not been able to come up with a great dry Flora, and what I want to do is to produce a sweet one, a Sauternes type. It is a hybrid, a cross between Gewürztraminer and Sémillon, and hybrids tend to have some peculiar characteristics, such as too much tannin, that are not compatible with high quality. Flora has a tremendous nose, but the finish is always coarse. Now, one of my favorite wines is Sauternes. I'm a great lover of them. People don't understand the great effort put into a Sauternes.

When you stop to think that all those berries are picked off one by one, and the rarity and the magnitude of complexity in a Sauternes, it's got to be the greatest value in the world. So after being unsuccessful with producing a decent dry Flora, I said maybe the Flora could be a Sauternes type wine. The sugars in the Flora go up to 30 Balling or more! And the grape has a thick skin like the Gewürztraminer. You can leave them on the vine until December without too much decay, and someday soon I'll leave them on the vine for a longer time and with higher sugar try to produce a sweet wine similar to my favorite Sauternes.

Which red wines do you make?

In reds, we make Cabernet Sauvignon, Pinot Noir, Gamay Beaujolais, Petite Sirah, Zinfandel and Burgundy.

How many cases a year do you produce now?

This year we will reach 50,000 to 60,000 cases. Our goal is 100,000; our operation is geared to 100,000 which we hope to reach within three years.

When did you start the winery?

My father started it. He was born in San Jose. He went back to the old country, northern Italy, at the age of six and remained there until he was 16. Back there he worked in the vineyards and in a winery for his father. When he was 16, he chose to return to California with two brothers and one sister. He came to San Francisco and, having no money to start a winery, started in the grape market. He would come to the country, buy grapes and sell them to home winemakers in the city. On one of his trips north to Cloverdale in Sonoma County, he met my mother. My mother was born in Cloverdale; I was born in the same home she was born in.

During Prohibition my father built a winery in Cloverdale and sold sacramental wines. But land was very expensive there and he decided to move north to this ranch in the Ukiah Valley which was partially planted in grapes and walnuts. In 1931, he and his four sons commenced construction of the present winery. However, the winery wasn't finished until the latter part of 1933. We were still selling grapes on the Eastern market to the home winemakers, 35 to 40 carloads of grapes a year were sold on the Hoboken market. But you had to ship the grapes to a receiver and the receivers charged $25 a car to receive the grapes. So my father sent me back there to be the receiver—I was 14 years old at the time and I received them and sold the grapes. I left Ukiah on the 4th of July and stayed back there until the 28th day of February. This was during the Depression, and I had quite an education. I saw the bread lines on Grand Avenue in New York City, I saw 4,000 cars of grapes a day sold on the Hoboken market. I learned a great deal. During this time, my father and a group of north coast farmers started a winemaking co-op. They had the privilege of hiring Dr. Edmund Twight from the University of California, who was one of the outstanding oenologists of the day. I worked under him for five years. After the war, I became winemaker and have been here ever since.

You own the winery now with your brother George, don't you?

Yes, in 1964 George and I purchased the partnership from our younger two brothers and our father, and went into production of varietal wines. That was quite a shift, because it had been a bulk winery before then. We brought in an investor, Teachers Management and Investment Corporation, a company which invests in real estate, mutual funds and so forth for school teachers. TMI has a majority interest in the winery, so you might say George and I own it along with about 2,000 teachers from TMI.

What is your total vineyard acreage?

We have about 400 acres of our own. We buy approximately one third of our grapes from other growers. All our vineyards are within six miles of the winery and all within a mile or so of the Russian River.

Are all the vineyards on the floor of this valley?

Not really on the floor, but on the bench approaching the hills, and our home ranch vineyard at the winery is on a plateau in the hills at about 700 feet in altitude.

What kind of soil runs through those vineyards?

All very light, gravelly, red soil. We don't have any river bottom soil. They are well drained soils and are low producers—four and a half to five tons to the acre.

Are these vineyards giving distinct characters to your wines?

Absolutely. This home ranch makes the richer wine, fuller flavored, probably because it produces fewer grapes per acre and is on a more reddish soil.

What is the yield per acre at this ranch?

About four tons per acre here compared with five and a half at the Talmage ranch and probably seven tons at the Largo ranch.

What is the climatic region here?

I think it is classified as Region III, but sometimes I think we're a little cooler than that.

Isn't it usually thought that it's too hot here, though, to grow varietals like Pinot Noir and Chardonnay?

The answer is no! We were the first to plant fine varietals in Mendocino County in 1964 and we produced wines from those plantings in 1969. How can anyone judge the quality of grapes or wines from an area that has never produced any varietal wine, especially from the largest county in California, with dozens of heat summations and micro-climates? It will take a long time for the vines to mature and then to evaluate wines from the different areas. At this point we have no track record to convince us we have the right area or the right variety. In 1964, we planted nine varieties on our Talmage ranch to determine which varieties produced well and made the best wines. We feel that Chenin Blanc, Chardonnay, Cabernet and Sylvaner produce excellent wines, and we've won awards to verify it. However, we're still waiting for the full maturity of our vineyards before we're convinced which varieties do best.

Do you think these micro-climate areas should be defined and serve as appellations of origin on labels?

Yes, I am a great believer in micro-climate definitions. If an area is found to produce an excellent wine consistently, my opinion is the area should be defined on the label for the benefit of the consumer and to encourage other growers in that area to plant the same variety. I believe the grower will only plant the variety best suited for his area when demands are made on him by the winery for specific varieties known to produce outstanding wines in that area. Those who enjoy European wines consistently purchase wines from certain chateaus or areas. California, with so many boutique wineries, could follow the same pattern as far as the demands of the consumer are concerned. Joe Heitz's Martha's Vineyard, Ridge with its many regions, Freemark Abbey's, Mondavi's and the many others that now use the area designations are already doing this and it's good for the welfare of the industry and the consumers.

Micro-climate designations tend to introduce a variety of wine styles, create more interest by wine enthusiasts, introduce new vineyards and areas, encourage a lot of comparative wine tastings which consume more wine and educate more people, and create more publicity. There are numerous other advantages. So, yes, I do believe micro-climate areas should be defined and serve as appellations of origin. We look forward ourselves to introducing wines from new areas in Mendocino County for the first time—Redwood Valley, Potter Valley, McDowell Valley, Ukiah Valley and others—that will someday produce outstanding wines, and if they don't the appellation won't be used.

Do you think it is adequate to have laws requiring only 51 percent of a varietal grape in varietal wines?

Now you've started a subject that really turns me on. For ten years I've said that if you are going to bottle a wine called Cabernet Sauvignon, it should be 75 to 95 percent Cabernet Sauvignon. Some vintners say, "What makes you think I can't make a better wine by blending a percentage of other grapes with the Cabernet Sauvignon?" and my response is, "I didn't say you couldn't, you can blend as you want but you should not put a Cabernet Sauvignon label on a bottle that is not predominantly Cabernet Sauvignon." That's misleading the public.

Would you favor an appellation control system which places restrictions on yield per acre?

No, I don't think we'll get down to such restrictions in California. You may see it on some small wineries just for prestige. I think we are already seeing Chardonnays advertised as coming from vineyards of only a ton and a half per acre. But you're fooling yourself. Those situations are not profitable, only the millionaires can play with something like that. As a commercial venture, I don't think that is going to happen in California. I do think the wineries are going to start asserting better control over the growers, forcing them to bring in grapes with better acid and sugar and so forth. That is where the restrictions on viticultural practices are going to come in.

Are your grapes mechanically harvested?

No, all hand picked, and the grapes are usually crushed within 20 or 30 minutes after they're picked. At the moment, I don't think mechanical harvesters are the answer for good wine production. However, mechanically picked and field crushed grapes will be the answer someday soon. But as long as we have the personnel and the transit force coming through seasonally, there is much to be said for staying with hand picking.

What do hand harvesters use to pick the grapes?

They use a little knife with a hook on it, put the grapes into little plastic or metal containers and from there they go into small bins that hold about 1,200 pounds. The minute the gondola is filled the truck picks it up and heads for the winery.

Do you pick the vineyards more than one time according to varying maturity in different sections?

No; except, of course, we leave the second crop on the vine.

What size staff do you have in the winery?

There is only a father and son and myself who handle any of the wine made in this winery. We have no other employees in the cellar. I'm the winemaster; Joe Monostori, who came over from Hungary, is cellarmaster and my assistant. His son Tom is learning the cellar work—two very dedicated individuals. They have been in our employ now for five years, a great team to be with.

Do you stem all the grapes as they're crushed?

Yes, we have an excellent crusher-stemmer. It runs very slowly, crushes about 25 tons per hour and doesn't shred the stems.

Do you ferment in stainless steel?

All in stainless steel. The whites will ferment between 45 and 55 degrees for about two to three months, and 85 to 90 degrees for most of the reds, although we like to have the Cabernet go over 90 degrees—between 90 and 100 degrees in its final stages.

I didn't think you could let it ferment that hot.

We let it go to 100 degrees only in its final stages for four or five hours. We find we extract more flavor and color by fermenting it that hot. With Pinot Noir, we've found something interesting: if we harvest the Pinot Noir early in the morning and crush it before it warms up, and put a coat of ice on the tank a day before, we can ferment the Pinot Noir for a week at cooler temperatures. We were never able to do that before. We're very pleased with that process. I was about ready to give up on it, because it's a very hard grape to work with. I predict California is going to make Pinot Noirs as great as those of France someday.

Do you start fermentation by inoculating with yeast?

Yes, we use Montrachet and Champagne yeasts. For many years we made wine by letting the wild yeast start the fermentation, but it's a little precarious that way. It is my opinion that the greatest wines will be made with the natural yeast, because in some years the yeast that predominates on those skins produces outstanding wines. But in other years it doesn't. I have found that if we have a rain before I pick the French Colombard, the wine isn't as great in nose as it would be if I picked before it rained. It's evident there is some yeast on the skins that is beneficial, and the rain washes it off. However, at present we inoculate with a yeast culture which proves to be quite successful.

How much sulphur do you add to stun the wild yeast before you ferment?

About 150 parts per million.

Do the reds go through a malo-lactic fermentation?

Always. I dislike wines that haven't gone through malo-lactic and ours go through it generally within their first year.

Do you frequently have to adjust the acid on your grapes?

Not frequently, but we do it if we have to. We have most of our own grapes, and if we have to pick them a little early sometimes to get good acid, we pick them. If we add acid, we use tartaric and malic—mostly tartaric.

Do you use any concentrate to raise the sweetness?

We never have used concentrate.

How heavily do you fine and filter?

We do a maximum of two filtrations on our white wines. I know that's pretty hard to believe. We fine them with bentonite. The main thing we do at this winery to get the wines clean is rack them. We rack our white wines every five degrees Balling as they ferment, then rack right after fermentation, and rack them twice more before the first three months until they are perfectly clear. Even when we fine the whites with bentonite, we rack them off the bentonite instead of filtering them off. Then we chill them to 30 degrees, no more than that, to precipitate out some tartrates. If that still leaves some it is just too bad. We filter them off the cold tank, then filter before bottling. Two filtrations.

No centrifuge?

No, we don't have a centrifuge in the winery.

And how are the reds treated?

All our special bottlings of reds are unfined and unfiltered. The only thing that has been done is to rack them. The regular red wines for distribution are refrigerated, filtered off the refrigeration and then filtered before bottling. Again, two filtrations.

Do you make any wines from the free run juice?

We have no press wine in any of our varietals. They are all 100 percent of the varietal, as close as we can manage, and they are all free run.

When you say free run, do you mean just lightly pressed, or actually free run juice?

Free run, drawn off the bottom. Our Burgundy is made from a combination of press wine from Gamay Beaujolais and press wine from Pinot Noir. Our white press wine goes into our jug Chablis. Once in a while, we take a very small amount of press wine and blend it back into some of the varietals if the year was bad and they turned out lacking tannin or color.

Do you produce a lot of the wines you call "special bottlings"?

Only 500 or 1,000 cases of each variety. We sell most of this wine to those who wish to lay wines away for further aging. We may give two cases or more to certain distributors who want to use it for promotional purposes. So it goes to the places where it does the most good. Most of it is sold here at the winery.

How long are the red wines aged?

Three years, minimum, in redwood. The Cabernets sometimes spend three to six months in oak. Pinot Chardonnay has three or four months of oak. The Petite Sirah has some oak, the Zinfandel none. And I have bottled some Cabernets with no oak at all.

What size is the cooperage?

It's 50 gallon barrels up to 1,200 gallon oak casks. It is all American oak. The redwood is 4,000 to 6,000 gallons.

In your opinion, are the best California wines as good as the best wines of Europe?

In my personal opinion, yes. Our best California wines can compete with those of Europe. Vintage for vintage, we would surpass them.

Temecula:

THE ICONOCLASM

The received wisdom about California wine is that fine wine grapes cannot be grown in Southern California—it's too hot. The fact is California winemaking started in the south. In the 1830s a Frenchman named Jean Louis Vignes tended a flourishing vineyard where the railroad station now stands in downtown Los Angeles. A handful of commercial wineries still thrive in the region. This has never impressed northern vintners: the wines, they have correctly observed, are far from great.

Temecula has now shattered that traditional thinking. Situated between Los Angeles and San Diego only twenty-three miles from the Pacific, Temecula is cooled by ocean breezes funneled through gaps in the coastal mountains. Its climate is more comparable to northern California than the traditional vineyard areas of the southland.

In typical southern California style, Temecula was "discovered" by a land developer, Kaiser-Aetna. It has turned once dusty grazing land into a huge, green new town called Rancho California. Real estate pages in Los Angeles Sunday newspapers carry full page ads wooing wealthy urbanites to the "country," a move which can include a new home on a large lot, a town shopping center with western style boardwalks and your own avocado grove or vineyard to boot. Aside from ex-urbanites dabbling in viticulture, there are serious grape growers at Temecula, away from the hubbub of development. The old Brookside Winery in Cucamonga now gets most of its grapes here, but the finest wines made so far are those of one dynamic man: Ely Callaway.

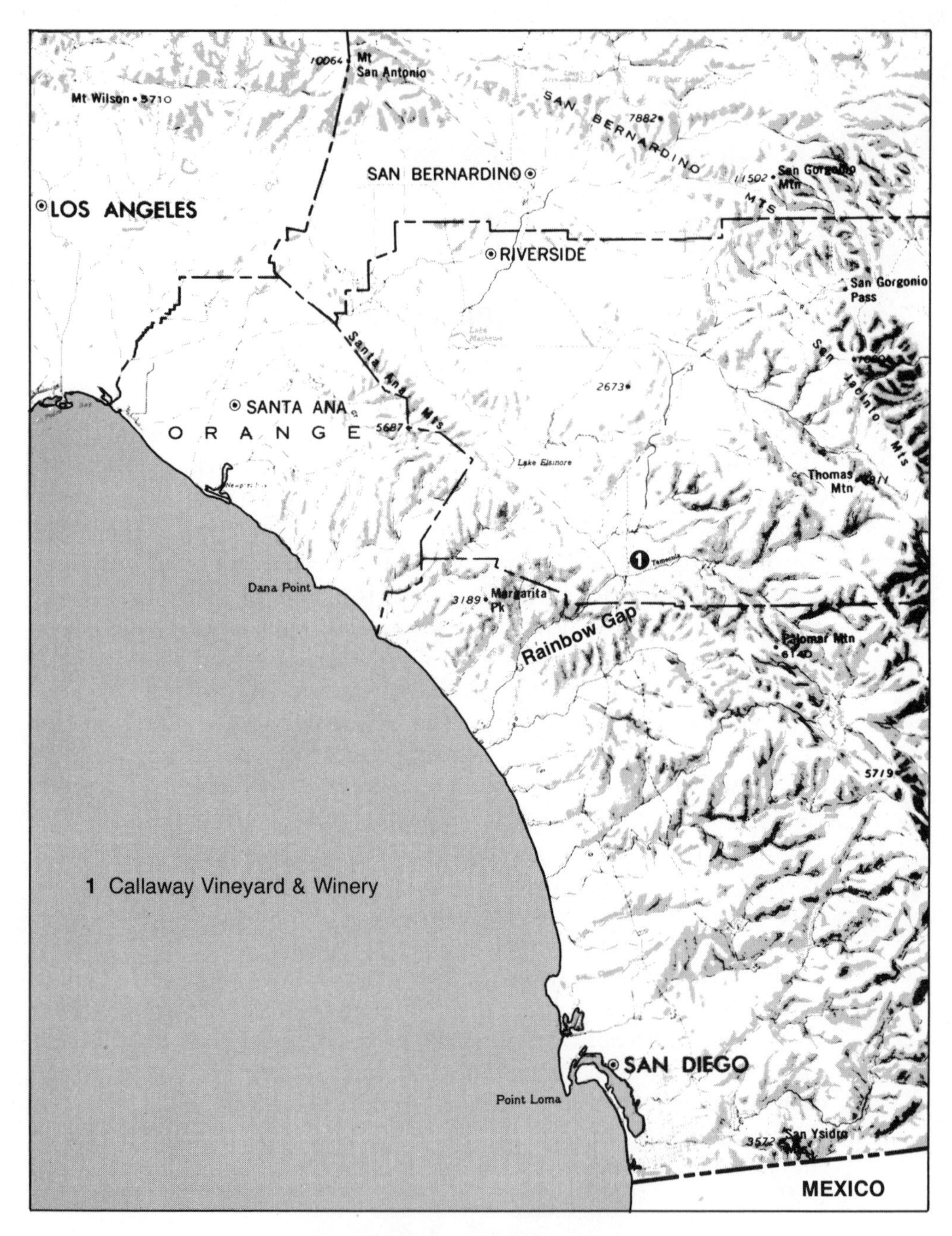

South Coastal Mountains
TEMECULA: The Iconoclasm

Ely Callaway

CALLAWAY VINEYARD & WINERY

Wine is a "story" business. Beer isn't. There's no back label with a story on a beer can.

If Temecula is the iconoclasm, Ely Callaway is the iconoclast who made it so. You know he is different when you learn he retired from the textile business as the president of Burlington Industries to start a winery in a place no one believed could produce fine wines. His native Georgia accent softened his peppery manner as he led me through the vineyard and winery, expounding the virtues of turning the California wine map on its head. He makes no secret that his nonconformity is designed to give Callaway wines "a story" appealing to the marketplace. And he is just as adamant that it is also designed to make some of the finest wines in the world. Though his wines have only been on the market since late 1975, there is already evidence they may achieve that goal. Their fruit is immense, their varietal character intense and rather unlike varietal character produced in other regions. His "Sweet Nancy," the first botrytised Chenin Blanc in the country, immediately was lauded by wine enthusiasts for its originality. The wine committee of the Pilgrims of the United States selected his White Riesling as the single wine to be served at a luncheon in honor of Queen Elizabeth on her 1976 Bicentennial visit to the United States. It was apropos: Callaway *is* a revolutionary.

Recommended wine to drink while reading this chapter:

CALLAWAY
WHITE RIESLING

Why did you build a winery in southern California so far from the known fine wine areas?

Here we are 600 miles south of the best known area in the United States for producing fine wine. History tells us that fine wine has come from areas relatively cool, for slow maturation of the grape—Bordeaux, Burgundy, certain parts of Germany, and parts of northern California. So why are we here in southern California? We're almost in Mexico! The answer is what you feel right now: the cool breeze. You can come here almost any day from May first to the end of November and 80 percent of the time, anywhere in my vineyards, you will find this ocean breeze. It starts around one in the afternoon and dies down around seven.

Why does that breeze come directly through this rather narrow area?

It's caused primarily by the influence of the desert, 60 miles east. We hired Dr. Krick, a meteorologist who was General Eisenhower's long range weather forecaster for the entire war. He lives in Palm Springs, and he has a weather forecasting company with headquarters in Geneva. I heard about him, went to see him, he came over with all of his key people, and we gave him a six month assignment. We wanted to know two things: are we likely to have smog here—after all we're only 40 miles from Riverside where they do have smog; and why is it so cool here? Dr. Krick said, "Mr. Callaway I can tell you pretty well right now, because I've been traveling from Palm Springs to La Jolla for 30 years. But let us study it." So he studied historical weather data, and concluded that we probably won't have smog unless there is a major change in our basic climatic conditions. He concluded that the reason the vineyard is cool is primarily because of the influence of the Salton Sea. The Salton Sea is generally the lowest pressure area in California, and it generally pulls air from the ocean which is a high pressure area. We happen to be in the pathway of the wind. The Rainbow Gap in the mountains to the west of us channels the wind directly across this vineyard. It's ironic. This is the first time, I suspect, that a desert influence has been beneficial to a fine wine vineyard. Fortunately, the desert is 60 miles away from here. Our wind is not only strong, about 15 to 17 knots at its peak every day, but it also contains moisture. That's why the Indians named this area Temeku—Temucula—meaning, according to local historians, "land where the sun shines through the white mist." At night during our growing season, 80 percent of the time, the relative humidity at vine level is between 65 and 80, a condition which gives us, among other things, a frequent botrytis cinerea.

Were you surprised at the botrytis you got here?

Yes, but we're no longer surprised. We get it all the time. I didn't even know what it was when I planted the vineyard.

Is that a problem for you, that it occurs so often?

It's not a problem because we're highly specialized and we know how to make botrytised wines. We also have tried to inhibit botrytis with a chemical on the vines at bloom time. But we don't have botrytis overwhelmingly all over the vineyard. It almost never affects our reds.

You talk abut its being cool. How cool does that make it in the Davis classification of regions?

We are supposed to be in Region III, but, in my opinion, that's irrelevant.

We have special climatic factors here, so it isn't necessarily significant what the thermometer reading is. The Davis scale is fundamentally based on thermometer readings. I can tell you what the thermometer readings are, and they're only moderately high. We have moderately warm days and very cool nights when compared to most fine wine regions in California. Our heat summation records show that my vineyard is in Region II or III. But the wind is even more significant, its rate of speed, moisture in the wind, moisture on the surface of the leaf and the resulting effect on the temperature of the leaf surface. Why are those more important? Because the name of the game is the rate of grape maturation—how even, how slow the maturation is. We think, based on observation here and some evidence from Europe, that the maturation rate is largely determined by the surface temperature of the leaf and of the grape skin. And that temperature can be substantially different from the thermometer reading—especially if there is convection cooling by the wind chill factor on the surface of the vine leaves and grape skins.

Have you measured the leaf surface temperatures?

No sir, we have not. We do not have the instruments. We understand they are available at certain places in Germany and we plan to buy them. We do know this: though we are 600 miles south of the coolest parts of the north coast, our grapes mature about the same time as comparable varietals in Napa, Sonoma or Mendocino. On some varieties we mature even later. In '75 we picked our Cabernet Sauvignon on November 18th and 19th, and we got an average Brix of 25.6. Another reason we don't have to pick early here is we normally don't have the threat of rain at harvest time. This gives us an opportunity which most in other areas don't often have—we can let the grapes hang on the vines until they are properly mature rather than pick them too early because of possible damaging rain.

How much rainfall do you get during the year?

About 15 to 16 inches, and it normally comes from December through May. We irrigate up to another 15 inches, depending on how hot and dry the season is. We didn't predict this. A lot of it was luck. I didn't realize when I planted the vineyard lack of rain would be a benefit, and we didn't even know about the influence of the wind chill factor. It rarely gets real hot at my vineyard. It might occasionally be as high as 98 to 100 degrees, which my thermographs showed happened last year on seven days only. That's pretty hot, but the nightime temperature during that heat wave dropped down to 58 to 62 degrees. Normally, the daytime thermometer readings will be in the high 80s, and the night temperatures will range in the mid to high 50s. So it's usually not very hot here and there are further mitigating climatic factors. First, the temperature stays at a peak for less time than in many other places which don't have our cooling wind. Secondly, we have this blanket of coastal mist that moderates the intensity of the sun's radiation. We have an instrument which measures the intensity of the sun's rays, and Dr. Krick told us the coastal haze acts as a moderating screen.

So you attribute the character of your fruit mainly to climate and maturation rate, then, or does the soil play an important part?

Both are important. Our soil is well-drained, nonfertile, with a large content of decomposed granite. This has a beneficial effect on the character of the fruit. I don't know how to quantify it, whether it's one-third or two-thirds of the grapes' character, or what. Someday when you talk to Andre Tchelistcheff again, ask him. He's been impressed with our highly granitic soil. He said he thought it was rather important. Soil, along with many other things, contributes to the distinctive character and aroma of our wines, but of course the climate is vitally important, too.

How many acres of vineyard do you have?

We have 135 acres planted. One hundred of the acres are in their seventh leaf year, and the rest are in their third leaf. We have Chenin Blanc, Sauvignon Blanc, White Riesling, Cabernet Sauvignon, Petite Sirah and Zinfandel. My neighbor, John Poole, has around 150 acres in the same varietals, and I have purchased quite a few of his grapes. He has the same elevation, soil, exposure, and the same vineyard manager, John Moramarco. Generally we select a section of Mr. Poole's vineyard from which we will buy grapes, and we determine the viticultural practices there.

What are those practices?

As an outsider coming into this industry I have been tremendously impressed with the importance of raw material to the quality of the end product. It's more important in the fine wine business than any product I know about. The influence of the vineyard and its fruit on the final product in the bottle is at least 50 percent, maybe more. So we spend just as much time, money, energy, and talent on the vineyard as we do in the winery. Essentially, it's a matter of attention to detail and deciding what your quality objectives are.

Is one of your principal objectives to hold down the yield?

Our objective is properly mature fruit. The weather helps give us that, as do soil and wind. But we could still come up with very ordinary grapes from these very same vines simply by letting the vines produce too much fruit. We prune and cluster thin, so each vine produces only that amount of fruit it will properly mature. And that's very costly and complex to do, but necessary since we want properly mature fruit.

What is the average yield per acre?

We've only been making wine for two years here, but our Chenin Blanc, generally a heavy producer, in the '74 vintage was two or two and a half tons an acre. In '75, the vines were older and we moved the yield up to two and a half to three tons. By limiting yield, you not only allow the vine to mature its grapes but you intensify the varietal character. Now our Cabernet Sauvignon was about two tons per acre in '75, and one and three-quarters in '74; in '76 we may move it up to two and a quarter. It depends on weather too. In '75 we picked the Cabernet at 25.6, fully mature fruit. The color just rolled out even on the first two or three pump overs prior to fermentation.

And what was the acid on those grapes?

I can't remember precisely. In the area of .70. Again I'm going to be different now, but I believe that's not necessarily so important. The important thing for our purposes is whether the fruit is properly mature.

But maturity is a matter of sugar and acid balance, isn't it?

Sure, sure, but it's also a whole lot of other things. We have some pretty good scientists here, and they will tell you it's taste. We pick by taste. Of course we measure sugar and acid. We even measure acid in the vineyard. Not only is it important to prune and cluster thin, but also most of the vines out there are in different stages of development, and this is a key point. They are six and a half years old and the vines will be individually in varying stages of development for another four or five years at least. So what do we do? We treat each vine as an individual, as they do wherever the finest wines are grown. That's why John Moramarco is one of the unique vineyard managers in the state. He brings a crew in to do the initial or gross pruning. Then his judgment factor comes in: how many canes and how long each cane should be. John makes the final judgment on each vine. There are not many people in California qualified to make that judgment. Then John finish prunes every vine in this place, with his own hands and shears. It takes him four months to do it. There are probably not 100 men in California who have the knowledge to exercise this judgment, and I bet there are not three who would actually do the final pruning personally as my manager does. This costs a lot of money.

Then in late May and June we come back and cluster thin. And of course the other thing we do at this vineyard is fertilize and irrigate it, as I told you. It's impossible for us to dry farm. But once we brought in the irrigation water, most of the apparant negatives of having a vineyard on this spot became pluses—including the lack of rainfall, because now we can usually control our rainfall. We don't want it to rain three or four weeks before harvest, or during harvest, so generally we don't have to pray, we usually don't have to worry, we normally don't have to pick too soon, we simply cut the water off, let the fruit mature, and thereby intensify the character of the grape. Irrigation got its bad name in fine wine in California mainly in the central valley where it was used to increase the yield. That dilutes the varietal character of the grape. We've learned that the proper utilization of water at the right time, and the elimination of water at the right time, is one of our most valuable tools. Of course it's silly to predict nature, but we probably have less chance of rain in the fall here on this vineyard than on most other varietal vineyards in the world.

You haven't planted any Pinot Noir or Chardonnay. Is that because when you put in the vineyard you thought it would be too warm, and might you put them in now that you know about the wind chill factor?

There are other vineyards in the area with Chardonnay and Pinot Noir planted and it looks pretty good, but nobody has ever made fine wine from those grapes so we don't know. We thought Pinot Noir was a little too difficult to work with. Furthermore in northern California there were a lot of great Chardonnays being produced. It seemed a little wiser from a marketing standpoint to go with other varieties. If I had to speculate I'd say we'd have as good a chance of growing fine Chardonnay and Pinot Noir on this spot as anywhere in California. But growing perfectly fine grapes is only 50 percent of the objective of growing very fine wine.

Do you think it's desirable for new areas, like Temecula, to be delimited and used on labels as appellations of origin?

I really think the only appellation that is significant is the name of the individual winery that produces the wine. Take the appellation "Napa Valley," for example. There are some marvelous wines produced in Napa Valley, and there are some ordinary wines produced there. The ordinary wines are generally produced by huge wineries using very different methods from those who produce the best wines. And yet all the wines can use the same "Napa Valley" appellation. So those who benefit the most from the existing system are those who are riding the coattails of the highest quality producers.

How are the grapes harvested?

That's the point at which we start making wine. We pick all by hand, and put the grapes into small gondolas. We pick selectively, because we're small and willing to spend the money.

Do you mean you pick the same varietal more than once, as it matures in different sections of the vineyard?

Yes.

Do the pickers use knives?

No, they use shears because during our first harvest in 1972 I walked out into the vineyard and saw them cutting with a hooked knife. The worker would grab the bunch and squeeze it while cutting it and some juice would run. I said, "I don't know anything about picking grapes, but I bet they'll be better if we use shears, so oxidation doesn't get started in the juice so early." Everything in this whole winery is designed, among other things, to minimize oxidation. We figure if we can have less oxidation than anybody in the world, we have a better chance of producing a finer wine, even if we don't do anything else better. We instruct every worker not to fill the gondola higher than this red mark. It's a two ton gondola, and we fill it only half full. This minimizes the juicing and therefore minimizes the oxidation. The crusher hopper which the gondolas are dumped into holds only one ton of grapes, so we have that quality control factor built into the size of some of the equipment.

What kind of a stemmer-crusher do you have?

Amos. Made in Germany. The grapes are fed into the stemmer-crusher evenly. This is very significant; I don't know whether you've examined the feeds on other stemmer-crushers, but this one feeds evenly and ideally. The grapes are destemmed and then pass through soft rubber corrugated rollers for crushing. Then the must falls into the hopper which is covered with a blanket of carbon dioxide. If it's red, we immediately pump into the fermentation tank. If it's white, it goes through the dejuicer first to separate skins from juice. Within three minutes the white grapes have been destemmed, crushed, pressed, and the juice is in the fermentation tanks.

You don't crush or ferment with any stems do you, for any wines? Some people do that.

No we don't. In Burgundy they do, and some over here do it on purpose. Our purpose is different. We want a different kind of wine—one which gives you the flavor and aroma of the grape, and the alcohols and glycerols, and all the elements which fermentation of the fruit alone produce. I don't like the taste of stems. They have a bitter taste. The Burgundians would say we're crazy. We don't even know of anybody with a stemmer-crusher exactly like this one which removes the stems first before crushing.

Yes, others in California have that kind.

Okay, fine. I think you'll find, though, that we have more fundamental differences, as a vineyard and winery combined, than any other place in the world. Another difference is we go to extremes to get our grapes from the vine into the winery fast. The total elapsed time from the moment the grapes are dumped into this hopper, are stemmed, crushed, pressed, dejuiced and pumped into their fermentation tanks inside the winery is about two and a half or three minutes. Now how long does a batch press take you? Some take a long time, during which time the juice may be oxidizing. So I think it's a factual statement that we have less oxidation than anybody in the world, up to this point. The total time elapsed from the time any grape is cut from its vine, white or red, and is in its fermentation tank, is 70 minutes. And this shows in the final wine. We bottle with less than one and a half ppm dissolved oxygen and extremely low levels of sulphur dioxide.

Do you make any wine from the free run juice?

Most of our wine comes from the so-called "free run," but our press is designed so that we use practically all the juice. We process the heavier press separately, and we ferment these juices in separate tanks. We centrifuge the white juice before fermenting.

Some winemakers resist the use of a centrifuge, although many more are getting them these days. Do you risk taking too much out of the wine with the centrifuge?

Not if one has the right centrifuge managed by experts. Karl Werner who consults with us is such an expert and so is Steve O'Donnell, our winemaker. We know our centrifuge is one of our most valuable tools in giving us the desired quality, and we would not do without it. Some people in the industry simply do not understand what the centrifuge does and what it can do. We centrifuge our white juice before fermentation, as I said. We also centrifuge at seven degrees Balling and this allows us to then continue fermenting our whites for another two or three months without developing "yeasty" aroma and flavor.

At what temperatures do you ferment?

Whites at maximum of about 55 degrees Fahrenheit. Reds at 65 degrees Fahrenheit maximum.

Do you pump over the cap of the reds while they're fermenting?

Yes, several times per day, and our grapes are generally fully mature, with very low yield per acre, so we get a great amount of our color even before fermentation begins. The normally dry days in the fall help obtain that maturity and full color which develops even though we ferment at a maximum 65 degrees Fahrenheit.

You've used the phrase "properly mature fruit" several times as a symbol of something unique here, but you obviously don't mean that vintners elsewhere are using immature fruit. What do you mean, is it that you get higher sugar in the grapes?

No, we don't always get higher sugar, although we may because we generally have more sunshine and it normally doesn't rain in the fall. I expect that we have a better chance of getting properly mature fruit—without "raisining"—than do most of the wine growers in areas of the world where fall rains are more likely, and where often the vines tend to be overcropped by independent growers. Our judgment of maturity is not based on sugar alone. You need proper balance of a combination of flavor components, skin pigmentation, sugars and acids. I'd say in Europe they certainly have mature fruit in a great vintage year compared with the fruit of just a good year, and it's that difference we have here.

Many wine growers might not want their grapes to be as mature or as ripe as we want. In making all of those comparisons, and citing all of the "differences" here, I'm not claiming that our wines are finer than others. But we want fine wines which are distinctively different from other wines, and so many of our practices in the vineyard and in the winery are different—not necessarily better.

Do you initiate fermentation by adding yeast?

Yes. We use populations of yeasts, with many strains, for our whites and a single strain for our reds. Our yeasts are obtained from Germany where they have been developing over many years to help achieve certain characteristics in aroma and flavor.

Do you fine all the wines?

Yes. But our real fining is in the juice stage on whites. The only fining we do in wine is to a very light degree, as a final "polish" using *Hausenblase* for white wines and fresh egg white for red wine. Both are very old practices of the finest wine growers in France and Germany. And are very costly.

Do you filter the wines?

We filter only once—a very light filtration immediately prior to bottling. We do not use the millipore type; we utilize low pressure from the pump, and our filter is very small.

You fine, filter, and centrifuge. There is a school of thought that would say "do one or two, but not all three of those procedures." They would say it takes too much out of the wine.

Of course many experts would say that. Those same people would also be likely to say "one cannot grow fine, dry table wine in Temecula, or Southern California." They would also very likely be the same experts who would hold that a winemaker cannot obtain sufficient color if the fermentation temperature is 65 degrees Fahrenheit maximum for red wine. Because the fruit from my vineyard is normally so mature, we have opportunities to do things differently in our winery. Much of our winery equipment is designed especially for our purposes. Furthermore, our objectives in quality and style are different. Therefore we can engage in practices and policies which, for others, might seem to be harmful. But in our particular case they are good and helpful.

We never claim our wines are better. But they *are* different; they are very carefully made; and we feel there is a special place in the market for them. Basically, we are striving to develop superior wines which have a distinct and pleasant character for the nose and palate, which will improve with age in the bottle for an unusually long time when compared with the same varietal made by others, and for which we can factually state the reasons they are different. Very rarely can you make a product of the absolute top quality—I don't care what it is, automobiles, clothing, food, steamships—and be able truthfully to say things about it that are distinct from anything else in the field. The combination is very rare. If we can do that, then we have something pretty special, don't we? We have a story. Wine is a "story" business. Beer isn't. There's no back label with a story on a beer can.

I'm interested in hearing about your different cooperage too.

We use German white oak from trees grown on Spessart Mountain. This is the highest mountain in Germany that grows oak. The reason we picked it is the oak grows slower there than anywhere in Europe. Therefore, the oak is harder and, especially after we steam leach it, imparts less of its tannin character to the aroma and flavor of the wine. We steam leach the barrels and casks to get out excess tannin that's naturally in German white oak. This is another thing we do which contributes importantly to the character of the wine. I don't think anybody steam leaches barrels and casks here in the United States, and yet I understand some do in Germany, in the quality operations. We don't want our wines to have the heavy effect of oak tannin, or stem tannin. We use the oak primarily as a vessel for controlled, slow oxidation—an exchange of air from the outside through the pores with the gasses inside. The whites are aged in ovals of 164 gallons and 337 gallons. The Riesling, Chenin Blanc and Sauvignon Blanc stay there until the winemaster decides they have had enough time; it's running two and a half to three and a half months now. Our Sauvignon Blanc Fumé stays in longer than the others; it's treated differently all through the winery, has more of the heavier press in it, is a bigger wine, and needs more wood to round it out. So we put more of that in the small 60 gallon barrels, and more in the small 164 gallon ovals. The other three whites will have also a little touch of the small barrels.

And your reds are all aged in those small 60 gallon barrels also?

Yes, all in 60 gallon German white oak barrels. We've been talking about differences all along, and there's another one. It's simply a fact that there has never been any Zinfandel, Petite Sirah or Cabernet Sauvignon in the world ever matured in German white oak 60 gallon barrels. Some winemakers would say, "Thank God I didn't do it, it's crazy to do it"; but we think it's very sound. There have never been any 60 gallon German white oak barrels made in the world before, except those right here and except for 13 that were ordered at the tail end of my order and were bought by one little winery which is not in California. The Germans don't make much red wine, and when they do I understand they put it in 90 gallon ovals. So the Germans never had made 60 gallon barrels of this type. But Karl Werner went to the smallest, oldest cooperage house in Germany, 300 years old, and had these made especially for us. We also have another difference in the room temperature of the aging room. We think that, ideally, red wines should mature in small barrels in a room about ten degrees warmer than white wines, so we separate these rooms.

How long does the Cabernet stay in the barrels, for instance?

Until its ready. The '74 stayed in about 14 months. Same with the Petite Sirah. And Zinfandel about eight months.

How many cases a year will you produce when you reach full size?

About 35,000. Right now, we're producing 18,000. We think that 35,000 is about as far as we can go and still maintain our quality. The operation will be financially successful at that level. One reason is that in California we sell directly to retailers and restaurants and don't go through wholesale distributors.

How many states are you selling wine in?

We now sell in 13 states. We started out with the idea of selling only in California, and in New York just as a showcase. But now—you've seen some of the publicity—we're getting calls from all over the country. And we've only had wines on the market for six months. Again, wine is a story business, and our story is apparently as interesting to wine drinkers in Boston or Phoenix or Dallas or Georgia as it is to those in Los Angeles. And that is very surprising and pleasing to us.

Is that going to tempt you to go beyond 35,000 cases someday?

No, in my opinion our quality would be compromised if we grow much beyond that size. Now we could still make relatively excellent wines even if we expanded beyond that, but this company will be a financial success at 35,000 cases and I don't need to be big personally. I've already had a pretty big job, and I like this small size even better.

I know you're referring to being president of Burlington Industries. What made you want to do such an outlandish thing as start a winery when you retired? Had you always been a wine buff?

No, I started being interested in wine when I was in Europe where we had a lot of operations. That's typical; many Americans get their first love of good wines in Europe. Then as I began to think about retirement I wanted an agricultural endeavor and investment I could turn into a merchandizable product. And I wanted one of high quality with a unique marketing position. That was my blueprint. Where else can you take an agricultural product and convert it into a highly sophisticated consumer packaged, high priced item? That narrows the field down pretty much. The wine business was like anything else. There is plenty of room at the top for anyone who makes an exceptional product and who knows how to merchanidize it. For a good while, I thought I would end up in the Napa Valley. This was in '69. I began to realize that if you do that and end up with a real fine winery in Napa Valley, you have something great but you're one among many. The marketing opportunities would have been very good, but wouldn't have been quite as good, or unique, as ours are now.

Are you sole owner of the winery?

Yes, I own all the operation personally—one of the few in the United States where one man owns vineyard and winery 100 percent; there are some, but not many. Most people have partners, even rich people, but I'm not rich and I don't have a partner yet. This is such a controversial business, with so many unknowns, that you wouldn't find many partners who would stand still for the controversial things we have done. And if you did, they would argue with you all the time.

In your opinion, do California wines equal the best wines of Europe?

Yes, although they are different, they do equal the best wines of Europe, at least when the vineyard is located in exactly the right spot in California, the wine grower does correctly everything within his control in the vineyard, the winemaker does correctly everything within his control in the winery, and provided the owner is patient . . . and lucky.

Winemaking Process at a Typical California Winery

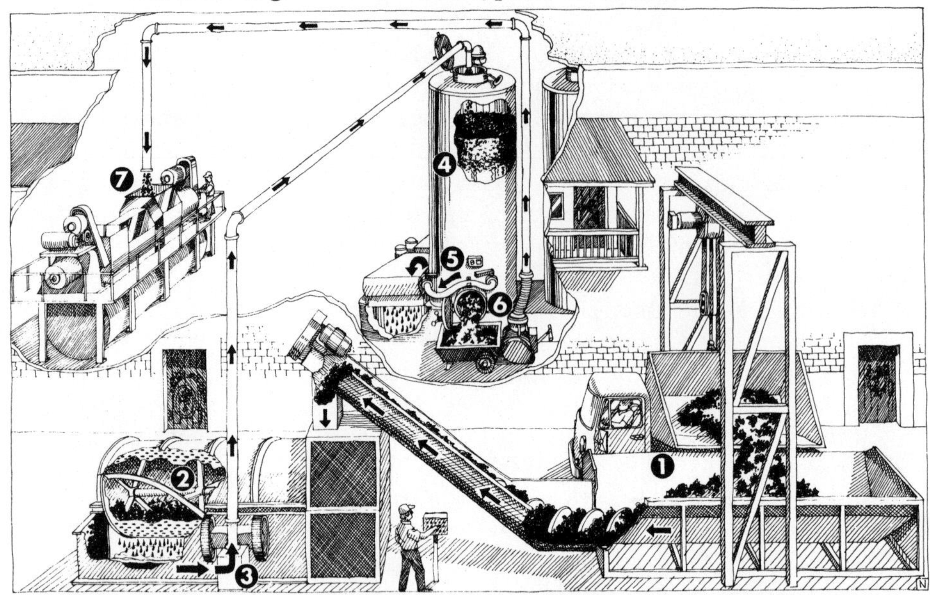

1 Grapes being received into stainless steel hopper.
2 Grapes being fed through crusher/stemmer.
3 Must (freshly crushed grapes) feeding into temperature controlled stainless steel holding tank.
4 Skins risen to form cap.
5 Free run juice being drained from skins and seeds to the dejuicer from where it will proceed to its final fermentation.
6 Portable transfer unit moving drained skins and seeds (pomace) through overhead pipeline to press (7).

Glossary

Amerine, Maynard A. Noted professor of oenology in the influential department of viticulture and oenology at the University of California, Davis. Retired 1974.

Appellation of origin. Name of a wine's geographical origin, as "Alexander Valley." Important because wines from different regions often reflect different characters. Though strictly regulated in Europe (barring fraud), appellations on American wine labels have been only casually controlled and there is currently a movement afoot to define them more precisely.

Balling. Standard of measurement used to calculate the amount of sugar in grapes or fermenting wines. Also called Brix. Balling and Brix were scientists who developed tables for measurement of dissolved solids, mostly sugar, in juice. It is important to know the sugar content of grapes in order to determine the right moment for harvest, to monitor the rate at which sugar is converted to alcohol and carbon dioxide during fermentation, and to calculate the amount of alcohol that will be produced in the final wine. A wine will contain a little over half as much alcohol as there was sugar present in the grapes. For example, grapes picked at 20 degrees Balling, or Brix, will produce a wine of about 11 percent alcohol.

Botrytis cinerea. A fungus which appears on certain grapes under special weather conditions, especially late in the season. Known as *pourriture noble* in France, *edelfäule* in Germany, and sometimes "noble rot" in America. Wine made from shrivelled, sugar-concentrated grapes affected with botrytis can represent the peak of sweet wine excellence, as in the great Sauternes of France or the *trockenbeerenausleses* of Germany.

Brix. See "Balling."

Cap. The thick mass of grape skins propelled to the top of the fermenting tank by the escape of carbon dioxide during fermentation. For greater extraction of color and flavor from the skins and to prevent bacterial development, the cap is regularly broken up, normally by "punching down" with a large paddle, or by "pumping over" the must through a hose from the bottom of the tank to the top.

Crush. When used as a noun, "the crush" refers to the annual winemaking epoch, commonly called "the vintage" in Europe. When used as a verb, "to crush" refers to the initial step in winemaking when grapes are crushed to release their juice. In this sense, it is not to be confused with "pressing" which is a later step. With red wines, the juice and skins ferment together, mainly to get the color from the skins, and the skins are then pressed, *i.e.* squeezed, for their remaining juice. With white wines, the skins are usually separated from the juice before fermentation and pressed for their remaining juice. See "press wine."

Fining. Clarification of wine with a substance which absorbs and precipitates suspended matter as it passes through the wine. Egg white, gelatin and a clay-like mineral called bentonite are typical fining materials.

Free run. The juice or wine that runs free before the grape skins are pressed. Compare with "press wine."

Generic wine. American wine said to be named after a generic type or class of wine, but usually carrying the name of a famous European wine region as Burgundy, Chablis, Chianti, Champagne, Rhine, Sherry—without regard to the standards set for the European wines whose names are borrowed. Use of such names, resented by European vintners and many American consumers, is on the wane among many wineries.

Goût de terroir. "Flavor of earth" perceptible in some wines, sometimes highly desirable, sometimes not.

Lees. The sediment which precipitates out of the wine during barrel or bottle aging.

Malo-lactic fermentation. Called "secondary fermentation" because it occurs after the first fermentation has converted grape sugar to alcohol and carbon dioxide. In the malo-lactic, a bacterial process, malic acid is converted to weaker lactic acid and carbon-dioxide. It reduces total acidity, softening the wine and, some say, adding complexity.

Must. A noun synonymous with "juice" in the winemaker's idiom.

Muté. Unfermented grape juice added to certain wines, typically Johannisberg Riesling, when some sweetness is desired. Instead of adding this "sweet reserve," or adding concentrate, some winemakers prefer to arrest fermentation before all the grape sugar is fermented.

Pomace. The solid residue of skins and seeds which is left after wine has been removed from the fermenter or the press.

Press wine. In white wine, wine made from the juice pressed from grape skins; in red wine, wine pressed from fermented or partially fermented red pomace after removal of the free run from the fermenting tank. Compare with *free run*.

Racking. Draining the wine from its sediment, when it is newly made and during aging, in order to clarify it and remove it from contact with dead yeast cells and other undesirable substances in the sediment.

Regions I-V. Temperature regions classified by professor Winkler and Amerine in the 1930s. Based on the observation that grapes do not grow when the temperature falls below about 50° Fahrenheit, the professors compiled data on the average daily temperatures above 50° during the growing season. They expressed these temperatures as "degree-days." Thus, a day with an average temperature of 80° would add 30 degree-days to the data. They took the summation of these degree-days to classify areas into Region I (cool, with 2500 degree-days or less), Region II (fairly cool, with 2501 to 3000), Region III (moderate, with 3001 to 3500), Region IV (warm, with 3501 to 4000), and Region V (hot, with more than 4001). Generally, fine wine grapes grow in the cooler regions. Although the utility of the classification, and its methodology, has sometimes been criticized, it has been very influential in California.

Topping. The practice of periodically filling barrels with wine to replace wine lost by evaporation through the wood pores.

Varietal wine. A wine named after the principal grape variety from which it is made, as "Chardonnay." Federal regulations have long permitted wines to carry varietal names even though they contain as little as 51 percent of the juice of the grape named. The government has recently shown some inclination to modify this deceptive labelling.

Volatile acidity. Small amounts of acetic acid, butric acid and propionic acid are present as desirable volatile acids in wine. However, if volatile acidity is too high the wine will smell and taste bad, usually like vinegar which is the acetic acid character.

Winkler, Albert J. Noted professor of viticulture in the department of viticulture and oenology at the University of California, Davis. Retired 1963.

INDEX

D

E

F

G

The wines of some of the vintners in this book may be hard to find. Here are the wineries' addresses for direct ordering:

Santa Cruz Mountains

Martin Ray, Inc. / 22000 Mt. Eden Road, Saratoga, California 95070
Woodside Vineyards / 340 Kings Mt. Road, Woodside, California 94062
David Bruce Winery / 21439 Bear Creek Road, Los Gatos, California 95030
Ridge Vineyards / 17100 Monte Bello Road, Cupertino, California 95014

Livermore Valley

Concannon Vineyard / P.O. Box 432, Livermore, California 94558
Wente Bros. Winery / 5565 Tesla Road, Livermore, California 94550

Monterey County

Chalone Vineyard / P.O. Box 855, Soledad, California 93960
Mirassou Vineyards / Box 344, San Jose, California 95121
(Vineyards in Monterey, winery located in San Jose)
The Monterey Vineyard / Box 650, Gonzales, California 93926

Napa Valley

Beaulieu Vineyard / 1960 Highway 29, Rutherford, California 94573
Mayacamas Vineyards / 1155 Lokoya Road, Napa, California 94558
Stag's Leap Wine Cellars / 5766 Silverado Trail, Napa, California 94558
Spring Mountain Vineyards / 2805 Spring Mountain Road, St. Helena, California 94574
Château Montelena / 1429 Tubbs Lane, Calistoga, California 94515
Chappellet Vineyard / Pritchard Hill, St. Helena, California 94574
Freemark Abbey Winery / 3022 St. Helena Highway, St. Helena, California 94574
Heitz Wine Cellars / 500 Taplin Road, St. Helena, California 94574
Sterling Vineyards / 1111 Dunaweal Lane, Calistoga, California 94515
Robert Mondavi Winery / P.O. Box 106, Oakville, California 94562
Louis M. Martini Winery / P.O. Box 112, St. Helena, California 94574
The Christian Brothers / P.O. Box 420, Napa, California 94558

Sonoma County

Davis Bynum Winery / 1580-A Solano Avenue, Albany, California 94706
(Retail address; winery located in Sonoma county)
Château St. Jean / P.O. Box 293, Kenwood, California 95452
Simi Winery / P.O. Box 848, Healdsburg, California 95408
Sebastiani Vineyards / P.O. Box AA, Sonoma, California 95476

Mendocino County

Fetzer Vineyards / 1150 Bel Arbres Road, Redwood Valley, California 95470
Parducci Wine Cellars / 501 Parducci Road, Ukiah, California 95482

Temecula

Callaway Vineyard & Winery / Box 275, Temecula, California 92390